American
Labor
Struggles

THE HOMESTEAD RIOT. The Pinkerton Men Leaving the Barges after the Surrender. *(Harper's Weekly,* July 16, 1892)

American Labor Struggles
1877-1934

SAMUEL YELLEN

PATHFINDER
NEW YORK • LONDON • MONTREAL • SYDNEY

ISBN 0-913460-33-8
Library of Congress Catalog Card Number 73-93633
Manufactured in the United States of America
Pathfinder edition, 1974
Sixth printing, 1997

PATHFINDER
410 West Street, New York, NY 10014, U.S.A.
Fax: (212) 727-0150 • CompuServe: 73321,414
Internet: pathfinder@igc.apc.org

PATHFINDER DISTRIBUTORS AROUND THE WORLD:
Australia (and Asia and the Pacific):
    Pathfinder, 19 Terry St., Surry Hills, Sydney, N.S.W. 2010
    Postal address: P.O. Box K879, Haymarket, N.S.W. 2000
Canada:
    Pathfinder, 4581 rue St-Denis, Montreal, Quebec, H2J 2L4
Iceland:
    Pathfinder, Klapparstíg 26, 2d floor, 101 Reykjavík
    Postal address: P. Box 233, 121 Reykjavík
New Zealand:
    Pathfinder, La Gonda Arcade, 203 Karangahape Road, Auckland
    Postal address: P.O. Box 8730, Auckland
Sweden:
    Pathfinder, Vikingagatan 10, S-113 42, Stockholm
United Kingdom (and Europe, Africa except South Africa,
    and Middle East):
    Pathfinder, 47 The Cut, London, SE1 8LL
United States (and Caribbean, Latin America, and South Africa):
    Pathfinder, 410 West Street, New York, NY 10014

TO MARY

CONTENTS

CONTENTS

INTRODUCTION

In the selection of the ten American labor struggles discussed in this book I have kept in mind a number of considerations, for these accounts are intended to be more than chronicles. Undoubtedly there have been many strikes equally important in the history of American labor, many also that were more exciting and would have made more stirring narratives. But I have tried to restrict my choice to those struggles which form the most revealing segments of the entire picture. For that reason, partly, only certain basic industries—transportation, steel, coal, textiles—figure here. The treatment of these struggles, moreover, has not been confined to a mere sequence of events and stratagems: one learns quickly that most strikes develop, mature, and expire in a definite pattern whose course can frequently be foretold. Rather I have attempted, although, of course, with no pretense of completeness, to analyze the causes underlying the development, to disclose the tactics and policies instrumental to the maturation, and to indicate the contribution left to the total current of the labor movement after the expiration of the struggle. Consequently, the emphasis has been placed on the weapons of industrial warfare devised and employed by labor and capital, the rôle of the government, and the attitude of social agencies. I have endeavored also to suggest, within the limits of the material, the growth of various ideologies and practices, the problems facing workers' organizations, the difficulties of the industries involved, and the general trend of the conflict between capital and labor in the United States.

The weapons of labor in its struggle against capital are

few, but powerful—the strike, picketing, the boycott, sabotage, mass protest and demonstration. However, changes have occurred in the form and the extent of their application. These changes have been the result, in large part, of labor's increasing awareness of the strength of the weapons and of a greater knowledge of their use; in part, these changes have been adaptations to aggressions or recessions by employers and to interference by the government or intrusion by social agencies. Thus a strike can be the spontaneous, scattered, and chaotic walkouts of the railroad strikes in 1877, or the disciplined and well-organized walkout of the textile workers at Lawrence in 1912; it can take the form of the localized and isolated protest by the southern Colorado coal miners in 1913, or the federated nation-wide drive by all the steel crafts in 1919; it can serve as a symbol of sympathy and support, like the refusal of the railway workers in 1894 to handle Pullman cars, or as a demand for the release of political prisoners, like the demonstration strike of 1912 in behalf of Ettor and Giovannitti, or as a mass defense against a concerted employer-offensive, like the San Francisco general strike of 1934.

Capital, on its side, likewise has developed methods of controlling labor during times of peace and of defeating it in times of strife. Some of these methods are overt, such as the lockout, the hiring of armed guards, and the importation of strike-breakers; others, like espionage and the blacklist, are covert. Furthermore, in welfare work and the company union, capital has found more subtle and insidious means of controlling labor, splitting its ranks, and dissipating its force. Any doubt concerning the effect of welfare work, whether so intended or not, is dissolved by a study of the absolute domination over labor gained by the Pullman Palace Car Company or the United States Steel Corporation through their welfare systems. Any uncertainty concerning the purpose of the company union, no matter what its alleged intention, is clarified by a study of the conception and birth of the Rockefeller Industrial Representation Plan during and after the Colorado coal strike of 1913-1914.

During the progress of the struggle between capital and labor, the government, whether city, county, state, or federal, has interfered often and has rarely proved itself impartial or neutral. Nor should this intervention be unexpected, if it is remembered that the government was established on the principles of freedom of contract (at least for labor) and private property. No amount of verbal artifice can conceal the fundamental opposition of organized labor to these two principles. When workers demand the eight-hour day or an increase in wages, they automatically invade the "right" of the employer to the full use of his property and the "freedom" of other workers to work a longer day or for lower wages if they so choose. When workers strike for recognition of their union and then picket in order to render the strike effective, they at once restrict the "freedom" of other workers to work where they please, with or without union affiliation, and the employer's "expectancy" (which has been decreed a property right by the Supreme Court) to hire workmen. It is not strange, therefore, that in protecting the principles of private property and freedom of contract the government, almost without exception, sends its police, sheriffs, militia, and federal troops to help crush strikes. Nor is it strange that the courts sustain the dispatch of the government's forces against the strikes, by causing the arrest of workers on such charges as vagrancy, picketing, contempt of court, riot, and rebellion. Even legislation, perhaps in a more oblique manner, frequently operates against labor during a strike; for example, the Sherman Anti-Trust Act and the Interstate Commerce Act, while ostensibly enacted to curb the monopolistic tendencies of industry and commerce, served to father the labor injunction at the time of the Pullman strike of 1894.

In the same way, such social agencies as the press, the radio, the pulpit, the movies, and the schools are conservative, in the sense that they act to *conserve* the existing economic and political set-up of society, and to defend the principles upon which it is erected. As a result, they assist in suppressing any serious outbreak of labor that occurs, whether in the deliberate and conscious manner of the council of newspaper publishers that directed the San Francisco press in its onslaught upon the general strike of 1934, or in the naïve and unconscious manner of the New England clergyman who, in vindication of the 12-hour day in the steel industry, cited the words of the "Toiler of Galilee"— "I must work the works of him that sent me while it is day; for the night cometh when no man can work."

The struggles of labor for better working and living conditions have led it to combine in organizations both for mutual assistance and for mutual protection. While many of these organizations were short-lived, as was the American Railway Union founded in 1893 by Eugene V. Debs, others existed over a period of years (and continue to exist) and exercised a steady influence upon the ideology and practice of organized labor in the United States. All degrees of attitude toward capital, the government, and society are represented in these organizations. The Brotherhoods of railroad workers, originally fraternal societies which slowly acquired the trade-union function of collective bargaining, have retreated gradually from the principle of collective bargaining to the policy of partial collaboration with capital and regulation by the government. Likewise, a large part of the American Federation of Labor has exhibited an inclination toward the idea of coöperation with capital and the practice of mediation and arbitration. On the other hand, the Chicago anarchists of 1886 and the Industrial Workers of the World renounced coöperation with employers and condemned arbitration as enervators and partitioners of the ranks of labor. Between these two groups there developed a sharp conflict; one group was conservative, the other radical, in the sense that it wished to get at the *root* of labor's difficulties in the existing society and, if necessary, to change the basis of that society. As a consequence, interwoven in the struggles of labor can be detected the influences of anarchism, syndicalism, communism, and other doctrines for the conversion of society. In other words, labor was led from its immediate desire for higher wages and fewer hours to an examination of causative defects in the structure of society.

Besides the primary cleavage in organized labor between the conservative and radical factions, other secondary cleavages appeared as new problems of procedure and theory arose, bringing with them corresponding differences of opinion concerning their proper solution. Tactics were tried, discarded, tried again. Violence was answered at different times with the boycott, sabotage, counter-violence. Mass picketing was the reply to the labor injunction, mass protest and demonstration to the partiality of the courts. Certain problems recurred again and again, and some of them still trouble American labor organizations. One is the question of the Negro. Unless organized labor can agree upon a method of including him in its ranks, he will continue to be, as in the steel strike of 1919, a depressor of wages and a potential strike-breaker. Another problem, even more pressing, is that of craft versus industrial unionism. Shall craft unions, like most of those in the steel industry, be the structural unit of a nation-wide organization of labor? Or shall all the workers in an industry, regardless of skill or special craft, be included in one industrial union, capable of united and simultaneous action? A third problem is dual

unionism. Dissatisfaction with the conservatism of existing
organizations, uneasiness concerning the "official scabbing"
induced by craft unionism, inability to get rid of the well-
established officialdom of trade-unions—all these have led to
the formation of rival unions. Thus in 1912, the I.W.W.,
in opposition to the existing United Textile Workers of
America, organized the workers in the entire textile industry of Lawrence, Massachusetts. More recently, the Communists have organized such dual unions as the National
Textile Workers' Union and the National Marine Workers'
Union.

I have attempted to trace the above-mentioned tactics,
principles, attitudes, influences, and problems in each struggle as it unfolded itself. At the same time, I have tried to
recount the story of the strike, its causes, its sequence of
events, its consequences. If there seems to be some repetition
in these accounts, it is attributable principally to the repetitions in the struggles themselves. Certain conditions—low
wages, long hours, favoritism, discrimination, company
stores, the speed-up, the stretch-out, the absence of collective bargaining—become unbearable to the workers in an industry; they organize, they strike, often they strike a second
time to defend their organization. Certain forces are brought
to bear upon them by employers, by the government, by
social agencies, even by other labor organizations. They resist these forces successfully and win, or they succumb to
them and lose. The story is simple enough. To a lesser degree, the repetitions are due also to the frequent failure of
labor to learn from its own history the errors of the past and
to rectify them. It may be that a political party or a single
nation-wide organization is essential for labor in order to
serve as the conducting medium for what has already been
learned by experience. Nevertheless, there has been no mere
cyclic recurrence of events in American labor history. There

has been an unmistakable and steady cumulative development, as can be seen from the wide difference between the conduct of the railroad strikes of 1877, soon after the United States emerged from the Civil War as a full-fledged industrial nation, and that of the longshoremen's strike on the west coast in 1934, with the accompanying general strike in the San Francisco Bay area.

It would be dishonest for me to pretend that these accounts are entirely free of prejudice or partiality, inasmuch as I think it impossible for any accounts to be so written, especially in history and the social sciences. If one fact taken by itself is malleable, and two or three facts permit a number of arrangements, the possibilities of interpretation and distortion, whether deliberate or not, in the handling of hundreds of facts are limitless. I have, however, endeavored to present all the facts which seemed significant to me, and to keep the emphasis as fair as I could. For evidence concerning the struggles themselves I have studied, wherever possible, government reports, other semi-official investigations, statements and decisions issued by the contestants, contemporary accounts in newspapers and periodicals, and other primary sources. For related material concerning the theories and results involved I have consulted such well-known authorities as I could find. In all cases I have presented my sources for quoted statements and figures.

I have attempted to present my exposition in simple and unadorned language. Aside from my talent or lack of talent for writing, I wished any eloquence in these accounts to derive from the facts, the figures, and the events themselves. I wished the material to speak for itself, and therefore avoided any personal comment. I found it necessary to resort to certain practices that may require explanation. For example, except in a few instances, I have used the word "crowd" rather than "mob" because of the dubious application of the latter by newspapers. At times, also, I have enclosed in quotation marks certain expressions, like "respectable elements," which carry overtones of emotional or social bias. Otherwise, I have tried only to order the material so that it would be clearly and economically expressed.

Acknowledgments: My gratitude to Mr. Henry David, of the College of the City of New York, for a number of emendations in the chapter on the Haymarket affair; and to the Northern California branch of the American Civil Liberties Union for the use of a pamphlet dealing with the state of civil liberties in San Francisco during the general strike of 1934. My deepest thanks to my wife for making the index and for her assistance, suggestions, and encouragement throughout the preparation of this book.

SAMUEL YELLEN

American
Labor
Struggles

I. THE RAILROAD UPRISINGS
OF 1877

1. Panic and grievances

The great railroad strikes which broke out spontaneously and spread with the speed of a plague in the summer of 1877 were the expression of a deep and accumulated discontent. Labor outbreaks had been common in the United States before this time, but had been confined to separate localities. Never before had industry and commerce been confronted with a nation-wide uprising of workers, an uprising so obstinate and bitter that it was crushed only after great bloodshed. The militia of the several states did not suffice; for the first time in the history of the country the federal troops had to be called out during a period of peace in order to suppress strikes. More than a hundred workmen were killed and several hundred badly wounded. For a full week the strikes crowded from the front pages of the newspapers all reports of the war between Russia and Turkey, then in progress, and of the campaign against the Sioux Indians in the Idaho territory. The general public, both workers and employers, became aware that a national labor movement had been born.

Although the strikes were primarily a protest against reductions in wages, they had a more profound origin in the depression that resulted from the panic of 1873. Stimulated by the Civil War, industry and commerce had prospered. For a number of years all kinds of business enterprise had been confidently undertaken. The first transcon-

3

tinental railroad had been opened in 1869. In the cities, factories had replaced home industry. Immigration had been encouraged and the population had increased. Corporations had sprung up and the foundations for vast fortunes had been laid. This hectic development, however, had been too rapid and was based too often on the wildest gambling and most corrupt scheming. Furthermore, the financial system of the nation was tottering, since paper money was widely circulated, with no provision for specie payment. When the inevitable crash came, hundreds of thousands were thrown out of employment, and many thousands lacked food, clothing, shelter, medical attention. Even those still at work suffered, inasmuch as wages were cut nearly in half during the next six years. All the remedial efforts of President Grant and Congress proved lamentably inadequate.

Notwithstanding optimistic predictions for a revival of trade, the year 1877 was the trough of the depression. The railroads, which had cut wages steadily, prepared for another reduction, in order that freight rates might be lowered. The Pennsylvania Railroad led the way with a 10 per cent cut to take effect June 1. On many other lines—the Erie; Lake Shore; Michigan Southern; Indianapolis and St. Louis; Vandalia; New York Central and Hudson River —a similar reduction was announced for July 1. These notices threw the men, already earning barely enough to support their families, into despair. When they protested against the cuts, their committees were summarily discharged and their small unions dissolved. With thousands of jobless men begging for places, the railroad officials felt certain that the workmen, no matter how intense their dissatisfaction, would be afraid to walk out.

But the railroads failed to calculate the sharp popular feeling against them. Farmers throughout the country resented the high, almost confiscatory freight rates; and the

National Grange of the Patrons of Husbandry, formed in 1867, had grown by 1874 into the Granger Movement, with 22,000 granges and over 800,000 members, distinctly hostile to the railroads. Workers were sullen because of continued wage cuts and unemployment, and the railroads, as employers of the largest number of men, stirred up great ill-will. Besides, scandals like that of the Crédit Mobilier and the Union Pacific had disclosed to the public a fraction of the bribery, corruption, and financial thieving that had gone into the building of the railroads. The *New York Times* remarked:

The great misfortune of the railroads is not that business is dull and comparatively unprofitable, but that they are required to face hard times burdened with the consequences of former errors of management. They are organized on a basis which presupposes a continuance of the era of inflation. They added enormously to their bonded debts, entailing fixed charges from which there is no escape save through bankruptcy. They entered into leases and guarantees which now are so many millstones about their necks. To crown all, they capitalized their stock according to the then inflated values and the exceptional amount of their earnings. The stock thus largely "watered" naturally craves dividends; and as one of the conditions of good credit, a company spares no effort to enable itself to pay them. Hence the exigency from which direct and indirect reductions of wages proceed.[1]

By means of fake companies, improper consolidations, premium bonds and certificates, stock dividends, and other financial maneuvers, the railroads had succeeded in erecting tremendous capitalizations, as much as seven-ninths water, upon which they demanded their "just and reasonable" dividends. Charles Edward Russell estimated, for example, that of the $89,257,450 capitalization of the New York Central and Hudson River Railroad in 1877, more than $50,000,000 consisted of security gifts made by Cornelius Vanderbilt to himself and his family.[2]

During the darkest years of the depression the railroads had continued to pay high dividends on their enormous and liberally watered capitalizations. The New York Central paid 8 per cent in cash dividends each year, 10 per cent in 1875; and the other trunk lines, whose financial structure was akin, kept pace. These cash payments were not all the dividends; for there were substantial surplus earnings each year, to be issued subsequently as free stock dividends, so that the New York Central actually paid 15 per cent on its capital, "as that virtually is what the Central is now doing, and to which exception is taken." [3] In 1877 the Pennsylvania, as a result of the Pittsburgh fire in which it suffered heavy losses, regretted that a cut in dividends from the usual 8 per cent to 6 per cent was prudent. And the *Commercial and Financial Chronicle*, despite the "relatively unsatisfactory business" in the first half of 1877, was able to report:

The largest decrease in gross earnings in June, 1877, as compared with the same month of 1876, is shown by the Central Pacific—mainly in consequence of the drought which has prevailed to so great an extent in the San Joaquin Valley and some other parts of California. The Central Pacific, however, deals in large figures, and as the company has been paying 8 per cent dividends on upwards of $54,000,-000 stock, nearly all held by the original projectors and builders of the road, the bondholders in New York or London may regard a rise or fall in the gross earnings, within a moderate limit, as a matter of comparative indifference.[4]

Yet when the *Springfield Republican* suggested that the New York Central might pay 6 per cent instead of 8 per cent in dividends and distribute the difference of $1,780,000 as increased wages, the *Commercial and Financial Chronicle* protested:

But it is intimated that Mr. Vanderbilt is paying for labor less than the present market price, or less than it is to be in a short time, and is thus, by squeezing his employes, keeping up the dividends for his stockholders—that all property has depreciated, and that he should be willing to accept the general depreciation, and pay smaller dividends. We must again object to a treatment of this question which makes Mr. Vanderbilt the exponent or representative of all the shareholders. The Central's stock is widely held, and by investors but poorly able to lose any portion of their income— "widows and orphans," the two classes which are so often mentioned with pronounced sympathy by our political newspapers, are largely represented.[5]

Even though only a small section of the picture was visible to them, the farmers and laborers realized that, through higher freight rates and lower wages, they carried the burden of the financial manipulations.

Aside from the question of wage reductions, the workers had other grievances against the railroads. They were, for example, always subject to call, although there was but three to five days' work a week. When they were on the job, they toiled excessively long hours, as many as 15 to 18 hours per day. On many roads their pay was several months in arrears. The trackmen of the Erie Road, who lived in shanties on land alongside the tracks, where they raised little patches of potatoes and cabbages, were commanded suddenly by the company to pay ground rent of $20 to $25 a year or vacate their homes.[6] Many roads also deprived the men of the passes that carried them to and from their jobs; hence one worker on the Lake Shore line at Collinwood, Ohio, was paid 16 cents in wages to take a train to Cleveland, but then had to report back to his superior at Collinwood at a cost of 25 cents in fare.[7] Most provoking of all to the men were the downright hostility of the companies to their mild fraternal Brotherhoods, the blacklisting of union members, and the refusal to treat with their grievance committees.

To defend themselves against such abuses and antagonism, the workmen had no organization except the weak Brotherhoods, three in number at that time and but recently formed. They were entirely fraternal organizations, devoted to ritualism and to mutual insurance, with no trade-union functions, such as collective bargaining for wages and conditions of work. Two of them—the Brotherhood of Railway Conductors, formed in 1868, and the Brotherhood of Locomotive Firemen and Enginemen, formed in 1873—were extremely feeble and remained inactive throughout the period of strikes. The Brotherhood of Railway Conductors, in fact, forbade its members to strike on penalty of expulsion, and acted as strike-breaker during the railroad uprisings. The third, the Brotherhood of Locomotive Engineers, which dated from 1863, favored a more energetic attitude. It was the first to protest openly, and conducted two strikes against wage reductions in April, 1877, one on the Boston and Albany, the other on the Pennsylvania. Both strikes failed. And when President Gowen of the Pennsylvania and Reading Railroad ordered his locomotive engineers to withdraw from the Brotherhood or be fired, they had to submit, since a surprise strike, set by them for midnight of April 14, was frustrated through the agency of Pinkerton detectives. The engineers were temporarily defeated.

After the Pennsylvania wage cut went into effect June 1, the employees at Pittsburgh sought desperately some organization which would protect them more vigorously than the Brotherhoods did. Through the efforts largely of Robert A.

Ammon, a young brakeman, a number of the men at Allegheny City organized secretly on June 2 the first lodge of the Trainmen's Union. This was to include all railway labor —engineers, conductors, brakemen, firemen, trackmen, shopmen—in one solid body. Ammon became general organizer and the union soon extended to the Baltimore and Ohio, the Pennsylvania with all its leased lines radiating from Pittsburgh, the Erie, and the Atlantic and Great Western. A simultaneous strike was resolved upon for noon of June 27, but at a meeting held the preceding night dissension arose and the plan collapsed. Again an organization had failed. Nevertheless, the accumulated rancor of the men was so acute that the slightest additional provocation was sufficient to set off a severe spontaneous and unorganized outbreak.

2. The Baltimore and Ohio breaks the camel's back

The spark was furnished by the Baltimore and Ohio when President Garrett announced on July 11 that beginning with the 16th all wages over $1 per day would be cut 10 per cent. Inasmuch as the same reduction had already been made by other main roads, Garrett expected no difficulties from his men; and he listened politely to the complaints of the firemen and brakemen on the freight trains. If the reduction went into effect, the men pointed out, first-class firemen would receive $1.58 per day and second-class $1.35, while brakemen would receive even less. With the average of four days' work a week, they would have at the best $5 or $6 as weekly earnings, out of which they had not only to support their families, but also to pay their living expenses while on the job. However, Garrett remained firm.

There was much grumbling among the men, but the company, with a good number of applications on hand for vacant positions, felt prepared for a strike, if it should come. On Monday morning, July 16, the first day of the new

wage scale, the trains were manned as usual, and it seemed
that the men's dissatisfaction had quieted down, except that
some 40 firemen and brakemen on the freight trains in Baltimore refused to work. They were quickly replaced by other
men. The strikers gathered at Camden Junction, three miles
outside the city, stopped a freight train, persuaded the fireman to leave, and would not let another take his place. A
force of 40 policemen dispersed them. Seven freight trains
were started, with the strikers replaced, and all appeared
peaceful once more.

Disturbing reports, however, were received by the company from other points along the line. At Martinsburg,
West Virginia, an important freight junction, 25 or 30 firemen abandoned their trains and a large crowd of sympathizers assembled. The mayor arrested the leaders among
the strikers, but the crowd released them by force. He then
attempted to start the trains with new men, but was prevented. By morning the strike had assumed "alarming proportions." The brakemen of the freight trains joined the firemen at Martinsburg, and although passenger trains were not
interfered with, all freight was halted. Vice-President King
of the Baltimore and Ohio sent representations to Governor
Matthews of West Virginia, who called out immediately the
two companies of militia stationed at Martinsburg; and Colonel Sharp, general master of transportation, known for his
stern and autocratic demeanor, was ordered by Garrett to
the scene.

After one short skirmish the militia fraternized with the
strikers, among whom were relatives and friends, and refused
to fire upon them. Angered by this disobedience, Governor
Matthews set out personally from Wheeling at the head of
two more companies of militia, but he abandoned them at
Grafton because of the hostility of the citizens. Everywhere
along the line the people were completely in sympathy with

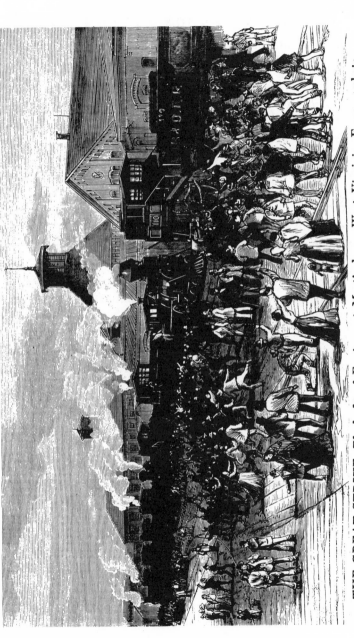

THE GREAT STRIKE. Blockade of Engines at Martinsburg, West Virginia. From a photograph by D. Bendann. (*Harper's Weekly*, Aug. 11, 1877)

the strikers, nor could the troops be depended upon to act against them. The *Baltimore Sun* wrote:

There is no disguising the fact that the strikers in all their lawful acts have the fullest sympathy of the community. The 10 per cent. reduction after two previous reductions was ill-advised. The company for years has boasted of its great earnings and paid enormous dividends. All that it could save of the reduction upon the wages of the 300 men, averaging about $6 dollars [sic] per week, would be less than $10,000 per year. The losses of the company already [because of the strike] have been estimated at $100,000. The firemen evidently have worked hard and suffered much on very small pay. They are chiefly old employes, married, and having families dependent upon them. The more intelligent seem content to appeal to the public, and ask if wages that do not now permit over $5 per week to go to the housing, clothing, and feeding a family are more than sufficient as a remuneration for experienced labor, full of danger and responsibility. The singular part of the disturbances is in the very active part taken by the women, who are the wives or mothers of the firemen. They look famished and wild, and declare for starvation rather than have their people work for the reduced wages. Better to starve outright, say they, than to die by slow starvation.[8]

The strike spread to Keyser, Grafton, and Wheeling, other junctions on the road, until 500 men were out. These were further reinforced by 200 striking boatmen on the Chesapeake and Ohio canal. At Martinsburg the freight blockade contained 70 trains with 1,200 cars, many of them loaded.

When the company saw itself checked by the default of the militia, it searched for other means of breaking the strike. It was Colonel Sharp's unprecedented "master stroke" to urge that a wire be sent to President Hayes at

Washington requesting federal troops.[9] Governor Matthews instantly did so, and his petition was supported by Garrett with a long telegram. On Wednesday evening 400 U. S. troops left Washington and Fort McHenry, Maryland, for Martinsburg on a special train provided by the Baltimore and Ohio. The company was anxious to have the blockade broken on the following day because commercial firms in Baltimore were calling for the delivery of the grain, live stock, coal, and petroleum needed to fill their steamer and ship engagements.

Upon the arrival of the federal troops in Martinsburg the company made up two test trains, on the morning of July 19, one to run east to Baltimore, the other west to Cumberland, Maryland. The strikers looked on. When they pleaded with the engineers not to run the trains, the troops drove them off with bayonets, and their leader, Dick Zepp, was arrested on charges of rioting. With troops on board the two trains reached their destinations safely, although people demonstrated all along the road in protest. Thus far the strikers had acted entirely without organization; that night committees from the various divisions met at Grafton, resolved to stand by one another, and offered to negotiate with company officials for a compromise agreement. To this offer Garrett replied that the company would hold to its ultimatum, and ordered that all faithful employees be rewarded with medals and that their names be placed first on the list for promotion. The next morning the company, under the protection of the troops, moved 13 trains out of Martinsburg, and officers were out to arrest the leading strikers.

But fresh freight clots appeared at Cumberland and at Newark, Ohio. The company asked for more troops. Governor John Lee Carroll of Maryland tried to avoid the mistake of Governor Matthews in calling out local and friendly militia, and decided to send troops from Baltimore. On Friday, July 20, the Fifth Regiment of the Maryland National Guard and three companies of the Sixth were mustered at their armories. As evening approached, crowds, composed of strikers, sympathizing workmen, and unemployed, gathered to protest the sending of the militia. At about 7 o'clock the Fifth Regiment marched with fixed bayonets to Camden Station, trailed by shouting and jeering citizens. The troops entered the waiting train, but the crowd drove the engineer and fireman from the locomotive, so that the regiment was stranded.

As the three companies of the Sixth likewise set out for Camden Station, they were followed by another crowd, perhaps 2,000, determined to prevent their departure. There resulted a running battle from the Centre Market up to the corner of Baltimore and St. Paul Streets, in the course of which at least 10 in the crowd were killed. "The determined temper of the soldiers is evinced by the circumstance that all the men killed were shot through the head or heart." [10] Although the troops reached the station with no loss, they were beleaguered by a great infuriated crowd. Governor Carroll called upon President Hayes for federal troops, and two companies of artillery and a detachment of infantry were dispatched from New York. For three days the rioting continued, and only on Monday, July 23, was an armed peace established. Baltimore was a military camp, particularly at Camden Station, where 700 soldiers guarded the company property with two Gatling guns and several field pieces. The total casualties of the affrays were 13 killed and about 50 wounded.

A week had now passed. The Baltimore and Ohio freight was still tied up at Cumberland and Keyser; but it became merely a matter of time until the company could get enough troops at each junction along the road to break the blockade and crush the strike. On July 26 a committee from the

strikers waited on Governor Carroll with an offer of arbitration. Vice-President King of the Baltimore and Ohio, while
he hoped that the "difficulties can be adjusted," refused to
discuss the wage reduction. Two days later the company
began aggressively to open one section after another with
the aid of the troops. President Hayes had to send hundreds
of marines and infantry. Bonuses were offered to men willing to run the trains, $50 each to those who brought the first
two trains from Grafton to Cumberland. Every striker found
approaching any of the men on the trains was arrested. It
was a bitter struggle, and the troops often had to shoot into
the crowds of strikers and sympathizers. On July 28 the
company moved 23 freight trains between Baltimore and
Cumberland. Opening the road between Keyser and Grafton
took three days of fighting. By August 1, after 16 days, the
strike on the Baltimore and Ohio began to dwindle.

3. Fire and riot at Pittsburgh

Even more violent was the strife that arose between the
Pennsylvania Railroad and its workmen, culminating in a
riot at Pittsburgh bloodier than any the country had experienced since the Civil War draft riots of New York. The
men had accepted the wage reduction of June 1 with its consequent hardships, but other grievances excited them. They
complained that the company had broken faith with them
on several of its lines. On the Pittsburgh and Fort Wayne
road, for instance, the brakemen had been cut in 1873 from
$1.58 to 85 cents per day of 15 to 18 hours; seeing that their
wages were already so low, the company had agreed that the
10 per cent reduction of June 1 would not apply to them;
and yet on July 6 posters appeared lowering their pay to
75 cents a day retroactive to June 1.[11] More objectionable to
the men was the "double header" edict of Superintendent
Pitcairn to go into effect on July 19. Freight trains, which

up this time had consisted of 17 cars and one locomotive, were now to have two locomotives and 34 cars or more; whereas the crew was to remain the same. This meant harder labor, extra danger, an indirect wage cut, and, above all, the laying off of nearly half the brakemen and flagmen. The company declined to bargain.

On the morning of July 19 the workers at Pittsburgh, goaded by the company's attitude and infected by the reports from the Baltimore and Ohio, left their trains without prearrangement and took command of the switches. Soon they numbered 500. Sheriff Fife of Allegheny County was unable to disperse them. The company officials wired Governor John F. Hartranft, who ordered out the Sixth Division of the militia at Pittsburgh. But the troops merely looked on while the workmen met all freight trains entering the yards and persuaded the crews to join the strike. The inhabitants of Pittsburgh—including many business men, who felt that they were discriminated against in freight rates—were in accord with the strikers. The moribund Trainmen's Union sprang to life, held a large and enthusiastic meeting of the strikers at Phoenix Hall, and demanded that the wage reductions of June 1 be restored, that the "double headers" with the exception of coal trains be abolished, and that all the strikers be reëmployed. More than 900 loaded cars stood idle the next day on the track between the Union Depot and East Liberty.

As soon as Governor Hartranft understood that the local militia were rendered ineffective by their fraternization with the strikers, he called for troops from Philadelphia, evidently depending on the ancient rivalry between the two cities. In fact, the Philadelphia Hussars boasted that they were going to clean out Pittsburgh.[12] The Pennsylvania made all arrangements for transporting the militia from Philadelphia, and ammunition was shipped from the state arsenal at

Harrisburg. The detachment of 1,000 troops, including a battery of artillery, arrived in Pittsburgh at noon Saturday, July 21, the day following the Baltimore shooting; and toward 3:30 began to march out Liberty Street to Twenty-eighth to disperse the strikers. A crowd of men, women, and children collected. Two or three stones were thrown by boys. Instantly the militia—whether ordered or not is uncertain—fired a volley into the crowd. A second volley was deliberately ordered. Twenty persons were killed and 29 seriously wounded, among them three small children and a woman.

The news passed swiftly through the city and caused high excitement. Great crowds gathered at the corners of the principal streets. The Philadelphia troops retreated to the Pennsylvania roundhouse and were soon surrounded by 20,-000 enraged men and women. Three militiamen who tried to escape were shot. By 1 A.M. the city was in the hands of ungovernable crowds, joined by the unemployed and the hungry, who were quite ready for looting. Arms and ammunition shops were raided and three pieces of ordnance were captured from Knapp's Battery. The besieged militia replied to the fire and many were killed and wounded. Finally, after a burning car, loaded with coke and saturated with petroleum, was run against the roundhouse where they were corralled, the militia shot their way through the crowd, killing 20 more and losing two or three men, until they were able to escape to Sharpsburg.

Meanwhile a fire started in the freight cars lined up outside the Union Depot from Washington Street to Thirty-third and spread uncontrolled till it had destroyed 500 freight cars, 104 locomotives, and 39 buildings, including shops, engine-houses, depots, offices, and the Union Depot and Hotel. The total loss to the Pennsylvania, according to its president, Colonel Thomas A. Scott, exceeded $5,000,-000. For two miles along the road there was wreckage and smoldering ruin. Food, clothing, and other materials were carried off from the smashed freight cars by looters. At this time Sheriff Fife disappeared and was reported dead. However, when peace was restored on Tuesday, July 24, he turned up alive and unharmed to quarrel with the authorities over the payment of special officers. The disturbances abated on Monday, and by Tuesday the streets were patrolled by strikers and citizen volunteers. With the strike still intact there was no freight movement, and the city began to suffer a shortage of provisions, particularly in fuel, milk, and truck.

Other cities became affected by strikes—Altoona, Easton, Harrisburg, Reading, Johnstown, Bethlehem, Philadelphia—and freight was tied up on the entire road. The Coal and Iron Police were brought into action. Colonel Scott refused to come to Pittsburgh to arbitrate, but put all in the hands of state and federal authorities until the strikes were broken. Governor Hartranft, who was away on a vacation, started immediately for home, telegraphing ahead to order out every militia regiment in the state, calling upon the President for federal troops, and reassuring Colonel Scott that he would open up the Pennsylvania. President Hayes dispatched General Hancock with 3,000 U. S. regulars. A special train was furnished by the Pennsylvania, from which Governor Hartranft directed military activities. He instructed his troops to fire into every crowd until it scattered. The rebellion throughout the state was to be crushed at any cost.

For nearly two weeks after the Pittsburgh rioting Governor Hartranft traveled from city to city with his troops and conducted a warlike campaign. Since no engineers could be found for the troop trains, it was frequently necessary to transport the militia in wagons. The difficulties were further complicated by strikes of miners in the Lackawanna Valley,

at Wilkes-Barre and Scranton, for a wage increase of 25
per cent. At Philadelphia, where marines were landed, all
meetings of strikers and of the Workingmen's Party were
prohibited. At Johnstown troops were stoned and many
workers shot. At Reading on Monday night, July 23, soldiers
killed 10 and wounded 40; and another slaughter was avoided
the following morning when the Easton Grays were prevented from shooting into a crowd only by the threat of the
Morristown Company to cross-fire. Later this Morristown
Company stacked its arms and refused to shoot strikers,
whereupon Governor Hartranft replaced it with 600 U. S.
regulars. At Pittsburgh, where food became scarce, Mayor
Phillips proposed to the strikers that if they would deliver
the freight to him personally, he would pay them for their
labor and would depend upon the railroad officials to reim-
burse him in the future. The men offered to bring the freight
up the river by boat and deliver it to him, but Mayor
Phillips declined furiously: he wanted the trains moved.

Aggressive operations against the strikers were now begun. More than 10,000 troops were concentrated along the
60 miles of road between Pittsburgh and Blairsville; then
Governor Hartranft, applying the technique used on the
Baltimore and Ohio, started west from Harrisburg and
opened the divisions in succession. In every city the strike
leaders were arrested and held without bail. On July 28
Governor Hartranft entered Pittsburgh commanding four
troop trains, with a Gatling gun mounted on a gondola car
in front of the first locomotive. By nightfall 3,000 troops had
arrived in the city. In spite of stubborn opposition the
freight blockade was slowly broken. The Pennsylvania issued
a notice that commencing with Monday, July 30, all its lines
would be open for passengers and freight. General Hancock
sent this dispatch to the War Department:

The quiet occupation of Pittsburg and opening of the Pennsylvania Railroad, I think, settles the question of order in this division, and the only trouble that seems to remain is that connected with the miners in certain points in the coal districts, such as Scranton. Possibly that may require similar treatment as that of the railroad.[13]

Governor Hartranft was free on August 1 to devote himself to the strikes in the mining districts around Kingston, Plymouth, Nanticoke, Scranton, and Wilkes-Barre. He set forth with federal and state troops, and announced that he would show no mercy.

Notwithstanding the lifting of the freight embargo, it was well into August before the Pennsylvania Railroad ran with its former regularity. Strike-breakers replaced many of the old men, troops guarded the trains, and arrests of strike leaders continued, until the strikes were thoroughly suppressed. The company was then able to concern itself with the question of damages for the freight property destroyed at Pittsburgh. It contended that Allegheny County was alone responsible and that the consignors would have to collect from the county. The shippers, small farmers, and traders prepared to sue the company. Vanderbilt and the New York Central, taking skillful advantage of this disagreement, opened a competing freight line, the Blue Line, direct to Philadelphia and began to capture the disgruntled customers of the Pennsylvania.

4. "I am proud of the men of the Central Road"

In New York State, because of the tactics employed by railroad officials, the strikes took a different course. The troubles began at Hornellsville July 20, the day following the walkout at Pittsburgh, with a strike on the Erie Railroad of freight firemen, brakemen, and trackmen. Instantly the officials wired all trains to stop, in order to prevent the gathering of strikers and a jam of cars at this junction. Besides their opposition to the mandate, mentioned above, to pay ground rent on their shanties, the men accused the company of breaking a promise made by Superintendent Bowen, that, providing the 10 per cent reduction of July 1 were peacefully abided by, all those who had been discharged for serving on grievance committees would be reinstated. Nevertheless, although the reduction had been accepted by the men, 14 committee members were not reinstated, on the grounds that they had been discharged not for serving on a grievance committee, but for leaving their posts without permission and other "flagrant violations of discipline." The men felt outraged, and the examples of the Baltimore and Ohio and the Pennsylvania were enough to bring them to strike.

The situation at Hornellsville was peculiar in that the Erie road was in receivership and anyone interfering with the train service could be charged with contempt of court. Receiver Hugh J. Jewett asserted that, rather than make any concession whatsoever, the road would shut down. Determined to halt all freight movements until their grievances were adjusted, the strikers organized effectively under the leadership of Barney Donahue. With the exception of the stoppage of freight, they intended to use no force; they closed the saloons and maintained order in the town, hoping by their conduct to escape the current abusive language of the newspapers. (In a single issue, July 26, 1877, the *New York Times*, for instance, referred to the railroad strikers in the following terms: disaffected elements, roughs, hoodlums, rioters, mob, suspicious-looking individuals, bad characters, thieves, blacklegs, looters, communists, rabble, labor-reform agitators, dangerous class of people, gangs, tramps, drunken section-men, law-breakers, threatening crowd, bummers,

ruffians, loafers, bullies, vagabonds, cowardly mob, bands of
worthless fellows, incendiaries, enemies of society, reckless
crowd, malcontents, wretched people, loud-mouthed orators,
rapscallions, brigands, robber mob, riffraff, terrible fellows,
felons, idiots.) Three attempts by the company to move the
freight failed, for the strikers greased the tracks on the up-
grades, boarded the engines, and ran the trains back into the
yard.

Two separate attacks on the strikers were initiated. For
one, Governor Lucius Robinson adopted the policy, familiar
by now, of calling out the militia in districts remote from
the scene of trouble. For the other, Receiver Jewett swore
out a warrant before Judge Donohue of the Supreme Court
of New York against Barney Donahue and several other
leaders of the strike, charging them with contempt of court.
The Twenty-third Regiment of Brooklyn, numbering 1,200,
occupied Hornellsville on July 23. That evening Barney
Donahue was arrested while he was eating alone at the
Nicols House. His bail was fixed at $2,500. Beemis and Haw-
ley, counsel for the strikers, argued that the writ was illegal
and advised Donahue not to recognize it by procuring the
bail. Donahue went to the village lock-up, but was later removed to the depot under military guard. After four more of
them were confined with Donahue and held incommunicado,
the strikers arranged to meet secretly for fear all their leaders would be arrested in a body.

Accompanied by the 110th Battalion and a wrecking crew,
a freight train was started east from Hornellsville on July
24, with two postal cars at the rear, so that the U. S. mails
would have to be obstructed before any car could be detached.
The strikers, proceeding about two miles in advance of the
train, tore up the tracks and blocked the road with freight
cars; but the wrecking crew cleared and patched the rails,
and the train finally reached Elmira. A westbound train be-

tween Corning and Hornellsville encountered even greater
difficulties, and took eight hours to make the trip of less
than 40 miles. No other trains were started this day, and the
company declared itself willing to meet the strikers' counsel
for a compromise. An agreement was reached on July 25:
the wage cut was to be restored to the brakemen, but not
to the firemen; no men engaged in the strike were to be proceeded against or discharged, except those who had destroyed
company property; the reinstatement of the committee men
was to be left to the appropriate superintendents; and the
case against Donahue was to be further discussed, the impression being left, however, that the proceedings were to be
discontinued. On the sixth day after the walkout the men
resumed work.

In the meantime, the strike on the Erie had infected both
the New York Central and the Lake Shore at Buffalo,
where many factory laborers quit work in sympathy. While
the strikers placed an embargo on all freight, they wished
the passenger and mail trains to proceed as usual. But the
company devised the scheme of trying to start mixed trains
of passengers, mail, and freight. In order to disconnect the
freight the strikers were forced to stop the entire train and
thus became liable to punishment by the federal courts for
hindering the passage of the mails. When the attempts to
run mixed trains failed, the New York Central refused to
run any whatever. The strikers wired to the Postmaster-
General at Washington that the mails were being held up by
order of the New York Central officials. To the inquiries of
the Postmaster-General, Tillinghast, general superintendent of the road, replied that not before the strikers were dispersed by the government and order was restored would any
passenger or mail trains be run. Buffalo was patrolled by
1,600 militiamen, the regular police force, 1,800 veterans of
the Grand Army of the Republic, and 300 citizen volunteers.

In the street clashes eight soldiers were wounded and an equal number of workmen killed.

Rapidly the strike traveled eastward through Rochester and Syracuse to Albany. Here the employees of the New York Central at a mass meeting the night of July 23 threatened to strike at 8 o'clock the next morning unless they were granted an increase of 25 per cent in their wages. They maintained that the best mechanics in the shops at West Albany received only $1.20 a day, while the switchmen, trackmen, and laborers got 80 cents to $1. William H. Vanderbilt, president of the New York Central, said in an interview:

There is a perfect understanding between the heads of departments and the employes, and they appreciate, I think, so thoroughly the identity of interest between themselves and us that I cannot for a moment believe that they will have any part in this business. I am proud of the men of the Central Road, and my great trust in them is founded on their intelligent appreciation of the business situation at the present time. If they shall stand firm in the present crisis it will be a triumph of good sense over blind fury and fanaticism.[14]

When the workmen struck as they had decided, Vanderbilt sent them a telegram from his summer cottage at Saratoga: "The public interests should not suffer from any differences between the road and its employes. Keep at work until the excitement is over, and a fair conference can be held." [15]

Thereafter Vanderbilt followed the stratagem of ignoring the strike by insisting publicly that his men were too intelligent and grateful to strike, but that they were violently prevented from working by outsiders. When interviewed at Saratoga, Vanderbilt said that he was "not informed of any strike on the part of the Central employes. They had been driven out of the shops by a crowd of rioters, and had been forced to stop work."

Reporter—What about the demand for an increase of 25 per cent. in wages?

Mr. Vanderbilt—I have received no such demand from the men of the Central. A dispatch was received last night embracing something of that sort, but I would not insult the men of the Central by attributing it to them. No such demand has been recognized. It was not signed by anybody, and I have not paid any attention to it. The shops have been visited by a mob, and my men have been forced to quit work. The desperate men who have done this are not the Central men, but probably men out of employment who would like the situations of those who are at work. They belong to the "rough" element, and have coerced the Central employes to leave the shops.[16]

To all the demands for an increase in pay he replied that the company was losing money. In another interview he said:

Our men feel that, although I may own the majority of the stock in the Central, my interests are as much affected in degree as theirs, and although I may have my millions and they the rewards of their daily toil, still we are about equal in the end. If they suffer I suffer, and if I suffer they cannot escape.[17]

Notwithstanding his assumption that there was no strike, Vanderbilt asked for troops and Governor Robinson sent a militia force of 1,200 to West Albany. At a meeting in Capitol Park on July 24 the strikers were addressed by John Van Hoesen, a young brakeman, who said that the workers were fighting for bread, and if they were given bullets, they would give bullets in return. Governor Robinson himself arrived to lift the freight blockade and warned the strikers that, in accordance with a law passed by the legislature on May 10, 1877, any person willfully obstructing the operation

of any railroad or destroying its property was liable to 10
years' imprisonment and/or $1,000 fine. A reward of $500
was offered for information concerning such offenders, and
Van Hoesen and other strike leaders were arrested.

On July 26 a committee of two was sent by the strikers
at West Albany to Saratoga for a conference with Vanderbilt. He declined to discuss the wage reduction, saying that
it would set a bad precedent to succumb to the men before
they returned to work and perfect order was restored.
Within two more days the workmen grew discouraged because of the presence of the troops, the arrest of their leaders, the refusal of the engineers to walk out with them, and
the surrender of strikers on other roads. They agreed to
rely on the magnanimity of Vanderbilt. Mayor Banks of
Albany promised that he and other prominent citizens
would sign a petition to Vanderbilt for a restoration of the
former wage scale, but somehow no such petition was sent.
The company put up the following notice on the shops and
depots at West Albany:

*The employes of this department will report for duty
Monday morning, July 30, 1877, at 8 o'clock* A.M. *Those
that do not report for duty at the time above specified will
be considered as having left the service of the company,
unless a good excuse or reason be given why they do not.*[18]

The strikers voted to return to work and leave their pay demands to the citizens' petition and Vanderbilt. On August 1
Vanderbilt, in a bulletin regarding the pay demands, announced that the wage reductions were to continue in force,
but that the pay of the men was to be increased "the
moment the business of the country will justify it." As a
reward for their loyalty Vanderbilt ordered that all the
employees on the New York Central and Hudson River
road have $100,000 divided among them proportionately

to their positions. At this small cost, plus some $250,000 spent by the state to maintain the militia, Vanderbilt defeated the strike after one week and avoided the vast losses of the Baltimore and Ohio and the Pennsylvania.

5. Rebellion in Chicago and St. Louis

From the Baltimore and Ohio, the Pennsylvania, the Erie, and the New York Central roads the "striking mania" rolled westward. Once this stimulus was present, the discontent of railway labor everywhere disclosed itself. Within a week after the first walkout at Camden Junction near Baltimore, strikes had occurred on the Lake Shore; Michigan Central; Pittsburgh, Fort Wayne and Chicago; Pittsburgh, Cincinnati and St. Louis; Vandalia; Ohio and Mississippi; Cleveland, Columbus, Cincinnati and Indianapolis; Chicago, Alton and St. Louis; Canada Southern; and many lesser roads. A few railroads averted strikes by rescinding the orders for wage reductions, but most of them met the strikers' demands by calling for police and troops. In all sections of the country the people proclaimed their sympathy with the strikers. Yardmen and switchmen on the Wabash road in St. Louis raised $775 for the strikers on the Baltimore and Ohio. There were huge demonstrations and meetings in Boston and New York. At Washington crowds of workingmen, who gathered at the depots to watch the departure of trains, cheered whenever favorable accounts came from the junctions on strike. Not since the outbreak of the Civil War had there been such avidity for news.

So alarming were the reports that, beginning with July 20, for more than a week President Hayes conferred daily with his cabinet about military precautions. Troops and warships were ordered to Washington to safeguard public buildings. General Hancock, for Pennsylvania, and General Schofield, for West Virginia and Maryland, had the duty of breaking the strikes. When on July 25 practically all the roads in the central and western states joined the freight blockade, President Hayes forbade interference with the trains, attacks upon property, and any riotous conduct as rebellion against the government of the United States, and he threatened to declare martial law throughout the land and to occupy all disturbed territories with federal troops. The cabinet discussed with him the advisability of calling on the militia of one state to proceed against the strikers of another. An invitation was issued by the Pennsylvania Railroad to all the trunk lines for a meeting in New York for the purpose of combining against the Brotherhood of Locomotive Engineers and the Trainmen's Union, and of determining to employ no one, after a specified date, who belonged to a trade-union. Detectives were engaged to discover the leaders in the strikes with the intention of prosecuting them for impeding the transportation of freight over the railroads.

As the strikes moved westward they extended to other industries and in many localities began to assume the proportions of a general strike. Such a situation grew up in Chicago, commencing simply enough with a strike on July 24 at the Michigan Central freight yards. The wave passed from yard to yard, and then to factories and shops, until there prevailed what approached a general strike. In a sub-headline the *New York Times* announced: THE CITY IN POSSESSION OF COMMUNISTS. The following day the police attacked the strikers with clubs and guns at the Michigan Central freight yards and arrested their leaders; nevertheless the strike spread. All street cars were halted on the South Side. The sailors in the port walked out. A crowd of 8,000 at the Chicago, Burlington and Quincy roundhouse was dispersed only after three were killed and seven wounded. The "respectable elements" held a mass

THE GREAT STRIKE. Scenes of Riot in Chicago—Fight between the Military and the Rioters at the Halsted Street Viaduct. From sketches by C. and A. T. Sears. (*Harper's*

meeting at the Tabernacle, at which the Rev. Robert Callyer declared: "As God lives, and as my soul lives, I would rather die in 20 minutes in defense of order and of our homes against these men than live 20 years of as happy a life as I have lived these 50 years." [19] The Board of Trade dispatched to President Hayes and to Governor Cullom of Illinois urgent requests for troops, and enrolled 5,000 citizen volunteers as special deputies. Secretary of War McCrary sent couriers to General Sheridan, who was then campaigning against the Indians in the Sioux country, commanding him to return immediately with his forces to Chicago.

The Workingmen's Party in Chicago (the Workingmen's Party of America, founded in July, 1876, was especially strong in Chicago) appointed an Executive Committee and attempted to gain control of the strike movement.[20] It issued circulars declaring that the movement had the sympathy of the people, that all workers should unite with the strikers, and that all industrial establishments were to shut down. The leaders of the Party, among them Albert Parsons, urged the strikers to remain peaceable, but firm. Mayor Monroe Heath sent for Parsons, and told him to quit addressing the strikers and to go back to Texas, for "those Board of Trade men would as leave hang you to a lamppost as not." [21] On Thursday morning, July 26, a crowd of 10,000, assembled at the Halsted Street Viaduct, beat back a police attack with stones and bricks. Soldiers and mounted police arrived, with orders to make every shot tell. At least 12 workers were killed, and fully 100 leaders arrested. The city was patrolled by six companies of the Twenty-second Regular Infantry, the entire Ninth Regular, two regiments of state militia, a battery of artillery, several companies of cavalry, 5,000 special deputies, 500 veteran soldiers, and members of various patriotic organizations like the Ellsworth Zouaves, besides the regular police force. Each day additional federal troops returned from the Indian wars and marched into the city. In the street fighting, between 30 and 50 men and women were killed and about 100 wounded. On July 28 the first freight train was sent east under military protection.

During these same days a more complete general strike, almost revolutionary in character, was in force at St. Louis under the direction of the Workingmen's Party. The Executive Committee declared that for the strikers there could be no middle ground, either absolute victory or defeat. Delegations of strikers visited all shops, mills, and factories to call out the workers. Steamers were stopped on the Mississippi until their captains granted wage increases. Many concerns acceded to the demands of the Executive Committee: the Laclede Gas Works restored a 25-cent cut in daily wages made on July 1, and the coopers had the price for handmade barrels restored from 9 cents to 12. A mass meeting at Lucas Market demanded the eight-hour day, and charged all the bloodshed in the strikes to President Hayes for sending the army to put down men struggling for their rights. Mayor Overstolz closed all places of business until the strike could be suppressed, and called for citizen volunteers. Merchants and business men raised $15,000 to arm 1,000 volunteers; 8,000 muskets arrived from the Rock Island Arsenal.

When Governor Phelps threatened to declare martial law, a dispatch was sent to him:

To the Hon. John S. Phelps, Governor of the State of Missouri, and all Citizens:

We request your speedy co-operation in convening the Legislature, and calling for the immediate passage of the eight-hour law, its stringent enforcement, and a penalty for all violations of the same; the non-employment of all chil-

*dren under 14 years of age in factories, shops or other uses
calculated to injure them. Your attention is respectfully
called to the fact that a prompt compliance with our reasonable demands, and living wages paid to the railroad men,
will at once bring peace and prosperity such as we have not
seen for the last 15 years. Nothing short of a compliance to
the above just demand, made purely in the interest of our
national welfare, will arrest this tidal wave of revolution.
Threats or organized armies will not turn the toilers of this
nation from their earnest purpose, but rather serve to in-
flame the passions of the multitude and tend to acts of
vandalism. Yours, in the nation's welfare.*

EXECUTIVE COMMITTEE,
United Working Men of St. Louis.[22]

From Mayor Overstolz the Committee demanded food for
the starving workers and offered to pay for it. But the
Committee had overestimated the revolutionary trend of the
strikes elsewhere, and found itself isolated by July 27 and
28, facing the combined military forces mustered by Mayor
Overstolz, Governor Phelps of Missouri, Governor Cullom
of Illinois, and President Hayes. Police raided Schuler's
Hall, headquarters of the strike. The members of the Executive Committee were searched out and arrested on charges
of conspiracy, and bail was set at $3,000 each, so that they
had to remain in prison. The revolutionary organization
had been broken after five days of control.

On the first of August only a few stubborn localities remained on strike. At San Francisco, where the strike movement deviated into race riots directed against the Chinese
cheap labor that had thrown many out of work, the 3,000
vigilantes, who had been armed by a fund of $60,000 raised
among merchants and business men, were dismissed. The
Lake Shore men at Cleveland agreed to a compromise with

their employers that adjusted some of their grievances but left the wage reductions in effect. When the freight blockade on the Pittsburgh, Fort Wayne and Chicago Railroad was still unbroken at the end of July, Colonel Scott of the Pennsylvania Railroad requested federal troops from Secretary of War McCrary; and in spite of the absence of any formal request from Governor Williams of Indiana or from Governor Young of Ohio, General Hancock was sent from Pittsburgh. In St. Louis the Citizens' Guard was disbanded and on Monday, July 30, general business was resumed. Four members of the Executive Committee—Curlin, Cope, Fischer, and Lofgreen—were sentenced to five years in the penitentiary and fined $2,000 each. With the military everywhere in complete control the President was able to discontinue on July 29 the daily emergency conferences with his cabinet. The Russo-Turkish war began once more to share the front pages with the strikes.

6. The right to work

Practically all the strikes had been defeated after the two weeks' struggle from July 16 to August 1, but not before society saw plainly that the land of opportunity, with its traditions of the sanctity of private property and of freedom of contract, had been converted into the battleground for a bitter war between two essentially hostile economic classes. As the early stages of capitalism, in which numerous small competitive industries flourished and the relations between employer and employee were personal and individual, yielded to a more mature stage, that of the combination and monopolization of industry and finance, fundamental changes occurred in the economic structure of society and in the principles on which it was erected. For the first time in its history the country had been swept by a general-strike movement, and workmen had challenged their employers not as discrete local groups, but as a nation-wide mass. The supporters of the existing structure became frightened at the sudden vision of violent strife.

The immediate effect was the widespread demand by the press for the swift and relentless punishment of those strike leaders who had been arrested. The *New York Times* wrote:

There is a goodly number of the ring-leaders of last week's riots now in custody. . . . A lasting service can be performed at once to the class to which these men belong and to the interests of the community at large by making salutary examples of all who have been taken red-handed in riot and bloodshed.[23]

The *Nation* wrote:

The kindest thing which can be done for the great multitudes of untaught men who have been received on these shores, and are daily arriving, and who are torn perhaps even more here than in Europe by wild desires and wilder dreams, is to show them promptly that society as here organized, on individual freedom of thought and action, is impregnable, and can be no more shaken than the order of nature. The most cruel thing is to let them suppose, even for one week, that if they had only chosen their time better, or had been better led or better armed, they would have succeeded in forcing it to capitulate. In what way better provision, in the shape of public force, should be made for its defense we have no space left to discuss, but that it will not do to be caught again as the rising at Martinsburg caught us; that it would be fatal to private and public credit and security to allow a state of things to subsist in which 8,000 or 9,000 day-laborers of the lowest class can suspend, even for a whole day, the traffic and industry of a great nation, merely as a means of extorting ten or twenty cents a day more wages from their employers, we presume everybody now sees.[24]

Furthermore, the press called for a stronger and more efficient military force. The weakness and unreliability of the state militia, many of whom had refused to fire upon the strikers, were now recognized. The *New York Times* wanted a better organized militia and a greater liberality in its support by the states. Both the *New York Times* and the *Nation* asked for an increase of at least 25,000 in the regular army, which was trained, dependable, and impersonal in its action. In an article printed by the *North American Review*, September, 1877, President Thomas A. Scott of the Pennsylvania Railroad urged that federal troops might be called out even without the governor's request, and that the government redistribute its forces more strategically throughout the nation so that they might be moved instantly to any point. The construction of the strong armories in the larger cities dates from this year.[25]

At the same time the employers opened an attack upon all labor organizations, whether fraternal, political, or trade-union in function. Even the compliant Brotherhood of Railway Conductors, whose members had acted as strike-breakers during the railroad uprisings, suffered the opposition of the railroad officials. At its annual convention in the autumn of 1877, it appointed a committee to wait on the officials of the Pennsylvania, the Philadelphia and Erie, and other roads in the East, with the purpose of explaining the innocent objects and principles of a fraternal order, and of reminding them of the Brotherhood's loyalty during the recent strikes. Grand Chief Conductor Wheaton headed the committee, which set a date for an interview with President Scott of the Pennsylvania. Twice the committee journeyed to Philadelphia to keep the appointment and twice it was humiliated by being refused admittance. After that Wheaton wrote a letter of explanation, to which Scott replied curtly.[26] Many workers were forced to pledge that they would join no labor organization. Trade-union members and labor leaders were mercilessly blacklisted. The courts, moreover, revived the doctrine of malicious conspiracy as applied to labor combinations, and conspiracy laws aimed at labor were enacted by many state legislatures.[27] Labor confronted a powerful and well-organized movement to suppress all its attempts to unite, either for reform of, or bargaining about, conditions of work.

In the course of the strikes and their aftermath workingmen grew steadily more aware of the dilemma which faced them whenever they made a concerted attempt to improve their condition. Ultimately they came into conflict with the principles of private property and freedom of contract. If they accepted these, then they had to submit peacefully to whatever conditions their employers imposed upon them; for no strike could be effective without picketing as long as the employers had a bottomless reservoir of unemployed workers—a reservoir artificially created by the encouragement of immigration—to replace the "disaffected elements." The right to strike was meaningless without the right to picket. And to picket, there could be no doubt, was to assault both private property and freedom of contract. Such was the rigor of the logic underlying the struggle between the workmen and their employers, and no compromise seemed possible.

This conclusion, pressed upon the strikers by their recent experiences, was reinforced by the tone of the comments in the press, on the platform, and in the pulpit. The right to strike, for example, was conceded by the *Nation*, but not the right to picket, without which the strike remained an ineffectual weapon:

It is worse than useless to dignify these transactions by calling them disputes between labor and capital. The right to strike is conceded by everybody. The right to seize other people's property and to prevent other men from selling their labor on terms satisfactory to themselves is denied by the law of every civilized country. Common sense does not allow any parleying over that fallacy, but insists that it be refuted with gunpowder and ball whenever it takes the shape of combined robbery and public tumult. Society does not owe any particular rate of wages to anybody.[28]

And the same principles were asserted by the Rev. Henry Ward Beecher in a sermon at the Plymouth Church in New York on Sunday evening, July 29:

We look upon the importation of the communistic and like European notions as abominations. Their notions and theories that the Government should be paternal and take care of the welfare of its subjects and provide them with labor, is un-American. It is the form in which oppression has had its most disastrous scope in the world. The American doctrine is that it is the duty of the Government merely to protect the people while they are taking care of themselves—nothing more than that. "Hands off," we say to the Government; "see to it that we are protected in our rights and in our individuality. No more than that." The theories of Europe in regard to the community of property we reject because they are against natural law and will never be practicable. God has intended the great to be great, and the little to be little. No equalization process can ever take place until men are made equal as productive forces. It is a wild vision, not a practicable theory. The European theories of combinations between workmen and trades-unions and communes destroy the individuality of the person, and there is no possible way of preserving the liberty of the people except by the maintenance of individual liberty, intact from Government and intact from individual meddling. Persons have the right to work when or where they please, as long as they please, and for what they please, and any attempt to infringe on this right, and to put good workmen on a level with poor workmen— any such attempt to regiment labor is preposterous.[29]

The dilemma of labor was inescapable, and strikes in their final stage had to contend against all the military and legal force of the nation.

Nevertheless, the moral effect of the strikes upon the working class was invigorating. A new spirit of labor solidarity was born and made national. The workers understood that the failure of the railroad strikes was due to their want of organization and to the refusal of all branches of railroad labor to act in unison. As a result of this realization, the four Brotherhoods (the Brotherhood of Railway Trainmen was formed in 1883) began to assume the trade-union function of collective bargaining in addition to their fraternal duties. Also trades councils, unions, and assemblies came into existence and multiplied rapidly in the principal cities. Many of these organizations had to remain secret because of the active opposition of the employers. In the next two years labor parties, like the Workingmen's Party, which late in 1877 changed its name to the Socialist Labor Party, gained thousands of members and put forth political candidates. The wars had only begun.

II. HAYMARKET

1. The eight-hour movement

The bomb which killed seven policemen and wounded 60 more near Haymarket Square in Chicago on the night of May 4, 1886, provoked a national convulsion of deeply fixed and violent prejudices. Press and pulpit let loose a stream of vituperation and terroristic incitement never before equaled in an industrial struggle in this land. When eight men were arrested and tried for the deed, they were frankly and openly convicted, not on any evidence of participation in the bombing, but because of the economic and social ideas they had preached. It then became clear to American labor that the courts were being used to convict labor leaders on tampered evidence. Working people in all sections of the country felt that they had martyrs to remember and avenge. So sharp and profound, in fact, was the split in public opinion concerning this affair that seven years afterward Governor Altgeld of Illinois, in his attempt to rectify what he believed a legal injustice, was made to sacrifice his political and financial career.

Two currents in the labor movement converged at Haymarket: the demand for an eight-hour day, and the introduction of a modified anarchism into labor theory and practice. The movement for a shorter working day was not new. As early as 1829 there had been a demand in the New York State general assembly for legislation on the reduction of hours, and toward the middle of the century Grand Eight-hour Leagues were formed in the principal cities and manufacturing centers of the North. Not until after the Civil War, however, did the demand grow vigorously. Nevertheless, even though 19 states and one territory had prescribed the hours of labor by 1886, the laws were rendered ineffectual by clauses permitting contracts for longer working days. As a result the average day was between 14 and 18 hours, rather than eight or 10. "In Minnesota, the legislature has found it necessary to impose a penalty of from $25 to $100, to be inflicted upon any officer or employé of a railroad company who compels a locomotive engineer or fireman to labor more than *eighteen* hours a day, except in cases of urgent necessity." [1]

Thus legislative action failed to bring about a shorter day. The eight-hour movement was too revolutionary to be fulfilled without the compulsion of a strong labor organization. The press ridiculed and abused the demand as outrageous; the *Illinois State Register*, for instance, declared that the ". . . one most consummate piece of humbuggery ever suggested in connection with the 'labor question' is the so-called 'eight hour movement.' The thing is really too silly to merit the attention of a body of lunatics . . . and the idea of 'striking' for eight hours is about as sensible as 'striking' for pay without the hours." [2] And what remained of labor organization after the railroad strikes of 1877 was well battered. It was limited to skilled workmen and was opportunistic, exhibiting neither class solidarity nor aggressiveness, each local striving alone. With the more rapid introduction of machinery in the early 1880's there was a great increase in the numbers of unskilled and semi-skilled workers, who, because of their lack of organization, possessed inferior bargaining powers. Wages went down and hours of work multiplied under the steady pressure exerted by certain economic factors: prices were forced down, for example, by the keen competition among wholesalers and jobbers. The reservoir of labor, furthermore, was flooded by the shift of population from country to city, by the peak wave of immigration for the century, and by the exhaustion of the public domain. In addition to the pressure of these factors, the worker faced the newly formed pools of the manufacturers in the chief industries. "American labour was now permanently shut up in the wage system." [3]

It was true that a widespread labor organization existed— the Noble Order of the Knights of Labor, founded in 1869 as a secret brotherhood, but made public in 1881. The Knights, it was also true, welcomed all workmen, irrespective of trade, and particularly the unskilled and semi-skilled. The leaders, however, were unwilling to take up so revolutionary a demand as that for a shorter day. It was left for the much younger and weaker Federation of Organized Trades and Labor Unions (forerunner of the American Federation of Labor) to assume the leadership of the national eight-hour movement. At its Chicago convention, October 7, 1884, it passed the following resolution and invited the Knights of Labor to coöperate:

Resolved, *By the Federation of Organised Trades and Labor Unions of the United States and Canada, that eight hours shall constitute a legal day's labour from and after May 1, 1886, and that we recommend to labour organisations throughout this jurisdiction that they so direct their laws as to conform to this resolution by the time named.*[4]

But the Federation failed to make effective preparation, either by collecting monies for strike benefits if needed, or by proper education and agitation. Without the help of the Knights of Labor, the Federation and its membership of less than 50,000 could not succeed.

Among the workmen throughout the country, embittered by wage reductions, long hours, and unemployment, there was an enthusiastic response to the resolution. A shorter day would furnish jobs for the unemployed and would provide the worker with leisure in which to educate and enjoy himself. Once more a feeling of solidarity spread among the working class, to be heightened by the depression of 1884-1885. Inasmuch as the Knights of Labor was already a numerous group, the unorganized masses flocked to it as the date for the struggle drew near. The Knights grew from 989 local assemblies with 104,066 members in July, 1885, to 5,892 assemblies with 702,924 members in July, 1886, the bulk of the increase coming after January 1, 1886.[5] The attraction of the Knights for the unorganized workers was made all the stronger by the militant boycotts which it conducted in 1885 against many establishments hostile to union labor, and by the successful strike which it led against the three Gould railroads—the Wabash; the Missouri, Kansas and Texas; and the Missouri Pacific—in March of the same year. Despite the reluctance of its leaders, the Knights of Labor found itself the spear-head of what promised to be a fierce drive upon capital.

As the eight-hour movement gathered momentum with the approach of May 1, the officials of the Knights of Labor tried to suppress it and withdraw from it. Already the boycotts conducted in 1885 had brought upon them the condemnation of the churches and a command forbidding Catholics from joining the Knights. The press animosity now evoked by the eight-hour demand frightened them: there was too much talk of socialism and revolution. The *Chicago Mail* wrote, April 29, 1886: "In addition to eight hours they wanted everything else that the craziest socialist or the maddest anarchist could suggest." The *New York Times*, May 1: "Strikes to enforce the demand for eight hours' work a day may do much to paralyze industry, depress business, and check the reviving prosperity of the country, but they cannot succeed." The *Philadelphia Telegram*, May 1: " 'The labor element' has been bitten by a kind of universal tarantula—it has gone 'dancing mad.' To think of inaugurating a great strike at this juncture for the eight-hour system!" The *Indianapolis Journal*, May 3: "Street parades, red flags, fiery harangues by scoundrels and demagogues, who are living off the savings of honest but deluded men, strikes and threatened violence mark the inauguration of the movement." [6]

At the General Assembly of the Knights of Labor in 1885 the officials had attempted to suppress the movement by granting little consideration to a resolution in its support. And then, almost on the eve of the struggle, March 13, 1886, Grand Master Workman Powderly issued a secret circular against the eight-hour movement:

No assembly of the Knights of Labor must strike for the eight hour system on May first under the impression that they are obeying orders from headquarters, for such an order was not, and will not, be given. Neither employer or employe are educated to the needs and necessities for the short hour plan. If one branch of trade or one assembly is in such a condition, remember that there are many who are in total ignorance of the movement. Out of the sixty millions of people in the United States and Canada, our order has possibly three hundred thousand. Can we mould the sentiment of the millions in favor of the short hour plan before May first? It is nonsense to think of it. Let us learn why our hours of labor should be reduced, and then teach others.[7]

Later this circular, when the rank and file learned of it, was to cost the Noble Order thousands of members, if not its existence. In the meantime the workers, unaware that their leaders had pulled their punch at the last moment, pressed on into the struggle in New York, Philadelphia, Chicago,

Louisville, St. Louis, Milwaukee, Baltimore. On May 1 at least 190,000 struck for a shorter day, while an additional 150,000 secured their demands merely by the threat of a strike. Thus the total number of workers in the movement was 340,000.[8]

2. Anarchism and the Chicago idea

Just as the panic of 1873 marked the birth of a national and self-conscious labor movement, it also marked the birth of a practical and realistic socialism, to replace the remote Utopian wishes of the earlier Socialists, contented with lofty intellectual conversations and romantic essays. From this time the Socialists, rather than hope idealistically for the morrow, began to act in the today by organizing hunger parades, unemployed demonstrations, strikes, mass meetings, and political tickets. At first they operated as the Working-men's Party of the United States, which was formed in 1876, and which played, as we have seen, a considerable part in the railroad strikes of 1877, especially in Chicago and St. Louis. After the failure of the railroad strikes the Workingmen's Party was reorganized as the Socialist Labor Party, with political action as its principal function, although friendly relations with trade-unions were to be maintained. When this change was made, the National Executive Committee of the Socialist Labor Party ordered the holding of mass meetings to present to legislative bodies resolutions for an eight-hour law, for the abolition of all conspiracy acts directed against labor, and for the purchase of railway and telegraph lines by the federal government.

But the socialist movement in America reflected the schism that had taken place in the First International, and split into two factions over questions of tactics and method. The Internationalists held for secret arming and direct preparation for the social revolution, with trade-unionism and politics as auxiliary activities to be strictly watched lest they led into the treacherous waters of opportunism. The Lassalleans, on the other hand, sought the gradual achievement of a new society through education, political organization, and parliamentary procedure. For a few years the Lassalleans controlled the policies of the party, and even Chicago, the stronghold of the trade-union and the revolutionary elements, dedicated itself to the ballot. A controversy soon arose, however, over the workingmen's military organizations. The largest of these, the *Lehr und Wehr Verein*, had been formed by the German Socialists in Chicago during 1875 as a protection against the physical intimidation of the older political parties at the polls; the need for its protection had further been shown during a strike of cabinetmakers in July, 1877, when the police raided peaceful meetings and attacked those present with outrageous brutality. A repudiation, therefore, of all such military organizations by the National Executive Committee of the Socialist Labor Party antagonized still more the Chicago revolutionary element. This hostility grew acute in 1880 after the discouraging slump of the Socialist vote in the elections; and the revolutionaries denounced the moderates for a compromise made that year with the Greenback Party. Moreover, the single Socialist alderman reëlected in Chicago was barred from taking his seat, through tricky manipulation by the Democratic city council; and the revolutionaries pointed out the futility of attempting to win a new society through the ballot-box. A great influx of refugees from the German anti-Socialist decree of 1878 augmented the revolutionary groups, and led finally to a convention of them in October, 1881, at Chicago.

Not until the arrival of Johann Most in America did the revolutionary groups precipitate into an active movement. The appearance of Most—disciple of Bakounin and Nechayeff, and founder of the anarchistic International Working People's Association, known then as the Black International —swept aside the parliamentary Socialists. In theory Most was not a pure anarchist; nevertheless, in practice he advocated the anarchist tactics of terroristic action against Church and State by the individual on his own initiative, so that the entire movement might not be endangered if the actor in any single deed were captured. Arms alone, he believed, secured for the worker some sort of equality with the police and troops. He issued a pamphlet: *Science of Revolutionary Warfare. Manual for instruction in the use and preparation of nitro-glycerine and dynamite, gun cotton, fulminating mercury, bombs, fuse, poisons, etc., etc.* He urged the formation of rifle corps and the extermination of the "miserable brood," the "reptile brood," the "race of parasites." In another pamphlet, *Beast of Property*, he declared that with existing society there could be no compromise, only relentless war until the beast of property "has been pursued to its last lurking place and totally destroyed."

Spurred on by the agitational energy of Most, representatives from revolutionary anti-parliamentary groups in 26 cities convened in Pittsburgh on October 14, 1883, to reorganize the International Working People's Association. Here again there were two distinct elements, united only by their opposition to political action. The delegates from New York and the eastern cities, led by Most, favored the individualistic tactics of anarchism; but those from Chicago and the western cities, under the guidance of Albert Parsons and August Spies, held for a mixture of anarchism and syndicalism that came to be known as the "Chicago idea." This modification actually approached syndicalism closer than it did anarchism, inasmuch as it recognized the trade-union as the "embryonic group" of the future society and as the fighting unit against capitalism. However, the trade-union was not to contend for the superficial and opportunistic benefits of high wages and short hours; it was to be satisfied with nothing less than the complete extinction of capitalism and the formation of a free society. In the struggle with capitalism it was not to resort to political action, was to distrust all central authority, and was to guard against betrayals by its leadership. All its faith was to rest in the direct action of the rank and file. Only two principles were lacking to make the "Chicago idea" conform with modern syndicalism: the general strike and sabotage, neither at that time theoretically developed.[9]

Since the western faction was by far the larger, the convention confirmed the importance of the trade-union. And direct action—force, violence—was the core of the tactics to be employed. The platform of the International, published in the *Alarm*, a Chicago paper edited by Parsons, read in part:

The present order of society is based upon the spoliation of the non-property by the property owners, the capitalists buy the labor of the poor for wages, at the mere cost of living, taking all the surplus of labor. . . . Thus while the poor are increasingly deprived the opportunities of advancement, the rich grow richer through increasing robbery. . .
This system is unjust, insane, and murderous. Therefore those who suffer under it, and do not wish to be responsible for its continuance, ought to strive for its destruction by all means and with their utmost energy. . . . The laborers can look for aid from no outside source in their fight against the existing system, but must achieve deliverance through their own exertions. Hitherto, no privileged class have relinquished tyranny, nor will the capitalists of to-day forego their privilege and authority without compulsion. . . . It is therefore self-evident that the fight of proletarianism against

*the bourgeoisie must have a violent revolutionary character;
that wage conflicts cannot lead to the goal. . . . Under all
these circumstances, there is only one remedy left—force.
. . . Agitation to organize, organizations for the purpose
of rebellion, this is the course if the workingmen would rid
themselves of their chains.*[10]

Here was a program advocating without camouflage the
annihilation of the existing economic and political order, a
program that could not be ignored.

In Chicago, thanks to the long history of police atrocities,
many workers joined the International, so that this city
alone had more than one-third of the 5,000 to 6,000 members.
Moreover, the most able and intelligent leaders were here—
men like Parsons, Spies, Samuel Fielden, and Michael
Schwab. In fact, the Internationalists in Chicago published
five papers: the *Alarm* in English, with an edition of 2,000
twice a month; in German, the daily *Chicagoer Arbeiter-
Zeitung*, edited by Spies, with an edition of 3,600, the
Fackel, and the *Vorbote*; and in Bohemian, the *Budoucnost*.
This revolutionary nucleus quickly penetrated the trade-
union movement. Under its influence the local Progressive
Cigar Makers' Union in June, 1884, called upon all the
unions in the city to secede from the conservative Amalgamated Trades and Labor Assembly and to organize a new
Central Labor Union with a militant policy. Four German
unions answered the call—the metal workers, butchers, car-
penters and joiners, and cabinetmakers—and a declaration
of principles was adopted: that all land is a social heritage,
that all wealth is created by labor, that between labor and
capital there can be no harmony, and that every worker
ought to cut loose from the capitalist political parties and
devote himself to the trade-union. From its inception the
Central Labor Union was in communication with the Inter-

nationalist group. The Socialist Labor Party, on the other hand, remained with the Amalgamated Trades and Labor Assembly.

For a year the growth of the new Central Labor Union was slow; nevertheless, by the end of 1885 it had 13 unions, whereas the Amalgamated Assembly had 19. Within a few months, however, by April, 1886, the Central Labor Union outstripped its rival and consisted of 22 unions, among which were the 11 largest in the city. It retained its contact with the International and united with it in processions and mass meetings. It began strong agitation for the eight-hour day, although its motives were different from those of the conservative Amalgamated Assembly and the Knights of Labor, since it regarded as paramount, not the attainment of the shorter working day, but the common labor front and the class struggle. It adopted the following resolution, introduced by Spies in October, 1885:

> *Be it Resolved, That we urgently call upon the wage-earning class to arm itself in order to be able to put forth against their exploiters such an argument which alone can be effective:* Violence, *and further be it Resolved, that notwithstanding that we expect very little from the introduction of the eight-hour day, we firmly promise to assist our more backward brethren in this class struggle with all means and power at our disposal, so long as they will continue to show an open and resolute front to our common oppressors, the aristocratic vagabonds and the exploiters. Our war-cry is "Death to the foes of the human race."* [11]

The initiative in the eight-hour movement in Chicago was left in the hands of an Eight-Hour Association, composed of the Amalgamated Assembly, the Socialist Labor Party, and the Knights of Labor, but the Central Labor Union co-operated energetically. On the Sunday preceding May 1 it organized a huge eight-hour demonstration, in which 25,000 took part, and at which Parsons, Spies, Fielden, and Schwab spoke. When the day of the struggle arrived, the main portion of the eight-hour movement in Chicago acted under the banner of the Central Labor Union and the International.

3. The bomb is thrown

The strike opened in Chicago with a display of great strength and much promise of success. Nearly 40,000 workers walked out on May 1 as prearranged, and the number jumped to 65,000 within three or four days.[12] Nor was this the full strength of the movement in the city: more than 45,-000 were granted a shorter working day without striking, the bulk of them—35,000—workers in the packing-houses.[13] In addition, there were already several thousand men on strike at the Lake Shore, the Wabash, the Chicago, Milwaukee and St. Paul, and other freight yards in protest against the hiring of non-union labor. With such a mass movement on foot, Chief of Police Ebersold apprehended difficulties and called upon the entire detective and police force to be on duty Saturday, May 1; and his force was augmented by Pinkerton detectives previously engaged by the railroads, and by special deputies, many of whom were selected from the Grand Army of the Potomac. In spite of these martial preparations, Saturday passed peacefully. The city, with hundreds of factories idle and thousands of strikers and their families promenading the streets, had a holiday appearance. There were processions and mass meetings, addressed in Bohemian, Polish, German, and English.

Faced with a strike of unexpected power and solidarity, the leading business men and manufacturers united to crush it. On April 27 the Western Boot and Shoe Manufacturers Association, with 60 firms represented in person and 160 by letter, was formed in Chicago for combined action. The chief iron and steel foundries, as also the copper and brass, declared that they would reject the eight-hour demand. A session of the principal planing mills was held on the morning of May 1 at the office of Felix Lang to determine procedure against the strikers. In the evening these were joined at the Sherman Hotel by all the lumber yards and box factories, and the lumber industry in concert decided to grant no concessions to the workmen. Nevertheless, by Monday, May 3, the spread of the strike was alarming. Lumber-laden craft blocked the river near the Lumber Exchange, and 300 more vessels with cargoes of lumber were expected to join the idle fleet. The building interests, then enjoying a boom, were suddenly paralyzed. The great metal foundries and the vast freight yards were tied up. To break the strike aggressive action was needed. On Monday police clubs began to scatter processions and meetings.

That afternoon serious trouble arose at the McCormick Harvester Works. The soreness here was old. It had begun in the middle of February, when Cyrus McCormick locked out his 1,400 employees in reply to a demand by the men that the company quit its discrimination against certain of their fellows who had taken part in a former strike at the plant. In the following two months strike-breakers, Pinkertons, and police had attacked the locked-out men with wanton savagery. Bogart and Thompson say of this period:

The police force of Chicago reflected the hostility of the employing class, regarding strikes per se *as evidence that the men had placed themselves in opposition to law and order. During these months of unrest it became a pastime for a squad of mounted police, or a detachment in close formation, to disperse with the billy any gathering of workingmen. The billy was an impartial instrument: men, women,*

children, and shop-keeping bystanders alike composed its
harvest. It was the police, aided by the "Pinkertons," who
added the great leaven of bitterness to the contest. To the
workingmen they furnished concrete and hateful examples
of the autocracy against which they protested.[14]

But a greater police provocation was reserved for Monday
afternoon, May 3. At this time 6,000 striking lumber-shovers
met near Black Road, about a quarter of a mile north of
the McCormick works, to appoint a committee to be sent to
the lumber-yard owners. While August Spies was addressing the meeting, a group of some 200 detached itself spontaneously from the crowd of strikers, marched to McCormick's, and heckled and attacked the scabs, who were just
then leaving for their homes. Within 10 or 15 minutes
there were more than 200 policemen on the spot. Meanwhile Spies, who was still speaking, and the strikers at the
meeting, seeing patrol wagons and hearing gunfire, started
toward McCormick's, but were met by the police. The clubs
and guns broke up the crowd; the police fired deliberately
into the running strikers, so that at least four were killed and
many wounded.

Spies, indignant at this fresh outrage, hurried to the
printing shop of the *Arbeiter-Zeitung* and issued a circular
in both English and German:

REVENGE!

WORKINGMEN, TO ARMS!!!

The masters sent out their bloodhounds—the police; they
killed six of your brothers at McCormicks this afternoon.
They killed the poor wretches because they, like you, had
the courage to disobey the supreme will of your bosses. They
killed them because they dared ask for the shortening of the
hours of toil. They killed them to show you, 'Free American

Attention Workingmen!

GREAT

MASS-MEETING

TO-NIGHT, at 7.30 o'clock,

AT THE

HAYMARKET, Randolph St., Bet. Desplaines and Halsted.

Good Speakers will be present to denounce the latest atrocious act of the police, the shooting of our fellow-workmen yesterday afternoon.

Workingmen Arm Yourselves and Appear in Full Force!

THE EXECUTIVE COMMITTEE

Achtung, Arbeiter!

Große

Massen-Versammlung

Heute Abend, ½8 Uhr, auf dem

Heumarkt, Randolph-Straße, zwischen Desplaines- u. Halsted-Str.

☞ Gute Redner werden den neuesten Schurkenstreich der Polizei, indem sie gestern Nachmittag unsere Brüder erschoß, geißeln,

☞ Arbeiter, bewaffnet Euch und erscheint massenhaft!

Das Executiv-Comite.

AN ANARCHIST HANDBILL. (The *Century Magazine*, April, 1893)

Citizens' that you must be satisfied and contented with whatever your bosses condescend to allow you, or you will get killed!

You have for years endured the most abject humiliations; you have for years suffered unmeasurable iniquities; you have worked yourself to death; you have endured the pangs of want and hunger; your Children you have sacrificed to the factory lord—in short: you have been miserable and obedient slave[s] all these years: Why? To satisfy the insatiable greed, to fill the coffers of your lazy thieving master? When you ask them now to lessen your burdens, he sends his bloodhounds out to shoot you, kill you!

If you are men, if you are the sons of your grand sires, who have shed their blood to free you, then you will rise in your might, Hercules, and destroy the hideous monster that seeks to destroy you. To arms we call you, to arms!

YOUR BROTHERS.[15]

A second circular called for a protest mass meeting the following evening in the old Haymarket on Randolph Street.

The morning of Tuesday, May 4, saw a police attack upon a column of 3,000 strikers near Thirty-fifth Street. Attacks upon gatherings of strikers continued during the afternoon, in particular one at Eighteenth and Morgan in the southwest part of the city. Mayor Carter H. Harrison, however, gave permission for the mass meeting that evening, and at 7:30 people began to assemble in Haymarket Square, the center of the lumber-yard and packing-house district. Between eight and nine o'clock about 3,000 persons were present, among them Mayor Harrison, who attended as a spectator to see that order was maintained. Only half a block distant was the Desplaines Street police station, where a good-sized detail of police was in readiness. The meeting was very quiet. Spies addressed the crowd from a wagon in front of the

Crane Bros. factory. Then Parsons spoke, confining himself
to the eight-hour demand; he was followed by Fielden. Toward 10 o'clock a threatening rainstorm began to disperse
the gathering; by that time Spies and Parsons had left.
Only Fielden remained to speak to the few hundred who had
not yet gone. Mayor Harrison, having found the meeting
peaceful and believing that all was over, left shortly after 10
o'clock, called in at the Desplaines Street station to report
that there had been no trouble, and went home to bed.

A few minutes after the mayor left, however, Inspector
John Bonfield, hated throughout the city for his record of
extreme brutality, led a detachment of 180 policemen to
break up what remained of the meeting. There was no excuse for this expedition, except Bonfield's desire for another
head-clubbing party, according to Governor Altgeld, who
declared ". . . that Capt. Bonfield is the man who is really
responsible for the death of the police officers." [16] The police
halted a short distance from the speakers' wagon, and
Captain Ward commanded the gathering to disperse. Fielden
cried out that it was a peaceable meeting. As Captain Ward
turned to give an order to his men, a bomb was thrown from
a point on the sidewalk a little south of the wagon. It exploded in the midst of the policemen and wounded 66, of
whom seven later died. The police immediately opened fire
hysterically and shot round after round into the crowd, killing several and wounding 200. The neighborhood was
thrown into terror. Doctors were telephoned. Drug stores
were crowded with the wounded.

Who threw the bomb is still undetermined. There are three
possibilities. (1) Governor Altgeld, in his pardon message
of 1893, contended that the bomb was thrown by someone
as reprisal for all the atrocities committed by Bonfield and
the police:

. . . it is shown here that the bomb was, in all probability, thrown by someone seeking personal revenge; that a course had been pursued by the authorities which would naturally cause this; that for a number of years prior to the Haymarket affair there had been labor troubles, and in several cases a number of laboring people, guilty of no offense, had been shot down in cold blood by Pinkerton men, and none of the murderers were brought to justice. The evidence taken at coroners' inquests and presented here, shows that in at least two cases men were fired on and killed when they were running away, and there was consequently no occasion to shoot, yet nobody was punished; that in Chicago there had been a number of strikes in which some of the police not only took sides against the men, but without any authority of law invaded and broke up peaceable meetings, and in scores of cases brutally clubbed people who were guilty of no offense whatever.[17]

(2) The possibility of an *agent provocateur* must not be dismissed offhand. The police officials in Chicago were at this time quite equal to such a scheme. On the morning after the bombing, Inspector Bonfield declared:

We will take active measures to catch the leaders in this business. The action of last night will show that their bombshell and dynamite talk has not been empty vaporings. . . . *The attack on us was brutal and cowardly. . . . [Roman mine.]* [18]

The emphasized sentence indicates perhaps an antecedent wish to prove that the "dynamite talk" was not "empty vaporings."

(3) There is a strong possibility that Rudolph Schnaubelt, an anarchist and brother-in-law to Michael Schwab, was guilty. The circumstance that he was twice arrested and

both times released, at a period when the police were arresting and holding all the anarchists and sympathizers they could lay their hands on, arouses the suspicion, almost the certainty, that the police wanted him out of the way, in order that they might be able to condemn the eight more important revolutionary leaders. In this connection Bogart and Thompson report:

In a statement now on record in the Illinois Historical Survey, made by Mr. Wallace Rice, June 25, 1919, and concurred in by Mr. Clarence S. Darrow and Mr. George A. Schilling, all of whom were in a position to know the inside history of the case, Mr. Rice says: "It was the impression of all the newspaper men informed in the premises that the fatal bomb was made by Louis Lingg and thrown by Rudolph Schnaubelt. Many of them believed further that this fact was also known to the police and that Schnaubelt was allowed to go after they had taken him into custody because he could not be connected in any way with the other men afterward condemned, with the possible exception of Lingg and of Michael Schwab, who was husband to Schnaubelt's sister. Lingg, however, was thought to be the only one of the defendants who had guilty knowledge of the bomb and its throwing. Schnaubelt, after his release by the police, went as far and as fast from the scene of the crime as he could, and when an indictment was found against him at last, was believed to be in southern California near the Mexican line, whence he could easily escape to another country. . . ." [19]

Judge Gary, when reviewing the case seven years after the trial, admitted the strong likelihood of Schnaubelt's guilt, and the release twice by the police of the man who was the chief actual suspect. Gary added: "But whether Schnaubelt or some other person threw the bomb, is not an important question." [20]

The newspapers, not only in Chicago, but everywhere, assumed an attitude of panic. They demanded the instantaneous execution of all subversive persons. Within a few days the police arrested the chief anarchists and revolutionaries in the city—Spies, Fielden, Schwab, Adolph Fischer, George Engel, Louis Lingg, Oscar Neebe; and many others, including the 25 printers in the *Arbeiter-Zeitung* shop, were taken into custody. The only one missing was Parsons, whom the police were unable to capture, notwithstanding a rigorous hunt. When the death of police officer Mathias J. Degan was announced, the press cried for speedy indictments by the grand jury. It kept fanning for weeks the feeling of terror aroused in the public. Its headlines screamed: Bloody Brutes, Red Ruffians, Red Ragsters, Bomb Makers, Red Flagsters, Dynamarchists, Bloody Monsters, Bomb Slingers, Bomb Throwers. The *Chicago Tribune* wrote, May 6: "These serpents have been warmed and nourished in the sunshine of toleration until at last they have been emboldened to strike at society, law, order, and government." The *Chicago Herald*, May 6: "The rabble whom Spies and Fielden stimulated to murder are not Americans. They are offscourings of Europe who have sought these shores to abuse the hospitality and defy the authority of the country." The *Chicago Inter-Ocean*, May 6: "For months and years these pestiferous fellows have uttered their seditious and dangerous doctrines." The *Chicago Journal*, May 7: "Justice should be prompt in dealing with the arrested anarchists. The law regarding accessories to crime in this State is so plain that their trials will be short." [21]

Stimulation of public hysteria became the main activity of the police. Inspector Bonfield and Captain Schaack, in particular, wanted to sustain the ferment of dread and hatred after the bomb-throwing, in order to keep the citizenry excited. Three years later, in an interview, Chief of

Police Ebersold confessed: "It was my policy to quiet matters down as soon as possible after the 4th of May [1886]. The general unsettled state of things was an injury to Chicago. On the other hand, Capt. Schaack wanted to keep things stirring. He wanted bombs to be found here, there, all around, everywhere. . . . *After we got the anarchist societies broken up, Schaack wanted to send out men to again organize new societies right away.*" [22] The police seized the subscription lists of the *Arbeiter-Zeitung* and instituted a long series of raids. Meeting halls, printing offices, and private homes were broken into and searched; everyone suspected of the remotest connection with the radical movement was held. The police saw to it that the raids were fertile. Each day there were discovered ammunition, rifles, swords, muskets, pistols, bayonets, billies, anarchist literature, red flags, incendiary banners, cartridges, dirks, bullets, bulk lead, materials for manufacturing torpedoes, bullet molds, dynamite, bombs, shells, percussion caps, infernal engines, secret trap-doors, underground rifle ranges. Each find announced by the police was well played up by the press. A rumor was spread that Herr Most was coming from New York, evidently to take charge of further assassinations; and the police even produced a show of detectives at the railroad station. A crowd gathered to await the dangerous arrival, but Herr Most did not appear. The proper atmosphere for the trial was being carefully prepared.

4. *"Let the voice of the people be heard!"*

When the grand jury met in the middle of May, it quickly indicted August Spies, Michael Schwab, Samuel Fielden, Albert R. Parsons, Adolph Fischer, George Engel, Louis Lingg, and Oscar Neebe, all prominent in the International, for the murder of Mathias J. Degan on May 4. The trial was set for June 21 at the criminal court of Cook County, with

Joseph E. Gary as judge. State's Attorney Julius S. Grinnell took command of the prosecution. The accused men were represented by William P. Black, William 'A. Foster, Sigmund Zeisler, and Moses Salomon. While the police were making their alarming finds, while the newspapers poured forth stories of anarchist plots for wholesale murder and the public clamored for the immediate execution of the indicted men, the trial opened. Just as the preliminary examination of talesmen commenced, the missing Parsons, who had baffled a police search for six weeks, walked into court and surrendered himself for trial, joining his comrades on the defendants' bench.

At the outset two circumstances prevented any approximation to a fair trial. First, Judge Gary forced all eight defendants to stand trial together, increasing the danger that all sorts of evidence would be admitted. Second, through an extraordinary device the jury was packed: the candidates for the jury were not chosen in the customary manner by drawing names from a box; instead, a special bailiff, nominated by the State's Attorney, was appointed by the court to select the candidates. A Chicago business man, Otis S. Favor, made affidavit that this bailiff had said to him in the presence of witnesses: "I am managing this case, and know what I am about. These fellows are going to be hanged as certain as death. I am calling such men as the defendants will have to challenge peremptorily and waste their time and challenges. Then they will have to take such men as the prosecution wants." [23] By the adroit questioning of the judge, many who openly admitted their prejudice against the defendants were pronounced fit for jury service and had to be peremptorily challenged by the defense. It took 21 days to select the jury: 981 talesmen were examined. Ultimately the defense exhausted all its peremptory challenges and the final 12 men were picked, among them a relative of one of the victims of the bomb.

The introductory speech by State's Attorney Grinnell, after the presentation of evidence began on July 14, assured the jury that the man who had thrown the bomb would be produced. This, of course, the prosecution was unable to do. It did at first, however, attempt to fabricate, by means of the testimony of two alleged anarchists who had turned State's evidence, a terroristic plot for the dynamiting of all police stations when the word *Ruhe* appeared in the *Arbeiter-Zeitung*. Under cross-examination the testimony of these two witnesses was largely impaired. When this failed, other strange evidence was disclosed. One witness named Gilmer, shown by cross-examination to be a professional liar who had in all likelihood been paid for testifying, swore that he saw an object resembling a bomb pass between Spies, Schwab, and Schnaubelt, and that he saw the latter throw the bomb among the police. Also several policemen tried to prove that Fielden had fired upon them from behind the speakers' wagon, but their assertions were contradictory. Regarding the witnesses and testimony produced by the State, Governor Altgeld said in his pardon message:

It is further shown here that much of the evidence given at the trial was a pure fabrication; that some of the prominent police officials, in their zeal, not only terrorized ignorant men by throwing them into prison and threatening them with torture if they refused to swear to anything desired, but that they offered money and employment to those who would consent to do this. Further, that they deliberately planned to have fictitious conspiracies formed in order that they might get the glory of discovering them. In addition to the evidence in the record of some witnesses who swore that they had been paid small sums of money, etc., several documents are here referred to.[24]

In spite of the generation of an emotional fog, the State, as Altgeld remarks, never discovered who threw the bomb. Nor was it able to show any specific conspiracy entered into by the accused men.

It soon developed that the eight men were on trial for their ideas, even though the defense was not permitted to introduce testimony concerning the theory of anarchism. On the grounds that the general principles of the anarchists urged the destruction of all capitalists, Judge Gary allowed the prosecution to establish a resultant specific conspiracy. The jury was deluged with readings from inciting articles in the *Alarm* and the *Arbeiter-Zeitung*. Furthermore, the police exhibited on a table before the jury-box all fashions of dynamite and bomb, with all their infernal mechanism, although these destructive engines were found often miles from the scene of the bombing and weeks afterward and had no association with the defendants. The display produced the desired effect: it aroused terror. Time and again the defense objected to the presentation of irrelevant evidence whose purpose was the evocation of emotionalism, but it was overruled by the court. In other ways too, as Altgeld later pointed out, Judge Gary revealed his bias. While he confined the defense in its cross-examination to the specific points touched on by the State, he permitted the State to wander to matters entirely foreign to those the witnesses were examined in. Besides, he made insinuating remarks in the hearing of the jury that proved much more damaging than anything the prosecution could have produced. Foster, of the defense counsel, pleaded that there existed no proof of the influence on the bomb-thrower of any spoken or written word by the defendants, nor of the instigation of the deed by the defendants. He persisted in conducting the case as one of homicide, since that was the charge; he confined himself to plain facts and law; and he wanted even to admit some criminal folly in the utterances of the defendants, but this they refused to permit.

The summing up before the jury began on August 11. It was concluded by State's Attorney Grinnell, whose final words were: "Law is upon trial. Anarchy is on trial. These men have been selected, picked out by the grand jury and indicted because they were leaders. They are no more guilty than the thousands who follow them. Gentlemen of the jury; convict these men, make examples of them, hang them and you save our institutions, our society." [25] As was foreseen, the jury brought in on August 20 a verdict of guilty and fixed the penalty at hanging for seven of the defendants, the exception, Oscar Neebe, being given 15 years' imprisonment. A motion by the defense in September for a new trial was denied by Judge Gary, and the convicted men were called upon to speak before sentence was pronounced. They delivered eloquent speeches lasting three days, addressed beyond the court to workers everywhere. After a long summary of his beliefs, Spies said:

Now, these are my ideas. They constitute a part of myself. I cannot divest myself of them, nor would I, if I could. And if you think that you can crush out these ideas that are gaining ground more and more every day, if you think you can crush them out by sending us to the gallows—if you would once more have people to suffer the penalty of death because they have dared to tell the truth—and I defy you to show us where we have told a lie—I say, if death is the penalty for proclaiming the truth, then I will proudly and defiantly pay the costly price! Call your hangman.[26]

George Engel said:

I hate and combat, not the individual capitalist, but the system that gives him those privileges. My greatest wish is

*that workingmen may recognize who are their friends and
who are their enemies.*[27]

And with the defiance he had displayed throughout the trial,
the twenty-one year old Lingg said:

*I repeat that I am the enemy of the "order" of to-day, and
I repeat that, with all my powers, so long as breath remains
in me, I shall combat it. . . . I despise you. I despise your
order; your laws, your force-propped authority. Hang me
for it!* [28]

On October 9 sentence, as decreed by the jury, was pronounced by Judge Gary.

Execution of the sentences was postponed while the case
was carried before the Supreme Court of Illinois. After several months of consideration, the Supreme Court, although it
admitted that the trial had not been free of legal error, affirmed in September, 1887, the verdict of the lower court. An
attempt to appeal to the Supreme Court of the United States
failed when that body decided that it had no jurisdiction.
Labor organizations everywhere asked for mercy for the condemned men; the American Federation of Labor adopted
such a resolution, while the Noble Order of the Knights of
Labor was prevented from doing likewise only through the
personal intervention of Powderly, who hated the anarchists
and wanted to clear his Order of any association with them.
During the last days Fielden and Schwab petitioned for executive clemency and asked for commutation of their sentence. The others demanded liberty or death. Governor
Oglesby commuted the sentence of Fielden and Schwab to
life imprisonment, and they joined Neebe in the State Penitentiary at Joliet. Lingg escaped the scaffold the day preceding the execution by exploding a dynamite tube in his

mouth. The remaining four were hanged on November 11, 1887.

The nooses were quickly adjusted, the caps pulled down, and a hasty movement made for the traps. Then from beneath the hoods came these words:

Spies: "There will be a time when our silence will be more powerful than the voices you strangle to-day."

Fischer: "Hurrah for anarchy—"

Engel: "Hurrah for anarchy!"

Fischer: "This is the happiest moment of my life!"

Parsons: "Will I be allowed to speak, O men of America? Let me speak, Sheriff Matson! Let the voice of the people be heard! O—" [29]

At the funeral 25,000 working people marched. William P. Black, who had been of the defense counsel, spoke over the graves:

. . . I loved these men. I knew them not until I came to know them in the time of their sore travail and anguish. As months went by and I found in the lives of those with whom I talked the witness of their love for the people, of their patience, gentleness, and courage, my heart was taken captive in their cause. . . . I say that whatever of fault may have been in them, these, the people whom they loved and in whose cause they died, may well close the volume, and seal up the record, and give our lips to the praise of their heroic deeds, and their sublime self-sacrifice.[30]

5. Collapse of the Black International

A portion of the public fury aroused by the Haymarket bomb was deflected against the eight-hour strike in progress. Confusion arose among the working people and their ranks were split. Using the alleged discoveries of anarchist plots as an excuse, the police attacked gatherings of strikers even more savagely than before. Labor leaders were seized without ceremony. Within a week after May 4 the strikers began

BETWEEN TWO FIRES. A cartoon by Thomas Nast. (*Harper's Weekly,* May 22, 1886)

to give in and return to their jobs. Many of them, particularly the freight handlers, found their places occupied by scabs. Nor was this disordered surrender of the shorter day movement confined to Chicago. *Bradstreet's* reported on May 22, 1886, that out of the original 190,000 strikers in the

United States, no more than 80,000 remained, many of these locked out. In Chicago only 16,000 were left of the former 65,000. While it is true that 42,000 of the 190,000 original strikers in the country won their demands and that 150,000, as has been stated, were granted shorter hours without striking, these concessions proved short-lived. As soon as the strength of the movement was spent, the employers retracted whatever they had granted. In one month the total still retaining the shorter hours either won or granted fell nearly one-third, from approximately 200,000 to 137,000.[31] By a lockout in October the Chicago packers took away from their 35,000 employees the eight-hour day that had been conceded without a strike in May. On January 8, 1887, *Bradstreet's* was able to report for the nation: "It may be fairly assumed . . . that so far as the payment of former wages for a shorter day's work is concerned the grand total of those retaining the concession will not exceed, if it equals, 15,000."

The eight-hour movement was not all that suffered under the steady barrage kept up by the press. For many years all radical theory and practice fell into disfavor with labor organization. Powderly expressed his extreme antipathy to the revolutionary elements:

A cardinal principle with the rampant Socialist and Anarchist is to propagandize on every occasion that presents itself. If a new society of laboring men is established these extremists become members of it, and attempt to force their ideas to the front. In canting phrase and with mock humility they will insinuate themselves into the good graces of men who would scorn them were they to disclose their real feelings, and once they gain the good will of such, they have inserted a wedge between the members of that society that sooner or later will drive them apart.

THE SMOOTH-TONGUED ADVOCATE OF ANARCHY *seldom does anything himself toward furthering the ends of the movement he is a part and parcel of. He secures the services of dupes who do his bidding, either through loyalty to principle or ignorance. That they will play on the ignorance of workingmen is but too true; that they despise every effort to lift the pall of ignorance that is lowered over the fortunes of the toilers, is also true. If the people become educated they will have no use for either anarchy or monopoly. . . .*[32]

The relentless abuse by the newspapers, periodicals, and pulpit was more virulent than Powderly's. Cartoons by Thomas Nast and others pictured bushy-bearded, foreign-looking, and villainous anarchists deluding the laborer, assassinating the respectable citizen, or hiding under a bed from the police. The *Nation* accused the eight convicted anarchists of petty cowardice, of being "chicken-hearted," for attempting to appeal their case, instead of hanging bravely and cheerfully like the more remote and romantic Russian Nihilists.[33]

Some of the assaults upon the radical factions were less crude, more subtle, veiled by an affected impartiality and objectivity. Such was the pseudo-scientific study by Professor Cesare Lombroso in the philosophical journal, the *Monist*, in which, after an impressive but dubious parade of tables, figures, and anthropological jargon, he concluded that anarchists and communists are of the criminal type. To arrive at this conclusion he analyzed the physiognomies of 100 anarchists arrested at Turin, of 50 photographs of communards, and of photographs in Schaack's book about the Chicago anarchists; and he found an abundance of proof in "exaggerated plagiocephaly, facial asymmetry, other cranial anomalies (ultra-brachycephaly etc.), very large jaw, exaggerated zygomas, enormous frontal sinus, dental anomalies, anomalies of the ears, anomalies of the nose, anomalous coloration of skin, old wounds, tattooing, neuro-pathological anomalies." [34] It was left for the convicted Michael Schwab, still confined in the Joliet penitentiary, to point out to Professor Lombroso certain fundamental errors: (1) that there most likely exists no anthropological and physical criminal type which is hereditary; (2) that crime is

ANARCHISTS' DRILL, NEW TACTICS. A cartoon by Thomas Nast. (*Harper's Weekly,* May 29, 1886)

in the main a product of the environment; (3) that in study-ing physiognomies, one's judgment is influenced by his emo-tional reactions; (4) that materials may easily and often unconsciously be selected to fit the desired conclusion; (5) that anarchism is not a distinct and definite term which per-mits the segregation of its supposed followers from those of communism, socialism, liberalism, etc.[35] Nevertheless, Pro-fessor Lombroso's study soon filtered down to the more pop-ular journals and newspapers, and furnished "scientific" support for the public attitude toward anarchists and revo-lutionaries.

Nothwithstanding this protracted wave of hatred, an Amnesty Association was formed in 1889 to campaign for the release of Neebe, Fielden, and Schwab. But Governor Fifer, who succeeded Oglesby, refused to consider the matter, and the Amnesty Association had to wait until 1893, when John P. Altgeld became governor of Illinois. A petition bearing 60,000 signatures was presented to him. If he had pardoned the three men as an act of mercy, on the grounds that they had already served seven years in the penitentiary, the community would probably have applauded Altgeld and its conscience would have been put at ease. Instead, he insisted on a thorough investigation and discovered that an irreparable and monstrous legal wrong had been done not only the three men still in prison, but also the other five who were dead. When he wrote his pardon message, with its unanswerable proof that the eight defendants had not been given a fair trial, and that the State had failed to establish any connection whatever between them and the unknown person who threw the Haymarket bomb; when he showed that the court, the jury, and the prosecution had yielded to the hysteria deliberately generated and intensified by the press and the police of Chicago, he actually charged the community with judicial murder. His pardon of Neebe, Fielden, and Schwab, therefore, brought a storm upon his head, second only to that suffered by the anarchists themselves. "But realizing at the outset that the Governor's legal position was impregnable, the outraged guardians of society rushed to their favorite weapon and turned upon Altgeld himself such an intensive and protracted fire of personal vituperation as few other men in public life have ever faced. If his arguments could not be answered, at least his motives might be impugned, his reputation blackened, his political and business fortunes ruined; and to such ends the press, actively or passively abetted by nine-tenths of the most highly respectable persons in American life, bent its efforts with an almost fanatical fervor and persistency." [36]

The radical factions in the labor movement were slow to recover from this period of persecution. After the Haymarket affair the Black International, as the workingmen withdrew in fear, soon dwindled to a small group of intellectuals. Although the modification known as the "Chicago idea" appeared again later, anarchism as a theory and a tactic never regained its hold on the labor movement in the United States. Workmen turned to the more conservative American Federation of Labor, which was able to point back with some satisfaction to the energetic part it had played in the eight-hour movement and to the resolution it had passed for the release of the eight condemned men. But the Noble Order of the Knights of Labor, both because of its official treachery in the strike and its official refusal to petition for the pardoning of the condemned men, was abandoned. Meanwhile, among the working class the executed anarchists were regarded as martyrs to the cause of labor, and their monument at Waldheim Cemetery became a shrine visited by thousands each year.

III. THE HOMESTEAD LOCKOUT

1. The angel of the workingman

For nearly five months in 1892 at Homestead, Pennsylvania, there was a severe clash between the steel manufacturers and the steel workers. This clash, during which 300 armed Pinkerton detectives attempted in vain to take possession of the mills for the manufacturers, reverberated through the nation, aroused sharp protests abroad, and helped defeat Benjamin Harrison and the Republican protectionists. At this time the steel manufacturers, completely triumphant, established a technique for quashing labor uprisings, shattered the union of the workmen, and laid down the unbroken rule that they would never again deal with that union nor any other union of the men.

The contestants in the struggle were the Carnegie Steel Company, Limited, forerunner of the United States Steel Corporation, and the Homestead lodges of the Amalgamated Association of Iron and Steel Workers. The newly organized Carnegie Steel Company controlled almost the entire steel market in this country; it owned and operated 12 steel and coke works in the vicinity of Pittsburgh, and employed 13,000 men. The Amalgamated Association of Iron and Steel Workers had 25,000 members, all skilled men, and was one of the most powerful trade-unions in the history of the American labor movement.

The borough of Homestead, scene of the struggle, rests on the left bank of the Monongahela River, seven miles east of Pittsburgh. It was then a dependent growth around the nucleus of steel works, where 3,800 of its 10,000 or 12,000 inhabitants were employed. Here were manufactured boiler plates, beams, structural iron of various kinds, and armor plate. The monthly payroll was $200,000, and wages ranged from 14 cents per hour for common labor to the peak of $280 per month for skilled labor, the great majority of the skilled workers, of whom there were only 800, getting $200 and less.

Ever since 1889, when the workmen had won a strike by turning back 100 deputies who had been sent from Pittsburgh to guard the steel works and permit the introduction of "blacksheep" or non-union men, the relations between the company and its employees had been unfriendly. An agreement had been signed for a sliding scale, whereby the basis for wages was to be the market price of 4 x 4 standard Bessemer steel billets. Wages were to rise and fall in accordance with the fluctuations of this market price, except that a minimum of $25 per ton of steel billets was arbitrarily set and wages were not to fall below the corresponding rate even though the market price sank lower. The agreement was to expire on June 30, 1892.

Throughout the three years of the contract the company, a dictatorial power with feeble rivals, chafed under the necessity of dealing with the Amalgamated Association and of subjecting its profits to a division with the men. Trouble was expected as the time approached for drawing up a new agreement. When Henry Clay Frick, known as the Coke King in the Connellsville district (50 miles south of Pittsburgh) was given the managing authority of the company, the workers realized that they would have to fight for the preservation of their union against the avowed and ruthless anti-union policy of the man who had already crushed several strikes by means of the Coal and Iron Police, the Pinkerton Detective Agency, and the state militia.

Before the appointment of Frick the men had believed somewhat in the friendship of Andrew Carnegie, poor immigrant boy from Dunfermline, donator of libraries and hospitals and music-halls, patron of the workingman and democracy and peace. He had written frequently concerning the relations of capital and labor; he had advocated trade-unionism and the peaceful arbitration of differences, and had deplored absentee capitalism and the violence of dispute. In an article in the *Forum* for April, 1886, he had stated:

The right of the workingmen to combine and to form trades-unions is no less sacred than the right of the manufacturer to enter into associations and conferences with his fellows, and it must be sooner or later conceded. Indeed, it gives one but a poor opinion of the American workman if he permits himself to be deprived of a right which his fellow in England has conquered for himself long since. My experience has been that trades-unions upon the whole are beneficial both to labor and to capital.[1]

And four months later in the same magazine:

While public sentiment has rightly and unmistakably condemned violence, even in the form for which there is the most excuse, I would have the public give due consideration to the terrible temptation to which the working-man on a strike is sometimes subjected. To expect that one dependent upon his daily wage for the necessaries of life will stand by peaceably and see a new man employed in his stead is to expect much. This poor man may have a wife and children dependent upon his labor. Whether medicine for a sick child, or even nourishing food for a delicate wife, is procurable, depends upon his steady employment. In all but a very few departments of labor it is unnecessary, and, I think, improper, to subject men to such an ordeal. . . . There is an unwritten law

among the best workmen: "Thou shalt not take thy neigh-
bor's job. . . ." [2]

When, therefore, during the disturbances at Homestead, contradictions between Carnegie's public humanitarian utterances and his private business practices were unveiled, the men felt as if they had been betrayed.

From Frick the workmen expected open hostility. But how to account for Carnegie's actions? Why had he declared himself so often in print for a liberal labor policy motivated by generosity and enlightenment? And after he had so done, then why did he let Frick, the notorious and unyielding enemy of trade-unions, assume full authority for the firm, and then himself hurry away to his castles and shooting boxes in Scotland?

A solution to this paradox was offered several years later by the man who had assisted Carnegie in his literary exploits and especially in his book *Triumphant Democracy.*[3] An organization like the Amalgamated Association, which demanded uniform wages for the same class of labor, acted to give Carnegie valuable aid against competitors whose plants were not so well endowed. His iron and steel works were situated in the Pittsburgh district, the very heart of coal and iron supplies, with unexcelled transportation facilities. If he could establish uniform wages throughout the nation, competitors in other regions, unable to cut further the cost of labor, would have to fall before the enormous natural advantages he possessed. There was no better ally to be found than a national trade-union, which maintained the cost of labor at the low level possible in the worst-equipped and least favorably located works. The growth and spread of the Amalgamated Association were to be fostered.

Once, however, the business rivals were beaten by this strategy, then the dangerous ally was to be annihilated before it grew large and powerful enough to interfere with and challenge successfully the despotism of the Carnegie firm. Although Carnegie turned this job over to Frick, there can be no doubt of his complicity, nor of his guiding spirit behind the action. On April 4, 1892, almost three months before the contract with the Amalgamated was to expire, Carnegie sent to Pittsburgh the draft of a notice to the Homestead employees. But Frick disapproved, and the notice remained unpublished until 1903. It read:

As the vast majority of our employees are Non-Union, the Firm has decided that the minority must give place to the majority. These works therefore, will be necessarily Non-Union after the expiration of the present agreement.[4]

Through the struggle that followed Carnegie wrote letters of support to Frick and the company officials; and when, after the bloody battle between Pinkertons and workmen, Baron Carnage-y—so he was named by the free-trade papers—was interviewed at his shooting box near Kinlock by an Associated Press correspondent, he said: "The handling of the case on the part of the company has my full approval and sanction."[5]

2. Fort Frick

Negotiations for a new agreement between the company and its employees opened in February, 1892, when a committee from the Amalgamated presented a scale to J. A. Potter, superintendent of the Homestead mill. Potter, in turn, handed the committee a scale from the company, providing for a reduction in wages and calling for a change in the date for the termination of the contract. The committee asked why a reduction was demanded, but no explanation was forthcoming.

The men haggled with the company for the next three

months, but the conferences brought no accord. Finally on May 30 the company issued an ultimatum that the men would have to accept its scale before June 24. After that date the men would be dealt with only as individuals. That this eventuality was not undesired by the company is evident from the letter which Frick wrote to Potter on the day of the ultimatum:

You can say to the committee that these scales are in all respects the most liberal that can be offered. We do not care whether a man belongs to a union or not, nor do we wish to interfere. He may belong to as many unions or organizations as he chooses, but we think our employés at Homestead Steel Works would fare much better working under the system [i.e., non-union] in vogue at Edgar Thompson and Duquesne.[6]

Meanwhile alarming preparations were being made at the Homestead works. A solid board fence was erected around the mill property. This fence was topped with barbed wire and was perforated at intervals, as if for rifles, although Frick testified before the Congressional investigating committee later that the holes were meant for observation; and in the mill-yard stood platforms equipped with searchlights. The workmen dubbed the mill Fort Frick.

In the proposal of the company there were three points to which the men objected. (1) A reduction in the minimum market price of the sliding scale from $25 to $22 a ton of 4 x 4 steel billets. (2) A change in the date for the expiration of the contract from June 30 to December 31. (3) A reduction in tonnage rates at those furnaces and mills where improvements had been made and new machinery had been installed.

The company defended each term of its proposal. (1) The market price of steel billets had declined steadily until it was

below $23 a ton. It was unfair for the workers to benefit from
a rise in the market price above $25, and yet not to share the
losses of the company. If there was no maximum to the sliding scale, there should be no minimum. (2) Commercial and
sales contracts terminated at the end of the year instead of
June 30. It would suit the company better to have its labor
contracts terminate to correspond with those of its customers, since it could then count on definite labor costs for the
entire year in settling its prices. (3) The improvements and
new machinery had been added at a great cost to the company, and had increased greatly the output of the mills.
Consequently the earnings of the men, dependent on tonnage, had risen without any additional expense or effort.
The company wanted to benefit fully from the investment in
the improvements and felt that the men were not entitled to
share in profits that had resulted simply from this invested
capital. Furthermore, the company contended, merely 320 of
the 3,800 employees were affected by the proposal, and these
suffered a reduction in wages of only 18 per cent.

The men, on the other hand, declared that since they had
no voice in the sale of the products, a minimum in the sliding scale was essential to protect them against collusion between the company and its buyers. Besides, when the company undersold on the market in order to defeat competition, the workers really paid by a reduction in wages, unless
there was some fixed minimum. The men charged also that
Carnegie had had a finger in the McKinley tariff bill, which
lowered the duty on steel billets, the only standard for
wages at Homestead; and that he had then deliberately
brought about a depressed market as a seeming consequence
of this specific reduction in duty. It was not true, the men
held, that a change in the date for ending the contract was
necessary. The Amalgamated offered to make a contract for
as long as the company wished, so that labor costs would be

calculated just as well in December as in June. Moreover, under the previous agreement the labor rates were changed each half year to correspond with the market price. To the men such a change in date meant much: in midwinter they would be powerless to resist a cut in wages or a corruption of conditions, since the severity of the season would make a strike almost impossible and would put them at the mercy of their employers.

Against the decrease in tonnage rates the men objected that they had been responsible for the suggestions resulting in many of the improvements and much of the new machinery, and that therefore they were entitled to a share in them. All improvements and new machinery, moreover, produced technological unemployment; hence those men who remained were, in fact, getting but a small portion of the former wages of those who were eliminated. In addition, the men found that they had to work with much greater concentration and increased expense of strength when new machinery was installed. Despite the contention of the company, said the men, all the 3,800 employees were affected by at least one of the three disputed points. Nor was the figure of 18 per cent for the reduction in wages accurate. W. T. Roberts, a leader of the workmen, calculated that the immediate reduction would be 26 per cent.[7] And although only 320 were instantly affected by the lowered rates, all the others would soon be forced to accept proportionate reductions.

At the request of the workers Frick met a committee from the Amalgamated in the company office at Pittsburgh for a final conference on June 23, the day before the expiration of the ultimatum. No agreement could be reached, even though the committee offered a reduction in the minimum to $24 and Frick, after the interposition of Superintendent Potter, offered to raise the minimum to $23. On the questions of date and tonnage rates both sides were adamant. Two days later the company issued a statement that its new scale stood, regardless of the union.

Throughout the conferences the men had been offended by the cold uncompromising attitude of the company and particularly by the fortifications thrown around the works even before the negotiations were at an end. Now they were angered by the obvious aggressiveness of the company, and understood fully that behind all the differences had been the single question of the preservation of their union. The company attitude rankled all the more because the men prided themselves on their Americanism and on the conservative policy and reasonable spirit of the Amalgamated. In this feeling the Congressional investigating committee later concurred with the men. It found that the workmen at Homestead were "very intelligent and highly skilled," that their work was of such a nature as to impair their eyesight rapidly and shorten their lives, and that therefore a reduction of 18 per cent to 26 per cent in their pay "warranted close scrutiny." Yet at the investigation Frick refused outright to state either the total cost or the labor cost of a ton of steel billets, on the grounds that he could not disclose such a trade secret to competitors. Concerning Frick the Congressional committee reported:

We conclude from all the surroundings that he, who is not the only manufacturer thus affected, is opposed to the Amalgamated Association and its methods, and hence had no anxiety to contract with his laborers through that organization, and that this is the true reason why he appeared to them as autocratic and uncompromising in his demands. If, as he claimed, the business of his company, on account of fall in the market price of the products of the works, required a reduction of the wages of the employés, he should have appealed to their reason and shown them the true state

*of the company's affairs. We are persuaded that if he had
done so an agreement would have been reached between him
and the workmen, and all the trouble which followed would
thus have been avoided.*[8]

Frick had patently tried to force the workmen into opposition, and he had succeeded.

Strained relations developed quickly. The workers hanged
Frick and Potter in effigy on the mill property, and turned
the hose on the men sent by Potter to cut down the effigies.
Using this incident as its excuse, the company began to shut
down the works on June 28, two days before the agreement
with the Amalgamated ended. By the morning of June 30
the entire force was locked out. The company had cleverly
forestalled the men and put them on the defensive.

3. The invasion of the Pinkertons

The workmen held a mass meeting, at which the mechanics
and common laborers, who numbered nearly 3,000 and who
were not members of the Amalgamated, determined nevertheless to stand with the 800 skilled union men against the company. To organize and direct the activities of the men, an
advisory committee was formed, and the leadership given to
Hugh O'Donnell, a young man of considerable intelligence
and swiftness of decision. His chief lieutenants were W. T.
Roberts, Hugh Ross, and John McLuckie, who was at the
time burgess of Homestead. The advisory committee soon
had full control of the town. A strict guard was kept day
and night around the steel works, and all approaches to both
town and mill were watched; no one could enter without the
consent of the committee. The men assigned to the different
posts reported regularly to the headquarters, and a system
of signaling was arranged, including rockets for the night,
so that 1,000 men could be had at any spot within five min-

utes. Furthermore, the committee communicated with Pittsburgh, Philadelphia, and other large cities to learn of any movement of "blacksheep" intended for Homestead. Meanwhile, through Burgess McLuckie, all saloons were commanded to check drunkenness and noisy gatherings. The committee was anxious to preserve order and decency: it wanted no excuse to exist for newspaper slander. They were no ignorant immigrants, no lawless vandals, no violent anarchists; they were good Americans, fellow citizens with Frick and Carnegie of a democracy, respectable men who were defending their moderate standards of living for their families.

When Superintendent Potter and several foremen attempted on July 1 to enter the mill, they were stopped at the gates by the locked-out men and induced to turn back. The workmen were determined to prevent all preparations for the intromission of scabs: their labor had built up the industry and the jobs were their right. Through its attorneys, Knox and Reed, on July 4 the company notified William H. McCleary, sheriff of Allegheny County, that 100 deputies would be needed to protect the mill property. McCleary went to Homestead to confer with the advisory committee of the workers. The committee pointed out to him that no one was trespassing upon the mill territory, and it offered to put in 100 to 500 special deputies under bail to watch the property; but McCleary refused on the contention that the deputies had to be men of his own choosing, men also who would act for the company, which had the legal right to use its property as it saw fit. After some discussion the committee agreed that he would be allowed to come with 50 deputies to take possession of the mill.

McCleary returned to Pittsburgh, but failing to assemble a *posse comitatus*, because the citizens refused to answer his summons to serve against the Homestead workmen, he was

compelled to send his office force of 12 deputies; he himself
did not accompany them. Upon arriving at Homestead, however, the deputies were met at the station by a crowd of 2,000
men, were permitted to see that the mill property was intact,
but were informed that they would not be let into the steel
works merely to provide entry for "blacksheep." To the
deputies the crowd seemed threatening and tense. It expected
a test of strength shortly. It was further excited by newspaper reports that Potter and 20 of his foremen were search-
ing in the large cities for the 260 skilled workers without
whom it was impossible to start the mill. As a result, the
deputies were escorted to the river, put on a tugboat, and
shipped back to Pittsburgh.

All this time Frick had been secretly active, making ready
to institute the next step in his offensive. If he could get a
force of armed Pinkerton detectives behind the fortifications
at Homestead, it would be relatively easy to fight off the
workmen and introduce the necessary scabs. As early as
June 20, even before the negotiations with the Amalgamated
were at an end, he had begun to deal with Robert A. Pinkerton, of New York, who had already once supplied him with
150 to 200 detectives during a similar difficulty in the Connellsville coke region. Yet he knew that the Pinkerton detectives were hated by the workmen for their strike-breaking
and their hired brutality, and that bloodshed was likely to
result from a clash between the two forces. Later, in an interview given the *Philadelphia Press*, Frick defended his action
—an action which, by the way, throws more light on his failure to come to any agreement with the Amalgamated—by
his doubt concerning the sheriff's ability to protect the company property, and cited the experience of 1889 when the
firm, then under the management of Abbott, had had to
yield:

*The posse taken up by the sheriff—something over 100
men—were not permitted to land on our property; were
driven off with threats of bodily harm, and it looked as if
there was going to be great destruction of life and property.
That frightened our people . . . an agreement was made
and work was resumed. We did not propose this time to be
placed in that position.*[9]

Again the Congressional committee, in its report to the
House of Representatives, censured Frick:

*There was nothing in the laws of Pennsylvania to prevent
Mr. Frick from employing Pinkerton men as watchmen in
the works at Homestead, yet we do not think, under the circumstances, he should have done so. He made no direct appeal to the county and state authorities for protection in the
first instance, but began to negotiate for the employment of
Pinkerton forces before the negotiations for the reëmployment of the workmen of the Amalgamated Association were
broken off.*[10]

A letter from Frick on June 25 gave detailed instructions
to the Pinkerton agency. Three hundred Pinkertons were to
gather at Ashtabula, Ohio, on the morning of July 5 and
were to proceed by rail to Youngstown. From there they were
to be transported at night by boat up the river to Homestead. Since it might prove illegal to bring an armed force
into the state, the rifles, pistols, batons, and ammunition
were to be shipped separately in care of the Union Supply
Company. The detectives were to be armed after they were
within the boundaries of Pennsylvania. Frick agreed to pay
$5 per day for each man. In the meantime two barges were
fitted up for the Pinkertons, one with bunks as a dormitory,
the other with tables as a large refectory, and two steamboats were engaged to tow the barges. The sheriff had been

informed by Knox and Reed on June 25 that the Pinkertons were to be brought, and was requested to deputize them. He had refused, and had offered instead to deputize the Pinkertons only after they were inside the steel works. Knowing so early of the impending battle, Sheriff McCleary nevertheless made no effort to prevent it, and was condemned by the Congressional committee as "a very inefficient officer," who displayed none of the "pluck and energy" expected of a sheriff. McCleary did, however, send to accompany the expedition Deputy Sheriff Gray, whose vague function it was to try to persuade the Pinkertons to turn back in case of violence.

In accordance with the plans, the Pinkerton train was met on July 5 at Davis Island Dam, five or six miles below Pittsburgh; and while the barges proceeded silently up the river, the detectives armed themselves with Winchester rifles and put on the blue Pinkerton uniforms. The attempt to introduce the Pinkertons clandestinely failed. The company had evidently hoped that the recent open request for deputies had diverted the attention of the workmen from any other preparations. This artifice of the company becomes clear upon an examination of dates. Frick's letter giving specific directions for the movement of the Pinkertons is dated June 25. The invasion was set for the night of July 5. On July 4 came the first public request for deputies. Since Frick, by his own admission, had no faith in the power of the sheriff's deputies, his purpose must have been only to mislead the locked-out men. But the detectives were sighted at 4 o'clock in the morning by a patrol about one mile below Homestead; soon whistles sounded a general alarm throughout the town, and a crowd of men, women, and children lined the river bank.

When the barges pulled up to the company beach, where the wire-topped fence had been brought down to the low-water mark so as to cut off all access by land, and the crowd on shore saw that the Pinkertons intended landing, it tore a gap in the fence and trespassed for the first time on the mill property. The workmen warned the detectives back, but both the Pinkerton prestige and the pay were at stake. A gangplank was shoved out and several Pinkertons started down it. Someone fired a shot. Who fired is unknown, each side later proclaiming its innocence. But it is certain that the Pinkertons then fired a volley into the crowd and brought down several workers. The women and children ran out of the range of the rifles to watch the struggle, while the men barricaded themselves behind ramparts of steel, pig iron, and scrap iron, and opened fire. The Pinkertons retreated into the shelter of their barges. The steamboat which had towed the barges took on board two or three wounded detectives and steamed away, leaving the invaders without means of escape.

This battle lasted from 4 o'clock in the morning of July 6 until 5 o'clock that afternoon; it resulted in three deaths among the Pinkertons and seven among the workers, besides many wounded. The news spread, and at 3:30 p.m. President Weihe of the Amalgamated arrived to stop the bloodshed. At first the workmen were hostile to any suggestion for the release of the Pinkertons. Only after a moving speech by Hugh O'Donnell did they agree to accept a surrender of the Pinkertons, who were to be handed over to the sheriff on charges of murder. But the promise of O'Donnell and the workers was of no avail. As the Pinkertons marched unarmed from the barges to the skating rink of the town, where they were to be kept, they were attacked and badly beaten, chiefly by the women. The advisory committee, in fact, got many bruises and scars in its endeavor to shield the surrendered detectives. The crowd also seized the guns and provisions left behind and burned the barges.

In the evening the Pinkertons were called for by Sheriff McCleary, taken to Pittsburgh by train, and sent back to their homes. The Carnegie Company had not succeeded in placing the Pinkertons by stealth within the fortifications, but it had succeeded in creating a state under which it could demand legal interference. On the same evening it issued a statement to the Associated Press: "We are not taking any active part in the matter at present, as we cannot interfere with the sheriff in the discharge of his duty, and are now waiting his further action." [11] The confidence of the company in the sheriff was now strangely and suddenly restored. The next day Secretary Lovejoy spoke again for the company to the press:

The Amalgamated people who committed these recent overt acts will probably find themselves in a very bad hole, for when the proper time arrives a number of them will be arrested on a charge of murder, and I need scarcely say, there will be no lack of evidence. . . .

This outbreak settles one matter forever, and that is that the Homestead mill hereafter will be run non-union, and the Carnegie Company will never again recognize the Amalgamated Association nor any other labor organization.[12]

The company thus suggested a future step in its action against the locked-out men, and published for the first time the non-union policy which it never thereafter retracted.

4. The militia at Homestead

The entire nation was swiftly stirred by the reports of the Homestead warfare. Unions in many states sent resolutions of support to the locked-out men and threatened sympathy strikes. In Pittsburgh the Window Glass Workers' Union of the South Side demanded that the city council return to Carnegie a gift of one million dollars for a free library, since the

gift represented workingman blood. Even in England workers made vigorous protests. Bourgeois opinion, however, was
against the Homestead workmen, either openly or evasively.
It is true that the Democratic free-trade newspapers assailed
Baron Carnage-y, seemed to befriend the workmen, and
blamed the whole struggle on the McKinley tariff bill and
protection. It is true, also, that Democratic senators and
representatives at Washington denounced the bloodshed,
and, as did Senator Vorhees, condemned Carnegie for pock-
eting his 55 per cent tariff on iron and 70 per cent on steel
and then cutting wages 10 per cent to 40 per cent. But these
appearances of support evaded the issue. A statement by
Daniel DeLeon, of the Socialist Labor Party of New York,
predicted this opportunistic friendliness:

*These troubles at Homestead will result in some extraor-
dinarily fallacious reasoning on the part of our Democratic friends; they will ascribe it all to the protective tariff,
forgetting or wilfully ignoring the fact that in free-trade
England workmen have been shot down like dogs in scores
of strikes. It is the old struggle between capital and labor,
which has been carried on and will be carried on in all parts
of the world for a long time.*[13]

A presidential election was to be held that fall, and Homestead served the Democrats and Cleveland with efficient
political ammunition against the protectionist Republicans.

The educated bourgeois opposition, whether liberal or
conservative, was based on the American guarantee of personal liberty. E. L. Godkin's *Nation* disapproved of the
workmen for attempting "to deprive rich men of their property and poor men of their right to labor."[14] The Hon.
William C. Oates, chairman of the Congressional investigating committee, objected to the "moral suasion" employed by
union men to prevent non-union men from scabbing, and

wrote: "The right of any man to labor, upon whatever terms he and his employer agree, whether he belong to a labor organization or not, and the right of a person or corporation (which in law is also a person) to employ any one to labor in a lawful business is secured by the laws of the land." [15] Neither the *Nation* nor Congressman Oates seemed aware of the dilemma of the workman: if he did not picket he was reduced to looking on while his job was given to a scab; if he did picket he transgressed the laws and ideals of the land.

While the country was roused to polemics, the Homestead men cared for their wounded and settled down to await the next move by the company. On the day after the battle the locked-out men repaired all damage done the mill, rebuilt the fence, and replaced the regular company watchmen on the property. The strict guard was not relaxed, for there were constant rumors that more Pinkertons were being assembled for another invasion. On July 7 two of the slain workers were buried, and Homestead remained quiet, wondering what the company would do and whether Governor Pattison would be persuaded to send troops. Sheriff McCleary began demanding on July 6 that the Governor call out the militia. He sent three telegrams this day and another on the 7th, but Governor Pattison replied: "Your telegram indicates that you have not made any attempt to execute the law to enforce order, and I must insist upon you calling upon all citizens for an adequate number of deputies." [16] The sheriff thereupon issued a proclamation, asking all good citizens to assemble at his office with arms and assistance, but made no further effort.

The Governor was annoyed by the apparent incompetence of McCleary and said to the newspaper reporters:

Why the Sheriff of Allegheny has not done a single thing.
He has neglected his duty and every citizen of Allegheny

County knows it. He has sent out a few notices, requests for people to become members of his posse, and his request has been virtually ignored. He will never get a posse by following that line of action. . . .

I am of the opinion that there would not have been a drop of blood shed if the proposition had been accepted to let the locked-out men guard the premises.[17]

Burgess McLuckie dispatched a telegram to Governor Pattison, reporting that the people were orderly and were keeping the peace, and that there was no need to send troops. A committee from Homestead went to Harrisburg and pointed out to the Governor that the workmen had only resisted an armed invasion of the town and were ready at any time to receive the sheriff and his deputies. The workmen began to feel certain that the militia would not be called out. Yet unexpectedly on Sunday, July 10, after keeping silence since July 7, McCleary telegraphed another request for troops; for some reason this time Governor Pattison complied and ordered Major General George R. Snowden to assemble the National Guard of Pennsylvania, numbering 8,000, and move to Homestead. On this same day Frick sent secretly a telegram to the Governor; but only a few days afterwards he was unable to produce this telegram for the Congressional committee, or to recall its contents.[18] It is possible now merely to guess at the probable pressure that brought about the Governor's decision.

The men at Homestead were dismayed and did not know at first how to receive the militia. Finally they decided to welcome the troops as fellow workers, and prepared a reception, including two brass bands and a speech by Burgess McLuckie. But the movements of the troops were not revealed, and on the morning of July 12 the militia arrived suddenly, took possession of the town, and encamped on the hills over-

THE FIRST TROOPS IN HOMESTEAD. Drawn by T. de Thulstrup after a sketch by F. Cresson Schell. (*Harper's Weekly,* July 23, 1892)

looking it. The officers refused to acknowledge the long-delayed reception: the bands did not play, the burgess delivered no speech. When O'Donnell and a committee from the town called on General Snowden, they were brusquely received. O'Donnell tendered the coöperation of the Amalgamated and the townspeople: "On the part of the amalgamated association, I wish to say that after suffering an attack of illegal authority, we are glad to have the legal authority of the State here." General Snowden replied: "I do not recognize your association, sir. I recognize no one but the citizens of this city. We have come here to restore law and order and they are already restored." [19] All attempts by the Homestead people to approach the troops as friends were suppressed by the officers. Sentries were stationed, and no civilians were permitted through the lines. Because of this unsympathetic attitude, the cooks and servant girls declined to wait any longer upon the military command, which was quartered at a club house called Frick Hotel; and the camp commissary had to be summoned to serve the officers.

Meanwhile a committee from the workers at Beaver Falls and the Upper and Lower Union Mills, branches of the Carnegie Steel Company, asked the company to arbitrate with the Homestead men. Secretary Lovejoy refused point-blank. Whereupon the Upper and Lower Union Mills quit work at noon, July 14, in a sympathetic strike, even though the Amalgamated scale at these mills had been signed by the company. The next day the Beaver Falls Mill joined the strike. The company, however, seized this opportunity to rid itself of these union contracts, and announced that the men at these three mills had until July 18 to return to work under a new non-union agreement.

As the locked-out men had anticipated, under the protection of the troops the company at Homestead began to prepare for the bringing of scabs. Cots and provisions were placed inside the mill-yard, and contracts were let for 100 houses to be erected within the mill enclosure. Outside the fence militiamen patrolled with fixed bayonets. A notice was put up on July 16 by the company, giving Homestead men until 6 P.M., July 21, to apply for work:

It is our desire to retain in our service all of our employes whose past record is satisfactory, and who did not take part in the attempts which have been made to interfere with our right to manage our business.[20]

None of the locked-out men applied. They felt confident that enough rollers, heaters, shearers, cutters, and other trained workers could not be found. Their treasury was still untouched, and they had many promises of help from other unions. Accordingly, two steamboats commenced on July 22 to convey small loads of "blacksheep," previously collected at Pittsburgh, to the mills at Homestead. The company issued eviction notices to all locked-out men occupying company-owned houses, whether the rent was being paid or not. The Beaver Falls and Upper and Lower Union Mills remained completely shut down.

5. Charges of murder, aggravated riot, conspiracy, and treason

The company prepared its final and overwhelming blow against the workmen. It had driven them into opposition by its attitude during the negotiations for a new agreement and by the untimely fortification of the mill. It had locked them out before the termination of the old contract and had assumed the aggressive. It had precipitated an armed conflict by sending the Pinkertons and had in this way procured the National Guard. It had brought "blacksheep" into the mill under the shadow of the militia. But it still had to weaken the resistance of the workmen and smash their unity, for it required the services of trained men and could not operate the mill with inexperienced scabs alone.

The legal prosecution of the Homestead men, long threatened by the company, was opened. On July 18 Secretary Lovejoy lodged informations before Alderman McMasters in Pittsburgh against Hugh O'Donnell, John McLuckie, Hugh Ross, and four other leaders of the workmen, charging them with the murder of Pinkerton detective T. J. Connors. Within the next few days the men surrendered themselves, and after spending a night in jail, all but one were released on $10,000 bail each. The workers retaliated on August 3 by lodging informations before Alderman Knight, charging with murder Robert and William Pinkerton, Superintendents Potter and Corey, and Frick, Lovejoy, Leischman, and Curry, officials of the company. All the defendants were admitted immediately to $10,000 bail each, without being subjected to the humiliation of passing a night in jail before getting a hearing in court. The difference in treatment enraged the workers. Lovejoy continued to have warrants issued, with the evident design of multiplying the amount of bail until the resources of the workmen were no longer sufficient and confinement could not be avoided. On August 30 he filed informations against 40 workmen, charging them with conspiracy and aggravated riot.

When the grand jury met on September 22, it returned 167 true bills against the Homestead men. There were six different indictments: three for murder, two for aggravated riot, and one for conspiracy. Hugh O'Donnell, Hugh Ross, and John McLuckie were defendants in all six indictments. The leadership of the men was buried beneath bail bonds. These legal proceedings bewildered the workmen. The nation, too, seemed to misunderstand them, to regard them not as honest and dependable laborers, but as murderers and rioters. The short-lived and treacherous political sympathy of the free-trade papers was dying. Deliberate lies were printed:

The 240 men who have been reduced were the head rollers or sub-contractors, who have been making, strange as it may seem, from $10 to $50 a day; some have made as much as $13,000 a year, all owing to the improved machinery which increases the output of piecework. These head rollers themselves employ men and are the leaders of the Association of Amalgamated Steel and Iron Workers. The reduction of these extravagant wages was deemed advisable and so was undertaken, with the present strike as a result. The reduction would still have left the head rollers a handsome pay.[21]

Actually the most extravagant wage paid during the peak month recorded was $280, and only one worker received this. Most of the skilled men received well below $200 a month, and that only during the season.

Then it was impossible to shoot those firing from the shore at the barges, because the strikers had made a breastwork for themselves by placing women and children in front and firing from behind them.[22]

This is George Ticknor Curtis's version of the deliberate volley by the Pinkertons into the crowd of men, women, and children on the shore.

Under the burden of martial law, the steady influx of "blacksheep," and the relentless arrests, the men began to show the first indications of weakening. In August the mechanics and day laborers, disturbed at the increasing number of scabs who were usurping their jobs, had to be urged to remain out. The sympathy strike at Upper Union Mills was broken, and the plant reopened as non-union. A similar strike at Duquesne was likewise broken with the aid of a regiment of militia. In the meantime an interlude had again thrown the Homestead trouble into the headlines and had brought a deluge of slander by the press. On July 23 Alexander Berkman, the young anarchist from New York, shot Frick at the company office in Pittsburgh and wounded him seriously. Berkman instantly surrendered himself and was jailed. At his trial he conducted his own defense and read a denunciation of the ruling class. The jury, without leaving the box, found him guilty, and he was sentenced to the maximum penalty of 21 years in the penitentiary and one year in the workhouse.

Early in October the workmen received another shock. Chief Justice Edward Paxson of the Supreme Court of Pennsylvania, without any open invitation from the local authorities, interfered in the Homestead case. Arriving at Pittsburgh, he ordered the arrest of 27 workers, members of the advisory committee, on charges of treason against the State of Pennsylvania. He announced, moreover, that he would instruct the grand jury, that he would hear applications for bail, and that, if the cases came to trial, he would act as judge. Pittsburgh was thus enabled to see the Chief Justice of the Supreme Court of the state sit in a court of Allegheny County and instruct the grand jury as to what constitutes treason. Paxson explained his unprecedented intervention by the extreme necessity for establishing an authoritative interpretation of the treason law in the Homestead cases. The grand jury, duly instructed by Paxson, returned true bills against the advisory committee members. Many of the indicted men were forced into hiding, since by this time their bail resources were exhausted.

Despite all its efforts, however, the company was routed in the courts. No jury would find the workmen guilty. The first case, that of Sylvester Critchlow, charged with the murder of T. J. Connors, was called to trial November 18. The Carnegie attorney Knox assisted the prosecution. After one hour's deliberation the jury acquitted Critchlow. Within the next four months the company appeared twice more in the courts, bringing O'Donnell and another to trial on charges of murder. When the company was twice defeated, an agreement was reached to drop all prosecutions on both sides. Nevertheless, the court victories had been costly for the workers. The men had been slowly crushed. Even though the last of the troops had left Homestead by October 13 and had been replaced by deputies, the mill had been gradually supplied with nearly 2,000 "blacksheep." The locked-out men began to realize that they were doomed to lose, and many of them moved from Homestead to look for other jobs. Interest in Homestead faded. The newspapers were filled with the election of Cleveland, the Corbett-Sullivan fight, the scare of a cholera epidemic, fresh strikes in Tennessee and New York. The locked-out men had spent their resources. They still made such feeble protests as withdrawing their children from the school that "blacksheep" children attended. On November 17, four and one-half months after the struggle began, the first break in their ranks occurred, when the day laborers and mechanics voted to return to work.

6. ". . . *to the unquestioned advantage of our employés*"

The actual collapse came as the Homestead lodges of the Amalgamated voted on November 20 to raise the prohibition against returning to work for the company. The vote was close, 101 to 91, and fewer than 200 of the original 800 members were present. Hugh O'Donnell and a number of the men were in jail at this time, others had abandoned Homestead to seek employment elsewhere, and many were too discouraged to appear at the last meeting. Only part of the men who applied for work were rehired. The company was glad to take back the skilled hands, and the new superintendent, Charles M. Schwab, not bound by the promises of

Potter, discharged many inexperienced scabs to make place for the indispensable services of the former workers; still there was not room for all. Many skilled men, also, were on the blacklist and could get work in no mill throughout the country. Those men, both skilled and unskilled, who failed to get reëmployment were destitute after the hardships of the lockout, and had to be helped by a relief committee and the Amalgamated.

Through the defeat not only was the Homestead plant lost to the Amalgamated, but unionism was eliminated in most of the mills in the Pittsburgh region. The struggle had been costly in money, lives, and time. Aside from the $600,-000 spent to maintain the militia at Homestead, the state paid the deputy sheriffs and the expenses for court trials. The workmen lost nearly $800,000 in wages during the 20 weeks of idleness, and perhaps again as much in savings and relief funds. The outlay of the company was never published, but its victory was relatively cheap. The hampering union was annihilated, and the workmen were reduced to absolute obedience, dependent now entirely upon the good will and magnanimity of the company. To be sure, Frick had once declared that the men would fare better under a non-union system:

The Edgar Thompson Works and our establishment at Duquesne are both operated by workmen who are not members of the Amalgamated Association with the greatest satisfaction to ourselves and to the unquestioned advantage of our employés. At both of these plants the work in every department goes on uninterrupted; the men are not harassed by the interference of trade union officials, and the best evidence that their wages are satisfactory is shown in the fact that we have never had a strike there since they began working under our system of management.[23]

But, as the men knew beforehand, these words were untrue and fruitless.

From this time forward the men had no voice in determining their hours and wages, the conditions of work, and the share they were to have in improved processes of production. They had no effective protest against any debasement of their standards of living, and as a result the standards were constantly forced lower. When Margaret F. Byington, some 15 years later, conducted for the Pittsburgh Survey an investigation into Homestead, she found conditions that made life and happiness nigh impossible. The men toiled long hours, nearly all working a 12-hour day, with a 24-hour stretch every two weeks when they exchanged day and night shifts.[24] There was no leisure, little family life, and little civic spirit; there were only hard work, poor food, and wearied sleep. Wages had fallen very low, especially for the fresh immigrant labor, with the usual consequences:

The analysis of expenditures indicates that the man who earns $9.90 a week, as do a majority of such laborers, and who has a family of normal size to support, can provide for them only a two-room tenement in a crowded court, with no sanitary conveniences; a supply of food below the minimum sufficient for mere physical well-being; insurance that makes provision which is utterly inadequate for the family left without a breadwinner; a meager expenditure for clothes and furniture, and an almost negligible margin for recreation, education and savings. Many can, to be sure, add to their earnings by working seven days a week instead of six; by working twelve hours a day instead of ten; but after all we are talking of standards of life and labor for an American industry, and common sense will scarcely sanction such a week of work. Many, too, as we have seen, take in lodgers, but do it at the cost of decency and health.[25]

That the absence of union control was largely responsible for the low wages is indicated by a comparison with the wages paid in the unionized bituminous mines of western Pennsylvania. In 1907 the organized common laborers in the mines received $2.36 for an eight-hour day, while the unorganized common laborers in the steel mills received only $1.65 for a 10-hour and $1.98 for a 12-hour day.[26] The earnings of the miners exceeded those of the steel laborers by two full days' pay a week. While the workmen in the steel industry sank into a state of slavery, the Carnegie Steel Company grew rapidly, accumulated more and more wealth, transformed itself into the United States Steel Corporation, and with its monopoly on steel production, established itself at the very heart of American capitalism.

IV. STRIKE AT PULLMAN

1. Model town

In the years following the extended and spontaneous rail-road strikes of 1877 there arose numerous local conflicts between the railroad companies and their workmen, but not until the spring and summer of 1894 was there another nation-wide alignment of labor against the power of the railroads. During the intervening 17 years labor had learned many lessons. It had seen state militia and federal troops employed to break strikes. It had come to expect the hostility of the courts and the vituperation of the press in its battles for better working conditions. It had experienced, as at Homestead, the crushing force of the corporation as a fighting weapon. It had been taught the necessity for unyielding solidarity in its ranks. When, therefore, the railroad workers undertook a second great struggle against the railroad companies, they were conscious of the significance of their struggle and of the dangers it involved.

The setting for the opening of this struggle was the town of Pullman adjoining the southern edge of Chicago. George M. Pullman had founded the town in 1880 as the site for the Pullman Palace Car Company. It was to rival similar constructions by Krupp at Essen in Germany and by Sir Titus Salt at Saltaire in England as a model town, a town, according to the pamphlet, *The Story of Pullman,* distributed by the company to all visitors, "that is bordered with bright beds of flowers and green velvety stretches of lawn, shaded with trees, and dotted with parks and pretty water vistas,

101

and glimpses here and there of artistic sweeps of landscape gardening; a town, in a word, where all that is ugly and discordant and demoralizing is eliminated, and all that inspires to self-respect is generously provided." The pamphlet closed by boasting that the town of Pullman "has illustrated the helpful combination of Capital and Labor without strife or stultification, upon the lines of mutual recognition." [1]

All the land and buildings in the town were the property of the Pullman company. The plant—the factories, foundry, shops, steel mills—stood on 200 acres. Another 100 acres were covered with homes, workers' tenements, and such public structures as a hotel, post office, bank, church, and arcade of stores. Here the company regulated with paternal solicitude the lives of its employees and conducted its highly profitable business of manufacturing and repairing its cars, which were operated under contract on 125,000 miles of railroad, three-fourths of the total mileage of the nation. Here the company was both employer and landlord for more than 5,000 workers, who with their families and a few shopkeepers made up the population of 12,000. As their landlord the company collected the rent, supplied water and gas, disposed of the sewage, accepted their savings in its bank, and permitted them to use its library at 25 cents a month. Nevertheless, the workers were dissatisfied with the ubiquitous guardianship of the company. They complained that the "green velvety stretches of lawn" were merely show places for visitors, while they had to live in overcrowded tenement blocks, with 300 to 500 persons in each, that there were only one closet and one water faucet for each group of five families, that there were no bathtubs, and that one barren space served as the only common yard for all the tenements surrounding it. In other parts of the town, they said, living quarters were even worse. Excessive rents, furthermore, forced them to take in lodgers.

In spite of their dissatisfaction the workers showed no organized resentment until the summer of 1893, when an economic depression settled over the country and the company laid off all except 900 men. Only in November, 1893, after it received contracts for new work and many cars were brought in for repairs, did it enlarge the force, so that during the winter about 4,000 of the original 5,000 to 6,000 were employed. This reëmployment, however, was offset for the workers by severe wage cuts, which averaged 25 per cent to 40 per cent between September, 1893, and May 1, 1894. Not only did the company reduce the wages in the departments manufacturing new cars, but it also made a corresponding cut in the repair shops, even though the railroads still paid the pre-depression rate of 2 cents per mile for the repair of each Pullman car. Pullman claimed that there were idle cars to store and repair, which increased the general repair costs, but all this testimony was, in the words of the United States Strike Commission, "in such loose and indefinite shape as to compel the conclusion that the reduction in the repair department was not made with reference to these depression results, but was part of a plan designed to reduce wages in every department to the lowest point possible to be reached in the department most seriously affected by the depression." [2]

Throughout this period no salaries of the officers, managers, or superintendents were reduced, and the company continued to pay its 8 per cent dividends on an exaggerated capitalization. For each year since its inception in 1867 the Pullman company had paid 8 per cent to 9½ per cent in annual dividends. By 1894 its total capitalization was $36,-000,000, much of it water.[3] In addition it had laid up a surplus of $25,000,000 as undivided profits, later to be issued as stock dividends. For the year ending July 31, 1893, the dividends were $2,520,000 and the wages $7,223,719.51. For the year ending July 31, 1894, although the wages fell to $4,471,701.39, the dividends rose to $2,880,000.[4] The economic depression became entirely the burden of the workers. Their pay was lowered to 4 cents an hour up to 16 cents, while inspectors and sub-bosses squeezed every available bit of work out of them.

It was impossible to live on such low wages. Often after two weeks' labor the men received checks from 4 cents to $1 over and above their rent, which was collected in advance by the employer-landlord Pullman. One blacksmith, who received 45 cents for six hours, quit work, preferring to starve without wearing out his clothes at the Pullman anvil. Another worker got for one month a pay check 45 cents short of covering his rent; a bill for the balance was sent to his house with a collector. The Rev. W. H. Carwardine, who was pastor of the Pullman Methodist-Episcopal Church for two years preceding the strike, reported:

After deducting rent the men invariably had only from one to six dollars or so on which to live for two weeks. One man has a pay check in his possession of two cents after paying rent. He has never cashed it, preferring to keep it as a momento [sic]. He has it framed. Another I saw the other day, for seven cents. It was dated September, '93. The man had worked as a skilled mechanic at ten hours a day for twelve days, and earned $9.07. He keeps a widowed mother, and pays the rent, the house being in his name. His half month's rent amounted to $9.00. The seven cents was his, but he has never claimed it.[5]

During the bitter winter of 1893-1894 the men fell deeper and deeper into debt for their very subsistence.

What aggravated the condition of the men was the refusal of the company to lower its rents in accordance with the wage reductions. It regarded its employer-function and its landlord-function as separate and distinct. No matter what the needs of the workmen, the rent collections were made. And no matter what the wages of the workmen, the rents remained the same. If the supposed aesthetic features of Pullman were discounted, the rents were from 20 per cent to 25 per cent higher than for similar accommodations in the neighboring towns of Kensington and Roseland. "The aesthetic features," comments the Senate report drily, "are admired by visitors, but have little money value to employees, especially when they lack bread." [6] To the charges that the rents were exorbitant the company replied that the men were not compelled to live in Pullman. This claim, however, was untenable, for the fear of losing their jobs tied the workers to Pullman. Whenever work was slack the company, to safeguards its rents, gave preference to its tenants. There could be no doubt that the company maintained its high dividends throughout the economic crisis by grinding its employees between high rents and low wages.

Aside from the high rents and low wages, the men had a number of long-standing grievances. For one thing, the company made additional profits by reselling them the water and the gas which it purchased from the city of Chicago. In fact, no service which the company furnished them was without its profit; even the sewage was used to fertilize the 140-acre farm of Pullman. For another thing, although the company paid an official physician and surgeon to provide injured employees with the necessary treatment and drugs, it was also his duty to urge the acceptance by the patient of any settlement offered by the company. "If suit follows, the doctor is usually a witness for the company." [7] The physician served in this way principally to protect the company against litigation. The sick and the injured received almost no compensation for time lost. At every point the company made itself felt, as if its workmen were medieval serfs. The officialdom was oppressive, and the superintendents and foremen were unfair, arbitrary, often insulting. A system of espionage kept the company informed of all that went on. There was much favoritism and nepotism, and there was a feeling of insecurity among the men, who felt that they were often discharged for slight reason. The blacklist was the reward of all who protested against any abuses, with the accompanying refusal of a recommendation of good character to another employer. Labor organizations were regarded with hostility. In the town it had built the company asserted its assumed right to regulate every phase of the workers' lives and to suppress any attempts at independence.

After a long winter full of hardship the resentment of the men came to a head, and on May 7, 1894, a committee chosen by the workers placed with Vice-President Thomas H. Wickes a formal demand for the restoration of the wage scales prior to the cuts of the preceding summer. Wickes asked the committee to meet with Pullman on May 9. At this conference Pullman declared that the company had taken its new work at a loss, merely to keep the shops open and furnish employment to the men. In fact, throughout the strike Pullman held that the company's purpose in keeping the shops open was philanthropic, and that a decrease in wages had been necessary in order to make lower bids for contracts possible. In the *Chicago Herald*, June 26, 1894, he said:

I realized the necessity for the most strenuous exertions to procure work immediately, without which there would be great embarrassment, not only to the employes and their families at Pullman, but also to those living in the immediate vicinity, including between seven hundred and eight hundred employes who had purchased homes and to whom employment was actually necessary to enable them to complete their payments.[8]

He mentioned 55 passengers cars manufactured for the Long Island Railroad at a loss of $300 each, and he offered to open the company's books for the inspection of the men. It was impossible, he contended, for the company to raise wages when it was building cars at less than cost. He refused to agree that workmen in the repair departments should not suffer the same cuts as those in the company's most seriously crippled department. He refused also to discuss the question of rents, and insisted that Pullman as employer was not to be confused with Pullman as landlord.

The committee of workers was chagrined at Pullman's reply to their requests. They suspected the genuineness of a poverty plea in a company that in 1892 had declared 8 per cent dividends of $2,300,000, besides a surplus amounting to $3,250,389; and in 1893 again 8 per cent dividends of $2,520,000 with a surplus of $4,006,448. They wondered if the company did not keep its shops open for some other purpose than the beneficent one announced by Pullman; perhaps it was to maintain the plant in running condition and thus prevent rapid depreciation, to secure the rent returns, and to continue the payment of dividends at the expense of the workmen. The U. S. Strike Commission confirmed the suspicions of the workers:

In its statements to the public, which are in evidence, the company represents that its object in all it did was to continue operations for the benefit of its workmen and of trades people in and about Pullman and to save the public from the annoyance of interrupted travel. The commission thinks that the evidence shows that it sought to keep running mainly for its own benefit as a manufacturer, that its plant might not rust, that its competitors might not invade its territory, that it might keep its cars in repair, that it might be ready for resumption when business revived with a live plant and competent help, and that its revenue from its tenements might continue.[9]

Nevertheless, upon Pullman's promise that none of the members of the grievance committee were to be discharged or discriminated against and that the shop abuses were to be investigated, the committee retired from the conference apparently satisfied with the good faith of the company's explanation.

2. Enter the American Railway Union

On May 10, the day following the conference between Pullman and the grievance committee, work went on as usual in the plant. Vice-President Wickes and other officials began the formal investigation of shop complaints. But suddenly the workmen were thrown into excitement and anger by the news that, in violation of Pullman's promise, three members of the grievance committee had been laid off. When charged later with breaking its agreement, the management disavowed any malicious intention in the laying off of the three men. What months of deprivation had failed to do, this breach of faith accomplished in a few hours. It was the signal for action.

The instrument for action was already in existence: during the preceding months of March and April the men at Pullman, seeking some relief from the distress they had suffered through the winter, had enrolled in the American Railway Union. Nearly 4,000 of them had become members in the 19 local unions organized. At that time the American Railway Union was rebuked harshly by the press for extending membership to the Pullman employees, who were not, strictly speaking, railroad workers. But the inclusion of all workers connected with any part of the railway industry in one solid vertical or industrial union was one of the principles

on which the American Railway Union had been founded by
Eugene V. Debs. Its amazingly rapid growth—150,000
members in less than a year—was due to this principle of
industrial unionism. For many years Debs had been Grand
Secretary-Treasurer of the Brotherhood of Locomotive Firemen and had grown steadily more discontented with the ex-
clusiveness, the jealousies, and the animosities of the four
railway Brotherhoods. After a switchmen's strike at Buffalo in 1893, when the Brotherhoods failed to help, Debs
resigned his position and devoted himself to the organization of a new federation of railway workers that would include unskilled labor as well as all the craft unions. In June,
1893, he formed the American Railway Union. In April,
1894, it sprang a surprise strike on the Great Northern
Railroad and won. By June, 1894, there were 465 local
lodges and 150,000 members. At this time the American
Federation of Labor had 275,000 members, the Knights of
Labor perhaps 175,000, and the four Brotherhoods some
140,000. The Brotherhood officials, of course, were decidedly
hostile to the new union.

The American Railway Union believed firmly that the interests of each of the 850,000 railroad workers in the United
States were the interests of all, and that one united organization was essential in the struggle for better working conditions. It was no longer to be possible for the employers to
foster the division of labor into crafts and to use one group
against another, as the Brotherhoods, for example, had been
used for strike-breaking during the railroad strikes of 1877.
The growing concentration of railroad capital and administration required a strong union of the workers for mutual
protection.

Often in the spring of 1894 the locals at Pullman had
appealed to President Debs and to Vice-President George
W. Howard to call them out on strike, but they had been

counseled to wait until the American Railway Union gained more strength and experience. With thousands idle and business in a slump, the time was inopportune for striking. However, when the Pullman company broke its promise to the grievance committee, 46 men, representing all the 19 local unions, met the entire night of Thursday, May 10, in a secret session and voted unanimously to strike on Saturday. Somehow, probably through a spy, the company discovered this plan early Friday morning and decided to declare a lockout at noon. But the strike leaders in turn learned about 9 A.M. of the company's decision, perhaps through a sympathetic telegraph operator, and word was passed along to the men to walk out. Immediately 2,500 employees left their machines and tools. About 600 remained until noon. By evening the entire force was out, demanding the reëmployment of the three laid-off men, the lowering of rents, and the restoration of the wage cuts made during the preceding year. The company replied by posting a notice that the plant was to be shut down indefinitely. It was nearly three months before the shops were again opened.

The conduct of the strike was given over to the Central Strike Committee, composed of representatives from each local union. Public meetings were held daily, and speakers urged the strikers to maintain their solidarity and to keep order. A cordon of workers was placed around the company property to protect it. The strikers wanted no violence, and the U. S. Strike Commission was able to report: "It is in evidence, and uncontradicted, that no violence or destruction of property by strikers or sympathizers took place at Pullman, and that until July 3 no extraordinary protection was had from the police or military against even anticipated disorder." [10] A relief committee was organized, and it appealed for food and money. Several business men contributed flour and meats, the *Chicago Daily News* donated the use of a storeroom, and the American Railway Union responded by assessing each of its members 3 cents per day to support the strikers at Pullman. For three weeks all remained quiet; even the brief notices of the trouble at Pullman disappeared from the newspapers, while the attention of the nation was occupied by the great coal miners' strike, the denouement of Coxey's march on Washington, and the disastrous flood at Johnstown, Pennsylvania.

The Pullman company settled down to starve out the strikers. After three weeks the families of the workmen began to suffer extreme privation. In the hope of conciliating the differences between the contestants, the Civic Federation of Chicago sent a committee, among whom was Jane Addams, to urge the Pullman company to arbitrate, but Vice-President Wickes replied point-blank that there was nothing to arbitrate. On June 3 the committee made a second fruitless attempt to secure arbitration. Meanwhile, on June 12, the first quadrennial convention of the American Railway Union opened in Chicago with all 465 local unions represented. Chief among the matters on the agenda was the strike at Pullman. Union members throughout the country were indignant at the imperious refusal of Pullman to arbitrate and were aroused by the sufferings of the strikers. There was talk of sympathetic strike and boycott.

It was the policy of Debs and Howard, however, to avoid both strike and boycott until every possibility of peaceful adjustment had failed. The constitution of the American Railway Union breathed moderation and conciliation:

The order, while pledged to conservative methods, will protect the humblest of its members in every right he can justly claim; but while the rights of members will be sacredly guarded, no intemperate demand or unreasonable propositions will be entertained. Corporations will not be permitted

*to treat the organization better than the organization will
treat them. A high sense of honor must be the animating
spirit, and evenhanded justice the end sought to be obtained.
Thoroughly organized in every department, with a due regard for the right wherever found, it is confidently believed
that all differences may be satisfactorily adjusted, that har-
monious relations may be established and maintained, that
the service may be incalculably improved, and that the necessity for strike and lockout, boycott and blacklist, alike disastrous to employer and employee and a perpetual menace to
the welfare of the public, will forever disappear.*[11]

Equal in importance with Debs's pacific nature was the fear
that the American Railway Union was still too young and
feeble to risk a dangerous conflict. Moreover, Debs undoubtedly wanted to win public opinion for the strikers by giving
the Pullman company every opportunity to damn itself in
refusing to arbitrate. In accordance with this policy the convention was instructed to send a committee to Pullman, and
in the meantime Debs did not permit strikes at the Pullman
works in Ludlow, Kentucky; Wilmington, Delaware; and
St. Louis, Missouri.

Wickes declined on June 15 to receive any communication from the American Railway Union committee, on the
grounds that it did not represent the Pullman strikers. Another committee, made up of the workers at Pullman, was
then sent, but Wickes again stated that there was nothing
to arbitrate. Thereupon the committee offered to submit the
question of whether there was anything to arbitrate to a
special board, to be composed of two men selected by Pullman, two selected by the circuit judges of Cook County, and
a fifth chosen by these four. Even though no worker was to
be on this board, the strikers agreed to abide by its decision
as to whether there was anything to arbitrate. Again Pull-

man refused to submit. Every effort made by Debs and the American Railway Union to bring about a peaceful settlement was shattered by Pullman's inexorability, concerning which the judgment of the U. S. Strike Commission was:

The policy of both the Pullman company and the Railway Managers' Association in reference to applications to arbitrate closed the door to all attempts at conciliation and settlement of differences. The commission is impressed with the belief, by the evidence and by the attendant circumstances as disclosed, that a different policy would have prevented the loss of life and great loss of property and wages occasioned by the strike.[12]

After the attitude of Pullman was made plain and the American Railway Union had demonstrated clearly its willingness to arbitrate, the convention, under pressure from the various local unions, voted unanimously on June 21 to give the Pullman company four days in which to treat with its employees. If by June 26 the company had failed to yield to mediation, then the members of the American Railway Union were to refuse to handle Pullman cars on any road.

3. White ribbons versus the red, white, and blue

As soon as they received the ultimatum, the Pullman officials sought and found a ready ally in the General Managers' Association, a voluntary unincorporated association which had been formed in 1886, with the 24 railroads radiating out of Chicago as its members. From June 22 to the end of the strike the General Managers' Association took charge of the struggle against the American Railway Union. It was an association organized for exactly such an occasion. It controlled over 40,000 miles of road, 220,000 employees, and two billion dollars in capital. Its function was to deal with problems of transportation, with the regulation of wages, and, above all, with labor difficulties. Whenever a wage controversy arose, the Association, rather than the individual road, handled it. If it became necessary the Association imported strike-breakers and directed activities.

No one, therefore, was surprised when at an emergency meeting on June 25, the day preceding the threatened boycott, the Association resolved:

That we hereby declare it to be the lawful right and duty of said railway companies to protest against said proposed boycott; to resist the same in the interest of their existing contracts, and for the benefit of the traveling public, and that we will act unitedly to that end.[13]

A few days later the Association issued the following statement to the press:

The railroad companies fail to see the justice of the position taken by the A.R.U. of fighting Mr. Pullman over the heads of the railroad companies, who have no control over Mr. Pullman's movements or his manufacturing business. The men who are now on a strike are considered as employes who have resigned their positions and who are not anxious for work.[14]

Employing the combined resources of all the roads, the General Managers' Association joined the Pullman Palace Car Company in a determined effort to crush both strike and boycott. Headquarters were established and John M. Egan was put in charge of breaking the boycott. A publicity bureau was started, agencies for hiring new men were opened, and communication was set up with civil and military authorities. When the boycott began on June 26, the Association ordered the discharge of every man who refused to switch Pullman cars. This order converted the boycott automatically into a strike, for as each switchman was discharged for cutting out Pullman cars the rest of the crew stopped work in a body. The men were quiet, but resolute: they were arrayed consciously against one of the most powerful combinations of capital in the nation.

The very day after the ultimatum expired the boycott was in full force on the Illinois Central and no Pullman cars were moved. By June 28 the Pullman traffic out of Chicago was completely paralyzed, and 11 roads were tied up by the automatic strikes that resulted. Furthermore, with remarkable speed the boycott spread west and south, and soon the Southern Pacific and the Northern Pacific were on strike. Debs issued an appeal calling upon all railroad workers to support the boycott of Pullman cars:

To the Railway Employes of America: The struggle with the Pullman Company has developed into a contest between the producing classes and the money power of the country. We stand upon the ground that the workingmen are entitled to a just proportion of the proceeds of their labor. This the Pullman Company denied them. Reductions had been made from time to time until the employes earned barely sufficient wages to live, not enough to prevent them from sinking deeper and deeper into Pullman's debt, thereby mortgaging their bodies and souls, as well as their children's, to that heartless corporation. Up to this point the fight was between the American Railway Union and the Pullman Company. The American Railway Union resolved that its members would refuse to handle Pullman cars and equipment. Then the railway corporations, through the General Managers' Association, came to the rescue, and in a series of whereases declared to the world that they would go into partnership with Pullman, so to speak, and stand by him in his devilish work of starving his employes to death. The American Railway Union accepted the gage of war, and thus the

*contest is now on between the railway corporations united
solidly upon the one hand and the labor forces upon the
other. . . .*[15]

Everywhere the workers displayed the confidence they felt
in Debs and the discipline they had learned from previous
strikes: they remained quiet, but they refused to work.

The country had never before seen a strike so well organized on so large a scale. The boycott was in effect at Minneapolis, St. Louis, San Francisco, Denver. The General Managers' Association in Chicago found it impossible to get men
to replace the strikers, and on June 30 Debs had to protest
to Immigration Inspector H. C. Bradey against an attempt
of the Association to import 2,000 men from Canada. The
officials themselves tried to make up a few dummy trains, but
moved them only with great difficulty.

With the exception of the *Chicago Times* and a few other
papers, the press was vehemently aroused by the amazing
success of the boycott and the unselfish solidarity shown by
labor. The cry was raised that the railroads were a public
institution and that any interference whatsoever with their
operation was an attack upon the general citizenry. What
was more, the boycott was an attempt by labor to blackmail
capital, an attempt virtually revolutionary in its implica-
tions. An editorial in *Harper's Weekly* declared:

*The brigand who demands ransom for his prisoner, with
mutilation or death as the alternative; the police captain
who sells for money his power to arrest the dealers in vice
and crime; the news-monger who gathers scandal in order
that he may be paid for suppressing it—these are the types
of blackmailers whom all the world loathes. The boycott
ordered by the railway union is morally no better than any
of these acts. It is an attempt at blackmail on the largest
scale.*[16]

The General Managers' Association called upon U. S. Marshal Arnold for special deputies, and District Attorney Milchrist wired to Washington for instructions. Attorney-General Olney replied that as many deputies were to be sworn in as were needed to prevent the obstruction of the mails. By July 1 Arnold had sworn in 400 deputies, and within a few days the number had increased to 3,600. These deputies were selected by Egan of the General Managers' Association, were paid by the railroads, and served both as United States officers and as railroad employees. The deputies were obtained by means of a stratagem that had proved successful in 1877. The mail cars were attached at the end of trains made up of Pullman cars deliberately to invite interference by the strikers. In cutting out the Pullman cars, the strikers necessarily obstructed the mails, and the federal government became involved.

With the introduction of the special deputies, violence first entered the conflict. A number of freight cars were burned in Chicago. The strikers, however, contended that the burning of freight cars and the instigation of violence were the work of *agents provocateurs* hired by the railroads, who feared that by peaceful means the American Railway Union would win all along the line. Mayor Hopkins of Chicago and Governor Altgeld of Illinois concurred in this opinion. Henry Demarest Lloyd wrote in his notebook:

E. W. Bemis was told that Mayor Hopkins before leaving office procured 40 affidavits showing that the burning of freight cars was done by railroad men; that the railroad men moved cars outside of fire limits, then burned them, inciting bystanders to participate. Hopkins, fearing these affidavits might be destroyed by some subsequent railroad mayor, took certified copies before leaving office.[17]

Partly to counteract the violence and rioting that began after the deputies were introduced and partly to solidify further the ranks of the American Railway Union, Debs asked all sympathizers and strikers to wear white ribbons. The Board of Trade in Chicago countered by distributing miniature red-white-and-blue flags for the lapel.

In spite of the presence of the special deputies, the strike grew steadily more effective. Debs issued an ultimatum on July 2 that any armistice with the Pullman company would have to rest on a basis satisfactory to the employees, that all strikers were to be taken back to their old positions with no discrimination and no wage cuts, and that the General Managers' Association and the Pullman company would have to settle together. The strikers were firm and intent on winning. The Association was thus far completely defeated, with the railroads paralyzed as long as they attempted to run Pullman cars. For the week ending June 30 the 10 trunk-line railroads out of Chicago carried 42,892 tons of east-bound freight; for the week ending July 7 the tonnage dropped to 11,600, and the Big Four carried not one ton, while the Baltimore and Ohio carried only 52.[18] The General Managers' Association began to demand troops, but it intrigued from the outset to keep out the state militia and to bring federal soldiers. In part, the Association distrusted Governor Altgeld and the use he might make of the militia; it may be, as Altgeld himself charged, that the Association feared lest the troops would really protect property and prevent acts of provocation. In part, the Association wanted federal troops in order to convert the conflict into one between the workers and the federal government. In addition, as was found in the strikes of 1877, federal troops were more dependable and impersonal than state militia and police. Only this intrigue of the Association can explain the absence of any request from Chicago, either from the local authorities or from the railroads, for state troops, notwithstanding the readiness with which Altgeld replied to requests for militia in other parts of the state.

The federal authorities responded almost eagerly to the intrigue of the General Managers' Association. As early as July 2 the federal garrison at Fort Sheridan, outside of Chicago, was instructed confidentially to make all necessary preparations. In the afternoon of July 3 President Cleveland received a request for federal troops from U. S. Marshal J. W. Arnold, supported by the signatures of Federal Judge P. S. Grosscup, District Attorney T. E. Milchrist, and Edwin Walker, who had been appointed by Attorney-General Olney to act as special counsel for the government during the railroad difficulties. Even though there had been no application whatsoever from either Governor Altgeld or the Legislature of Illinois, President Cleveland ordered out the federal troops. The troops, he asserted, were sent not to interfere with the state authorities, but to protect federal property, to prevent obstruction of the mails and interference with interstate commerce, and to enforce the decrees of the federal courts. At 10:15 A.M. on July 4, Independence Day, four companies of the Fifteenth Infantry marched into Chicago and camped on the lake front. By July 10 there were nearly 2,000 federal troops in Chicago under the command of General Miles, who established his headquarters in the Pullman building at Michigan Avenue and Adams Street.

When Altgeld learned of the arrival of federal troops in Chicago, he instantly wired a long and sharp protest to President Cleveland and demanded the immediate withdrawal of the soldiers:

I am advised that you have ordered Federal troops to go into service in the State of Illinois. Surely the facts have not

*been correctly presented to you in this case or you would
not have taken this step, for it is entirely unnecessary, and,
as it seems to me, unjustifiable. . . . So far as I have been
advised, the local officials have been able to handle the situation. Notwithstanding these facts the Federal Government
has been applied to by men who had political and selfish motives for wanting to ignore the State government. At present
some of our railroads are paralyzed, not by reason of ob-
structions, but because they cannot get men to operate their
trains. . . . The newspapers' accounts have in many cases
been pure fabrications, and others wild exaggerations. You
have been imposed on in this matter, but, even if, by a forced
construction, it were held that the conditions here came
within the letter of the statute, then I submit that local self-
government is a fundamental principle of our Constitution.
. . . As Governor of the State of Illinois I protest against
this, and ask the immediate withdrawal of Federal troops
from active duty in this State.*[19]

Cleveland replied with a short telegram that ignored the
issues raised by Altgeld and merely restated the statutory
authority on which the troops had been sent. Again Altgeld
dispatched a long telegram, on July 6, even sharper in tone
than the first. But Cleveland answered with contemptuous
brevity that the discussion would have to end.

The press meanwhile became enraged at what it regarded
as Altgeld's impudence in rebuking the President. It recalled
his pardoning of the anarchists Fielden, Neebe, and Schwab,
and named him the champion of anarchy. Its frenzy almost
exceeded that of the preceding year when Altgeld issued his
pardon message. In an editorial, "Gov. Altgeld and the
President," the *Nation* wrote:

*It should surprise nobody that Governor Altgeld of Illi-
nois came to the rescue of Debs and his fellow law-breakers*

*by protesting against the efforts of the federal authorities
to restore order in Chicago. He is the executive who pardoned the anarchists out of prison, and it is only natural
that he should sympathize with anarchists who have not yet
been sent to prison.*[20]

Altgeld was treated by the *Nation* and the rest of the press
as an anarchistic revolutionary, not as the honest liberal he
was. It was his sin to uphold the principles of the Constitution and the Bill of Rights at times when employers and
authorities wanted to set them aside. As for Cleveland's
second contemptuous reply, the *Nation* saw in it, not uncon-
stitutional behavior masked by dogmatic assurance, but the
answer of righteousness to anarchy:

*President Cleveland's method of dealing with Gov. Altgeld
is a model one. He wastes no time in arguing with him, or in
defending himself against his attacks, but in a few terse
sentences sets him before the country in his true light as the
friend and champion of disorder. Altgeld is probably as
unconscious of his own bad manners as he is of the bad odor
of his own principles; but boorish, impudent, and ignorant
as he is, he can scarcely fail to wince under the treatment
which he receives from the President.*[21]

In the clamor that arose the protest of Debs and Howard to
President Cleveland was lost.

The presence of the federal troops stirred up violence on
July 5, when they helped move the first train of Swift & Co.
meats from the Union Stock Yards. A crowd refused to
move from the tracks until driven away by bayonet and
cavalry charges. That night Mayor Hopkins issued a proclamation forbidding riotous assemblies, and Governor Altgeld,
upon the mayor's application, ordered out the five regiments
of militia stationed at Chicago. The city was now a military

camp, with at least 14,000 men under arms. For the first time since the calling of the boycott serious street fighting arose. U. S. deputy marshals on July 6 fired into a crowd and killed two. In the afternoon of July 7 at Forty-ninth and Loomis Streets, where a crowd collected in protest against the movement of a wrecking train by Company H, Second Regiment, Illinois National Guard, the militia opened fire and killed 20 to 30 persons. Similar trouble arose at Denver and San Francisco, where federal troops had been ordered out. State troops were called out in California, Iowa, and Michigan. Six companies of federal infantry from Fort Leavenworth, Kansas, and two from Fort Brady, Michigan, were ordered to Fort Sheridan so as to be near Chicago. President Cleveland issued a proclamation warning all citizens in Illinois and especially in Chicago against assembling after the noon of July 9. A second proclamation, to take effect at 3 P.M., July 10, applied to North Dakota, Montana, Idaho, Washington, Wyoming, Colorado, and California. The situation was grave.

But notwithstanding the military array and the presidential proclamations, the strike remained unbroken. Of the 24 roads in Chicago, 13 were entirely blockaded on July 6 and the others ran only mail and passenger trains. The Associated Press reported:

Despite the presence of the United States troops and the mobilization of five regiments of state militia; despite threats of martial law and bullet and bayonet, the great strike inaugurated by the American Railway Union holds three-fourths of the roads running out of Chicago in its strong fetters, and last night traffic was more fully paralyzed than at any time since the inception of the tie up.[22]

Debs still controlled the boycott and strike. At least 50,000 miles of railroad were directly involved, and many more indirectly affected. From all sections of the country came word of sympathetic walkouts of engineers, telegraph operators, firemen, switchmen, car cleaners and repairers. It is true that the officials of the Brotherhoods opposed the strike actively and expelled all members who joined it. Grand Master Frank P. Sargent of the Brotherhood of Locomotive Firemen announced as early as June 30 that any member who joined the Pullman boycott would be expelled.[23] Grand Chief E. E. Clark of the Order of Railway Conductors denounced the boycott and strike bitterly, as did Grand Master Wilkinson of the Brotherhood of Trainmen, who said: "The triumph of this railroad strike would be the triumph of anarchy." [24] Nevertheless, the membership of the Brotherhoods was strongly sympathetic. Indeed, many lodges—for instance, Lodge 233 of the Brotherhood of Locomotive Firemen in Chicago—turned in their charters and joined the American Railway Union. Debs conferred with the leaders of the trade-unions in Chicago, and a general strike for the city was announced to begin Wednesday morning, July 11, provided that Pullman again refused to submit to arbitration. A committee of seven, to whom Mayor Hopkins added four members of the City Council, called upon Wickes on Monday, July 9. He reiterated that there was nothing to arbitrate.

4. Government by injunction

The intervention of federal troops was not sufficient to halt the spread of the strike. Nor was this the only weapon employed against the American Railway Union. Even before Attorney-General Olney had ordered the swearing in of deputy marshals and President Cleveland had dispatched the federal troops, there were preparations for court action to break the strike. On June 30 Olney named as special counsel for the government the prominent attorney Edwin Walker, who, as the strikers protested, had been since 1870 the attorney for the Chicago, Milwaukee and St. Paul Railway, one of the roads involved in the strike. This salaried official of the railroads plotted with Olney and District Attorney Milchrist. Olney wrote in a letter to Walker: "It has seemed to me that if the rights of the United States were vigorously asserted in Chicago, the origin and center of the demonstration, the result would be to make it a failure everywhere else, and to prevent its spread over the entire country." [25] To block effectively the spread of the strike, Olney advised Walker and Milchrist not to rely upon warrants issued under criminal statutes against persons actually guilty of criminal action, but to use the injunction to restrain persons from anticipated criminal action.

Although the injunction was not a new instrument, this was its first important use against labor. Moreover, the Supreme Court, by its action in the Debs case after the Pullman strike, gave the injunction a firm legal basis; from the manner in which the Supreme Court searched for a plausible explanation, it would seem that the weapon was first used and found effective, and then the Supreme Court was given the task of justification.[26] When Olney first advised its use, he found his justification in the Interstate Commerce Act and in the Sherman Anti-Trust Act of 1890, both of which had ostensibly been enacted to prevent collusion and monopoly among corporations. This explanation by itself, however, did not suffice at the hearing before the Supreme Court several months afterwards. In order to legalize the injunction the Supreme Court had to establish two doctrines. First, it was necessary to show that the act to be restrained by the injunction would do irreparable injury to the complainant's property. This was a difficult problem, for injunctions were ordinarily issued to restrain strikes, picketing, and boycotting, and no physical property was threatened. The Supreme Court solved the difficulty by declaring that expectancies based upon the merchant-customer relationship and upon the employer-employee relationship are property. Thus a strike and picketing damage the employer's expectancy of keeping his old employees and hiring new ones; whereas the boycott injures the merchant's expectancy of retaining his old customers and obtaining new ones, an expectancy expressed in the principle of good will.

The proof that irreparable injury might be done to property, however, was not enough. By law there can be no recovery for losses due to the exercise by others of their legal rights; and if the strike, the boycott, and picketing were legal rights of the workers, then there could be no injunction issued to restrain them from injuring the expectancies of the employer. It was necessary, second, to justify the injunction as a procedure under equity—*i.e.*, extraordinary justice—and to show that the strike, the boycott, and picketing constitute malicious conspiracy against the complainant. Thanks to the peculiar interpretation made by Olney of the Interstate Commerce Act and the Sherman Anti-Trust Act, the principle of malicious conspiracy was readily established. The result of the deliberations of the Supreme Court was that the "malicious" interference of strikes, picketing, and boycotts with the "probable expectancies" of the employer could be restrained by court order.

This justification, it must be remembered, came months later. It was wholly on the initiative of the Department of Justice and on the instructions of Attorney-General Olney that an omnibus injunction was issued on July 2 in the United States Court of Judge Grosscup, restraining Debs, Howard, and all members of the American Railway Union from interfering with the mails, with interstate commerce, or with the conduct of the business of the 23 railroads specifically named. Even attempts to persuade railroad employees to quit work were prohibited, for the injunction enjoined:

Compelling or inducing, or attempting to compel or in-duce by threats, intimidation, persuasion, force, or violence, any of the employees of any of said railroads to refuse or fail to perform any of their duties as employees of any of said railroads, or the carriage of the United States mail by such railroads, or the transportation. . . .

Compelling or inducing, or attempting to compel or in-duce, by threats, intimidation, force, or violence, any of the employees of any of said railroads, who are employed by such railroads and engaged in its service in the conduct of interstate business or in the operation of any of its trains carrying the mail of the United States, or doing interstate business, or the transportation . . . to leave the service of such railroads.[27]

Under this injunction any form of picketing became a crime. This Chicago injunction was copied in other cities; one injunction, in fact, issued by Judge Phillips in the U. S. Circuit Court at Kansas City, Missouri, not only enjoined persuasion, but admonished the workers on the Santa Fe Railroad not to leave the service of the company.

Under the injunction, furthermore, there was no trial by jury. The judge became supreme arbiter, for he not only issued the injunction, but also punished all violators for contempt of court. In this way a kind of military law was established. The U. S. Strike Commission pointed out:

It is seriously questioned, and with much force, whether courts have jurisdiction to enjoin citizens from "persuad-ing" each other in industrial or other matters of common interest. However, it is generally recognized among good citizens that a mandate of a court is to be obeyed until it is modified and corrected by the court that issued it.[28]

Labor was placed in an awkward, even fatal, predicament. If it obeyed the injunction and waited for a court test, the strike was effectively broken in the interim, and the test, even providing the court brought in a favorable decision, came invariably too late. If it disobeyed the injunction, it faced arrest and summary punishment for contempt of court that served to disrupt the ranks of the strikers. Thus the court injunction proved itself a potent strike-breaking instrument, with the result that it has been employed ever since in strikes.

When the plans for a general strike in Chicago, however, progressed despite the injunction served on Debs and the officers of the American Railway Union, Judge Grosscup summoned a special federal grand jury which was to determine whether an insurrection against the government existed and, if so, what parties produced it. The jury assembled on July 10 and was instructed by Judge Grosscup in the meaning of insurrection. Any open and active opposition to the execution of the law, he declared, was insurrection; therefore, any interference with the passage of the mails, since the laws forbade such interference, was insurrection. Moreover, any conspiracy in restraint of interstate commerce, a restraint specifically prohibited by law, was likewise insurrection. He left no doubt in his instructions to the jury that the strike corresponded to a state of insurrection:

If it shall appear to you that any two or more persons corruptly or wrongfully agreed with each other that the trains carrying the mails and interstate commerce should be forcibly arrested, obstructed and restrained, such would clearly constitute a conspiracy. If it shall appear to you that two or more persons corruptly or wrongfully agreed with each other that the employes of the several railroads carrying the mails and interstate commerce should quit and that successors should, by threats, intimidation or violence, be prevented from taking their places, such would constitute a conspiracy. . . .[29]

Having been duly instructed by Judge Grosscup, the special grand jury returned indictments against President Debs, Vice-President Howard, Secretary Sylvester Keliher, and Director L. W. Rogers, all of the American Railway Union, charging them with conspiracy to obstruct the mails, to interrupt interstate commerce, and to intimidate citizens in the free exercise and enjoyment of their rights and privileges under the Constitution. The indictments were found on Tuesday, July 10, the day preceding the scheduled general strike in Chicago. The offices of the American Railway Union were broken into by federal authorities, and all papers and legal documents of the union were seized. Debs and the other three union officers were arrested, but were released on bail of $10,000 each.

While injunctions and conspiracy indictments were being issued by the courts, Debs persisted in his efforts to organize a general strike. It was his plan first to call out organized labor in Chicago, numbering 50,000 to 100,000, and then to proceed from city to city until the entire nation was paralyzed or the General Managers' Association and Pullman surrendered. But contrary to his hopes, the general strike in Chicago was slow in getting under way; on Wednesday, July 11 only 1,700 cigarmakers and 800 German bakers walked out. Even though the workers both in Chicago and St. Louis were in favor of the general strike, many officials of the American Federation of Labor failed to respond to Debs's plea, and as a result of this conflicting authority confusion arose. At the request of Debs a meeting of the 25 chief national officials of the Federation, among them Samuel Gompers, was held in Chicago on July 12. Debs strove for some united authority that would end the confusion of the workers, and he urged the calling of a general sympathetic strike. But Gompers and other officials opposed him on the grounds that such a strike would be "unwise and inexpedient." After two days of sessions the conference decided against ordering a general strike, though it did vote $10,000 to aid the American Railway Union officers in court defense. It recommended that the strikers return to work and abandon the attempt to win against the military forces already called out. It recommended also that labor organize more solidly and seek correction of industrial and economic ailments at the ballot box. The Chicago trade-unions rescinded their strike order, and the movement for a general strike was checked.

After the decision of the American Federation of Labor officials, Debs and the American Railway Union sent through Mayor Hopkins a proposal to the General Managers' Association to call off the strike and boycott, provided that all the men, with the exception of those convicted of crime, were restored to their former positions without discrimination. The proposal was returned unanswered. The General Managers' Association refused to treat with the strikers. It felt that the strikers were being defeated by the federal troops and court action, and it wanted labor to learn thoroughly the lessons of defeat. In reply to the obduracy of the Association, Debs announced that the strike would continue, and he began to strengthen the ranks of the strikers. Traffic was still tied up, and only on Monday, July 16, was the blockade in Chicago even partially raised. On July 17, however, Debs, Howard, Keliher, and Rogers, while out on bail for the conspiracy indictment, were again arrested, this time for contempt of court through information filed in the U. S. Circuit Court accusing them of open and continued disobedience of the injunction which had been served on them July 3. Bail was again set at $10,000. The four officers of the union decided to go to jail in order to force a test trial.

5. *The strike is defeated*

The court actions, in addition to the unprecedented concentration of federal troops, state militia, deputy marshals, deputy sheriffs, and police, began to discourage and disorganize the strikers in Chicago. The indictments were multiplied until every strike leader was hampered by court charges. On July 19 the federal grand jury returned 23 indictments in Judge Seaman's court and named 75 individuals for violating federal statutes. Debs, Howard, Keliher, and Rogers were named in nearly all the indictments. In all, during this period, 190 strikers were arrested under the federal statutes, and 515 were arrested by the police on charges of murder, arson, burglary, assault, intimidation, riot, inciting to riot, etc.[30] Moreover, the Brotherhood officials became more energetic daily in their strike-breaking activities. Grand Chief Arthur of the Brotherhood of Locomotive Engineers, for instance, not only ordered his men to work with scab firemen, but also recommended men to replace all striking engineers. Under such combined opposition the strikers began to weaken. The east-bound freight on the 10 trunk lines out of Chicago, which fell from the 11,600 tons for the week ending July 7 to the lowest point of 4,142 for the week ending July 14, rose to 29,146 tons for the week ending July 21. The corresponding tonnage for the week ending July 21, 1893, had been 47,359.[31] With this renewal of traffic the defeat of the strike in Chicago was foreshadowed.

Although the first train in 18 days reached St. Paul from the Pacific coast on July 17, the boycott and strike were still firm in the West, particularly at Sacramento, Oakland, and San Francisco. At Sacramento the strikers offered to furnish 3,000 deputies to see that no lawlessness was committed, provided that the railroads could find any crews to man the trains. It was necessary to employ both federal troops and the injunction to break the boycott here. The strikers were literally beaten into submission. On July 17 the Board of City Trustees of Sacramento adopted a resolution condemning "the tyranny and brutality which has characterized the conduct of the United States soldiers who have wounded and assaulted unoffending persons upon the streets." The trustees further condemned the troops "for the free and unprovoked use of their bayonets and guns and for the reckless wounding of innocent citizens." [32] On July 20 the federal troops were withdrawn from Chicago and sent west to smash the stubborn strikes still existing there.

The hearing of the contempt of court cases against Debs, Howard, Keliher, and Rogers opened on July 23. The trial was postponed until September 5 because of the illness of Edwin Walker, who was assisting District Attorney Milchrist with the prosecution. Among the defense counsel was Clarence Darrow. The prosecution argued that the defendants had conspired to restrain interstate trade, and produced as evidence telegrams, which had been seized during the raid on the American Railway Union office, directing workers in various parts of the country to go on strike. In turn, the defense contended that the strike involved no conspiracy, inasmuch as the American Railway Union was a voluntary organization and the members had voted unanimously of their own free will to go on strike. If the workers had the right to strike, then they could not be accused of conspiracy. On December 14 the U. S. Circuit Court, basing its decision on the Sherman Anti-Trust Act, found Debs and his associates guilty. An appeal to the United States Supreme Court resulted on May 27, 1895, as has been indicated, in a unanimous opinion upholding the legality of the injunction and of the contempt of court decision. Debs was sentenced to six months in the county jail at Woodstock, the others to three months each.

In the meantime, the Pullman company, sensing that the boycott and sympathetic strikes were failing, posted a notice, dated July 18, on the gates of its shops:

These shops will be opened as soon as the number of operatives taken on is sufficient to make a working force in all departments.[33]

Only some 325 men registered to return to work, and since Wickes needed a minimum of 800 workers, the shops remained closed. There was still no evidence of surrender at Pullman. A bicycle picket corps kept the strikers united, and only on August 1 was Wickes able to announce that the required 800 men had applied for work, of whom 300 were special policemen that had been guarding the plant. Mayor Hopkins asked Altgeld to recall eight of the 11 companies of militia at Pullman, which were costing the state $9,500 per day; it was clear that the shops could not get men to work. In contrast to the firmness displayed at Pullman, however, the American Railway Union now began to yield on all sides. Federal troops opened the Union Pacific road, and the American Railway Union was forced to declare the strike off in the West. Everywhere the railroads discriminated against the strikers. The Union Pacific dismissed all men who had been active in the strike. The Big Four at Cairo, Illinois, discharged 40 strikers; the Erie Road shops at Kent, Ohio, 35; the Chicago and Erie shops at Huntington, Indiana, 60. A pledge was required by the Southern Pacific that its men sever all connections with the American Railway Union, and that they join no labor organization during their period of employment. It was the death knell of the American Railway Union.

Debs concluded that it was suicidal to continue the hopeless struggle and called a convention of the American Railway Union to end the strike. When the convention met in

Chicago on August 2 only 53 delegates, nearly all from the West, were present. The American Railway Union had been crushed in the struggle. The strike in Chicago and throughout the country was called off on August 5. At Pullman the strike continued until September 6, and even then many workers refused to yield. The Pullman company announced that it would not give employment to members of the strike committee, nor to any others who had taken an active part in persuading workmen to strike or in encouraging them to stay out. Labor organization was taboo. For this stand the Pullman company was rebuked by the Strike Commission:

Since the strike, withdrawal from the American Railway Union is required from those seeking work. The company does not recognize that labor organizations have any place or necessity in Pullman, where the company fixes wages and rents, and refuses to treat with labor organizations. The laborer can work or quit on the terms offered; that is the limit of his rights. To join a labor organization in order to secure the protection of union against wrongs, real or imaginary, is overstepping the limits and arouses hostility. This position secures all the advantage of the concentration of capital, ability, power, and control for the company in its labor dealings, and deprives the employees of any such advantage or protection as a labor union might afford. In this respect the Pullman company is behind the age.[34]

Altgeld investigated matters at Pullman and wrote to George M. Pullman, urging him to relieve the starving people. He pointed out that the state had spent $50,000 to protect property at Pullman, and suggested that the company forego all rents in arrears and charge no new rent until October 1. Pullman did not reply, and Altgeld had to issue a proclamation calling for public contributions to aid the 6,000 workers with their families suffering at Pullman.

With the strike definitely lost, the railroads began to estimate its cost. The loss from incendiarism was less than $250,000.[35] Another $400,000 was spent for the hire of deputy marshals. The loss in income was $4,672,916, and there were, of course, additional losses throughout the country because of the paralysis of transportation. The workers, on the other hand, suffered about 25 persons killed and 60 badly injured. The Pullman strikers lost $350,000 in wages and the other railroad strikers $1,389,143.[36] After the conflict was ended, President Cleveland appointed a Strike Commission to study the Pullman strike. It took testimony for 13 days and examined 109 witnesses; and it recommended: (1) that there be compulsory arbitration for disputes between railroads and their workers with a permanent strike commission to judge; (2) that the separate states adopt systems of conciliation and arbitration; and (3) that labor organizations be recognized and dealt with by employers. These recommendations died of neglect.

Meanwhile, Debs and his counsel Darrow made every effort to bring to trial the conspiracy indictments of July 10. Finally on February 9, 1895, the trial opened before Judge Grosscup. Edwin Walker represented both the railroads and the government. Pullman was subpoenaed, but went East and refused to appear: he was not cited for contempt of court. The defense was hampered in every possible way; for one thing, it was not permitted to read in court the secret proceedings of the General Managers' Association to prove a conspiracy of the railroads, although the proceedings of the American Railway Union were introduced by the prosecution. Finally a juryman fell ill and the case was postponed. Darrow offered to read the testimony to a new juryman and continue the trial, but Walker refused. The case was postponed again and again on various excuses until at last it was dropped from the records. The 86 witnesses that

Darrow had ready to testify to deliberate violence instigated by the Association were never called. Thus faded out in the courts one of the most bitter struggles between labor and capital, a struggle in which were demonstrated new uses of the courts as a weapon against strikes and labor demonstrations. Hereafter the injunction, with its consequent contempt-of-court charges and summary punishment, serves in nearly every strike.

V. ANTHRACITE, 1902

1. *"Black stones"* and *"white horses"*

Before considering the protracted struggle between miners and operators in the anthracite coal fields of Pennsylvania during the summer and early fall of 1902, it is essential to understand the conditions then prevailing in the industry. In the United States anthracite coal, commonly called "black stones" by the early settlers, constitutes practically a natural monopoly. Almost the entire source of this commodity is restricted to an area of less than 500 square miles in eastern Pennsylvania, and 96 per cent of the nation's total output is produced in the five counties of Lackawanna, Luzerne, Carbon, Northumberland, and Schuylkill. The anthracite fields of this area are divided into three sections: the Wyoming region, including the Northern Basin and with its center at Wilkes-Barre and Scranton, which yielded in 1901 approximately 50 per cent of the nation's output; the Lehigh region, including the Eastern Middle Basin around Hazleton, which yielded 17 per cent; and the Schuylkill region, made up of the Western Middle Basin surrounding Shamokin and the Southern Basin surrounding Pottsville, which yielded 33 per cent. In 1901 a population of 630,000 in the anthracite areas was directly or indirectly dependent upon the production of the collieries; of this number 144,000 were mine workers.

From 1855 to 1875 anthracite coal was used in the blast furnace for the manufacture of pig iron, but it was then replaced by coke, obtained from bituminous coal. After this market was lost, anthracite found a new one in domestic consumption. For this purpose the large lumps had to be broken into smaller domestic sizes (grate, egg, stove, chestnut) and a great amount of unmarketable fine coal resulted. However, during the 1890 decade it was found that even the smallest sizes (pea, buckwheat nos. 1, 2, and 3) could be used, for making steam; thereafter the old culm banks were put through the washeries in order that the steam sizes might be reclaimed. The market for both domestic and steam sizes, it is true, was limited: the domestic sizes were consumed in the winter months, with the result that the collieries were most active in the fall and winter, while the spring and summer were slack seasons; the steam sizes, on the other hand, had to meet the competition of bituminous coal and at times had to be sold at prices below the cost of production. Nevertheless, the output of anthracite coal in 1901 was 60,242,560 long tons; and its value—$112,504,020 at the mines—exceeded that of any other metallic or non-metallic mineral product in the country, with the exception of bituminous coal and pig iron, and amounted to more than 10 per cent of the value of the entire mineral production.[1]

It was to be expected that capital would make an effort to control so valuable and profitable a natural monopoly. The development of a corresponding financial monopoly commenced in 1873, when the coal-carrying railroads, headed by J. Pierpont Morgan and the Philadelphia and Reading Railroad, invaded the anthracite fields to buy and lease coal properties. Through skillful purchasing and the making of contracts in perpetuity, the railroads practically eliminated the independent operators; the few that remained were at the mercy of the coal carriers whenever they had to get their product to the markets. By 1892 the Philadelphia and Reading alone controlled nearly 70 per cent of the total shipments of anthracite.[2] By 1902 the coal-carrying railroads owned or controlled 96.29 per cent of the anthracite deposits, of which they owned nearly 91 per cent outright.[3] But in order to achieve the desired consolidation and monopoly, the railroads were forced to burden themselves with immense debts, which were taken care of largely through the device of watering the capitalization. Difficulties arose, since:

. . . *the productive capacity of the mines was twelve to fifteen million tons greater [in 1890] than the market would take at satisfactory prices,—satisfactory, that is, not to the public, but to the companies, which desire prices that will return a profit, not merely on their mining operations, but also a surplus toward meeting the interest charges on the vast obligations incurred (perhaps not always wisely) in securing their enormous holdings of coal lands.*[4]

The rapid concentration of the anthracite properties in the hands of a few corporations was accomplished at the expense not only of the general public, which paid through higher prices and the waste of an essential commodity, but also of the mine laborers, who contributed to the increased dividends, interest rates, and profits through lower wages, longer hours, and poorer working conditions. Precautions were taken against the possibility of active opposition on the part of labor to the debasement of its standard of living. Whatever organization the mine workers formed for their mutual protection was destroyed by the operators. The Miners' and Laborers' Benevolent Association, which came into existence following the Civil War, was crushed in 1875 after the failure of a general strike. Two other organizations, the Knights of Labor and the Miners' National Progressive Union, arose within the next 15 years, but were not successful in their efforts to organize the miners. The operators, furthermore, imported large numbers of workers from Austria, Hungary, Poland, Russia, and Italy so as to have on hand an oversupply of unorganized labor which would both depress wages and, because of differences in custom and language, hinder an effective union of the miners. In 1880, for example, not 5 per cent of the anthracite workers were Slavs, whereas by 1904 the Slavs constituted 50 per cent.[5] The pressure of the immigrant reservoir was soon felt by the workers, particularly during the six years from 1893 to 1899, when they were given employment only 160 to 175 days in the year.

Wages were forced down until in 1902 the average wage in the coal fields was $22 a month.[6] In 1901 the average annual earnings of the contract miner, who was among the highest paid of all mine labor, were $560.[7] This rate, the miners maintained, was much lower than that prevailing in the bituminous fields and in other occupations requiring equal skill and training. And this rate was especially inadequate in view of the hazardous employment, with the liability to serious and chronic disease, the accidents, and the high death rate incident to it. The operators, on the other hand, insisted that the frequent accidents were due mainly to the carelessness of the workers, not to the character of the work. In this controversy the Anthracite Coal Strike Commission agreed with the men and recognized the dangers they were exposed to:

In considering the compensation to be paid for any class of labor, the danger to life and limb to those engaged should be taken into account. All kinds of mining work involve risk of accident considerably in excess of the average in manual labor. Coal mining is more hazardous than any other class of underground work, for in addition to the usual dangers from falling rock and premature blasts, the coal miner runs risk of fire, explosion, and suffocation. The temporary shutting off of the supply of air may place in jeopardy the life of every worker in a coal mine. The flame from a "blown-out" shot may explode a mixture of gas, or dust and air, and result in the death or injury of many men. The danger of tapping a gas pocket is always present, and constant vigilance is necessary in order to protect the safety of the coal miner. The occupation must therefore be classed among those of a hazardous nature, the fisheries, certain classes of railway employment, and powder manufacture being among the few in which the danger exceeds that of coal mining.[8]

Moreover, an increased cost of living and the spread of work among an oversupply of labor, the miners complained, made their real wages so low that their children were prematurely forced into the breakers, washeries, and collieries in order to help support the family. While the laws of Pennsylvania prohibited the employment of children under 14 years of age inside a mine and under 12 outside, they were ignored; and thousands of boys under 12 worked as slate pickers and sat over chutes and screens to pick impurities from the coal as it passed by. For this labor they received 27, 33, or 39 cents for a 10-hour day. The door-tenders, who worked inside the mine, got 67½ cents for a 10-hour day.[9]

Besides the low rate of wages, the mine workers suffered from injustices in the measuring and weighing of the coal they mined. The old Miners' and Laborers' Benevolent Association had secured in 1875 the passage of a law in Pennsylvania for the weighing of coal and the adoption of a standard ton. After the destruction of the union, however, the law was persistently violated and finally completely disregarded. Where the coal was still paid for by weight, the ton had grown from the standard 2,240 pounds to 2,800 and 3,190 pounds, while the operators still sold coal by the ton of 2,240 pounds. The difference was supposed, so said the

companies, to compensate for the impurities and small un-
salable sizes which were found in the coal as it came from
the mine. A weighmaster certified the amount of coal to be
paid for. Where, as in most mines, the coal was paid for by
the carload, the price paid the miner had remained the same,
while the size of the cars had increased gradually as though
they were made, so the miners put it, of live oak. Nor was
this all. The miner had to load from six to nine inches
of "topping" above the railing of the car. To increase the
confusion and unfairness, there were great variations in the
size of the mine cars. In the Phoenix colliery of the Philadelphia and Reading Coal and Iron Company, for example,
four different cars were used, ranging in size from 74.4 to
94 cubic feet, and each was paid for at five different prices,
ranging from 70 cents to $1.05, according to the difficulty
of the mining. As a result, the rate per ton varied from 30
to 56 cents, or nearly 100 per cent.[10] A docking boss, furthermore, deducted a round sum for impurities and underweight,
with no appeal for the miners from his arbitrary judgment.

As a remedy for the confusion in the measuring and weighing of the coal, the workers wanted first the right to employ
check-weighmen and check docking bosses, who would act as
inspectors to watch the weighing and docking of the coal.
Where such check-weighmen and docking bosses were employed, the percentage of dockage dropped as much as 50
per cent. In three collieries of the Scranton Coal Company
previous to the employment of check docking bosses the percentages of dockage were 3.11, 4.41, and 6.46. These fell
after the employment of check docking bosses to 1.77, 2.39,
and 3.13 respectively. Likewise, in four collieries of the
Temple Iron Company the percentages dropped from 4.94,
7.10, 4.62, and 4.03 to 2.34, 4.43, 2.08, and 1.29 respectively.[11] Second, the miners wanted the payment for coal by
weight and the adoption of the legal ton, for these would

lead to uniformity in wages. Incentives to cheating and dishonesty, both by operator and worker, would be removed. Unjust discrimination and favoritism would be prevented. Originally, also, the excessive ton had been adopted to compensate the operator for the smaller sizes of coal which were discarded, but since these sizes had become marketable for steam making, any except the legal ton was unfair to the worker.

In opposition to the desires of the miners, the operators contended that uniform wages could never be granted in the anthracite basins. Inequality of wages, they held, was the necessary result of natural variations and difficulties in the anthracite veins: variations in the thickness of veins from two to 100 feet, in the lay of the seams, in the impurity of the coal because of rock and slate, in the faults and flexures, in the quality of the roof, in the specific gravity of the coal; difficulties resulting from breakage of machinery, the presence of water in the chambers, the sulphur streaks, the failure of pumps, storms, and repairs.

Many other grievances were held by the miners. There was a shortage of mine cars, and their distribution was not fair, but was guided at times by favoritism. Miners, therefore, had to remain idle frequently while they waited for a car to load the coal into. The miners regarded the 10-hour day as injurious to health and life, as conducive to accidents and disease. Indeed, some of the workers—the engineers and firemen engaged in hoisting water—worked 12-hour shifts, with a 24-hour turn every other Sunday when the shifts were alternated. The workers wanted an eight-hour day. There were charges, moreover, that through company stores and company houses the operators profited "not only by mining coal but by mining miners." At the company store the worker had to pay exorbitant prices for inferior goods. From the company house the miner could be evicted during a strike.

Besides, the company doctors, whose salaries came usually from obligatory monthly deductions from the worker's pay, were inefficient and unsympathetic. For all these services, nevertheless, the miner had to pay. After the numerous deductions for purchases at the company store, rent, doctor fee, dockage, powder, tools, etc., were made, there was little left of the miner's wages. For months sometimes the men got no actual money from the companies. Often on pay day the miner would receive a "white horse" (as the empty pay envelope was termed) if not a statement of indebtedness to the company.

2. *Maneuvering for a hold*

Ever since the destruction of the Miners' and Laborers' Benevolent Association in 1875, the coal miners had recognized the need for a strong organization to counteract the growing monopoly over the coal fields, but their efforts had proved inadequate. It was not until January, 1890, when the District Assembly no. 135 of the Knights of Labor and the Miners' National Progressive Union combined at Columbus, Ohio, to form the United Mine Workers of America, that the miners saw promise of a widespread union. Even the United Mine Workers, however, during the first years of its existence appeared doomed to ineffectiveness and death; its membership had dwindled by 1894 to 13,000. But in 1897 the United Mine Workers, with only 10,000 members, conducted a stubborn 12-week strike in the bituminous fields of Illinois, Indiana, Ohio, and Pennsylvania, and won all its demands with, above all, official recognition of the union. From this time on the United Mine Workers remained dominant in the bituminous fields. Meanwhile the organizers sent to the anthracite fields in eastern Pennsylvania by the United Mine Workers encountered numerous difficulties. There were some 20 nationalities in the anthracite basin, and mutual distrust had been bred among them. There still existed, also, the memories of former failures at organization. Moreover, there was fear of reprisal against union members, for the few operators who dominated the anthracite fields were able to formulate a common labor policy and exercise a rigid blacklist. Yet, although the organizers were rebuffed, they felt certain that thousands of miners would participate in a strike to increase their wages and alleviate their grievances, provided the strike were general enough.

Despite these difficulties, the United Mine Workers succeeded in setting up organizations in the three anthracite districts, all of which together had fewer than 8,000 members. As the discontent of the anthracite miners with their working conditions increased during the fall and winter of 1900, the United Mine Workers called for a convention at Hazleton in July. Here demands were drawn up, principally for an increase in wages, for the abolition of the company stores and the discontinuance of the company doctors, and for a reduction in the price of powder, which the men were obliged to buy from the companies at $2.75 a keg, while the same keg sold for $1.10 in the open market. An invitation was sent to the operators for a joint conference with the mine workers in August. The invitation was ignored. Whereupon, in an effort to evoke some attention from the operators, the United Mine Workers called upon them to reply to the miners' demands within 10 days. There was no reply, and a strike was therefore declared on September 17. That this was the will of the mine workers is seen from the fact that, notwithstanding the actual union membership of fewer than 8,000, between 80,000 and 100,000 men and boys obeyed the strike order on the first day, and within two weeks 90 per cent of the 144,000 employees quit work.

Most likely the operators would have attempted to crush the strike by concerted action, but the time was inopportune: a presidential election was impending. Senator Mark Hanna, chairman of the National Republican Committee and campaign manager for President McKinley, intervened, and on October 3 the operators posted notices of a 10 per cent increase in wages, refusing, however, to make the proposal directly to the miners, lest that would imply tacit recognition of their organization. Since the notices contained no statement of how long the increased wages were to be paid and said nothing of their other demands, the workers decided to continue the strike. After two weeks of silence the operators, under pressure from Senator Hanna and the Republicans, posted new notices. There were to be a 10 per cent increase in wages and a reduction in the price of powder, but this reduction, amounting to 6 or 7 per cent of the total wages, was to be subtracted from the advance in wages. The wages were to be paid semi-monthly, and the other demands were to be adjusted later. Again the operators refused to make the proposals directly to the miners and so left the road open for a future attack on the miners' organization. Nevertheless, the United Mine Workers, satisfied with the concessions and with the progress it had made in the anthracite field, ordered work resumed on October 20.

Neither the miners nor the operators regarded the settlement of October 20, 1900, as final, the former because it was a temporary proposal without recognition of the United Mine Workers, the latter because it bound them to certain concessions to their employees. Sooner or later, both sides understood, there would have to be a more decisive and permanent settlement. In preparation for the approaching struggle the operators adopted an aggressive policy. Stockades were constructed around many of the collieries, and depots were erected for the storage of coal. Workers were discouraged from joining the United Mine Workers, and, according to John Mitchell, president of the United Mine

Workers, agents of the company entered the union to spy and disrupt. Irritation developed among the mine workers. In spite of these preparations and the discontent on both sides, when April, 1901, arrived, the operators proposed to renew the unwritten agreement for another year and the workers accepted. But as the time approached for the end of the renewed agreement, the miners began to prepare to secure some recognition of the principle of collective bargaining. On February 14, 1902, President Mitchell addressed a letter to the operators inviting them to join in a conference with the miners at Scranton for the purpose of drawing up a wage scale for the year beginning April 1, 1902. However, since such a conference would have meant acknowledgment of the existence of a miners' organization, the presidents of the coal companies declined the offer unanimously.

Aware that, with the termination of the 1900 settlement close at hand, the continued refusal of the operators to attend a conference portended the long-expected struggle, the anthracite mine workers met in convention at Shamokin from March 18 to 24. Here they passed resolutions embodying four demands: (1) An increase of 20 per cent over the wages paid during 1901 to employees performing contract or piece work. (2) A reduction of 20 per cent in hours of labor—*i.e.*, from the 10-hour day to the eight—without any reduction in wages, for employees paid by the hour, day, or week. (3) Payment for coal by weight wherever practicable, with a minimum rate of 60 cents for the legal ton of 2,240 pounds and the continuation of the differentials then existing at the mines. (4) The incorporation of wages, conditions, and satisfactory machinery for the adjustment of disputes in a written agreement between the United Mine Workers and the anthracite coal companies. The convention served notice that after April 1 the miners would work only three days a week until the operators came to some agreement with the

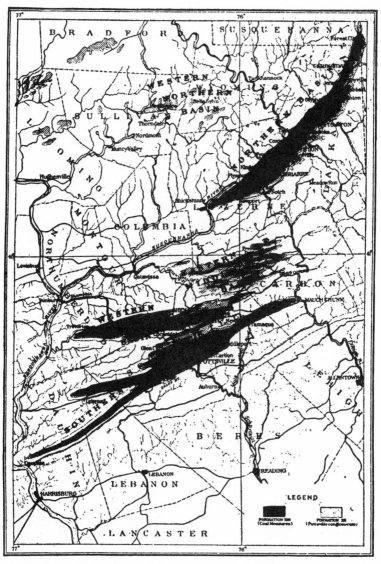

PENNSYLVANIA ANTHRACITE COAL FIELD. (*Report to the President on the Anthracite Coal Strike of May-October, 1902, by the Anthracite Coal Strike Commission*)

workers. What other action would be taken the convention did not say. Mitchell, like most of the officials, did not favor a strike, since he foresaw that it would be long and severe. He hoped for arbitration and appealed to the National Civic Federation to assist the miners.

The motivation for the maneuvers on both sides was the demand of the miners for recognition of the United Mine Workers, to which the operators were unalterably opposed. To a telegram from Mitchell requesting a conference on the resolutions passed by the Shamokin convention, George F. Baer, president of the Philadelphia and Reading Coal and Iron Company, the Lehigh and Wilkesbarre Coal Company, and the Temple Iron Company, and the authoritative spokesman for the operators, replied that he was willing to meet his own employees as individuals, but not the officers of the union. The operators voiced many objections to the miners' union. First, the majority of the union members were employed in the bituminous fields, and the officers, who came from the bituminous fields, were unacquainted with the problems peculiar to the mining of anthracite. Second, the bituminous and anthracite industries were sharp competitors in the steam-producing market, and if a single union embraced both regions, each industry might foster strikes in the other's collieries in order to gain advantages in the market. Third, the voting of boys, wanting in judgment and a sense of responsibility, was permitted in the local union. And fourth, the United Mine Workers engaged in and encouraged violence and lawlessness.

To these objections the miners replied that the officers of the three anthracite districts in the United Mine Workers were all former anthracite miners and comprehended the problems of the industry; that unity was necessary among all coal miners, whether bituminous or anthracite, to preserve the strength of the organization and to prevent the use of one against the other; that if the boys were old enough and responsible enough to work 10 hours a day, they were old and responsible enough to cast a half-vote in the local union; and that whatever lawlessness and violence existed in the anthracite fields were due chiefly to the employment of the Coal and Iron Police. The union, contended the men, would improve their conditions, keep discipline among them, and preserve peace in the settling of disputes.

The National Civic Federation, in an attempt to reconcile the difference between the operators and the miners, appointed a conciliation committee with Senator Hanna as chairman. On April 1 the United Mine Workers agreed to a 30-day truce, so that the conciliation committee might have ample time to bring about an adjustment. Certain of the operators were invited by Senator Hanna to meet the officers of the United Mine Workers and the committee of the National Civic Federation for a discussion of the miners' demands. At this time the operators submitted the following propositions as the basis for the conference:

First. The anthracite companies do not undertake in the slightest manner to discriminate against members of the United Mine Workers of America, but they do insist that members of that organization shall not discriminate against nor decline to work with non-members of such association.

Second. That there shall be no deterioration in the quantity or quality of the work, and that there shall be no effort to restrict the individual exertions of men who, working by the ton or car, may for reasons satisfactory to themselves and their employers produce such a quantity of work as they may desire.

Third. By reason of the different conditions, varying not only with the districts but with the mines themselves, thus rendering absolutely impossible anything approaching uni-

form conditions, each mine must arrange either individually or through its committees with the superintendents or managers any questions affecting wages or grievances.[12]

Following a discussion of these proposals, which were unacceptable to the union, the conference was adjourned, and was not resumed until April 30, the concluding day of the truce. Although the newspapers spoke of the probability of an agreement, nothing came of the second conference. When reporters asked President Baer of the Philadelphia and Reading whether peace was closer than before, he replied evasively: "The great peacemakers, the members of the Civic Federation, will try to make peace. Blessed are the peacemakers, for they are the children of God."[13] In the meantime, the operators stored up enough coal during the truce to carry them through the dull summer months and to enable them to withstand a strike for two or three months without difficulty.

Mitchell notified the Executive Committee of the three anthracite districts of the United Mine Workers that the negotiations of the National Civic Federation had failed, and the members assembled at Scranton on May 7. All day the Executive Committee debated, but could reach no decision, because of Mitchell's reluctance to call a strike. Concerning this evident unwillingness to call a strike, the *New York Times* reported:

The Board of Directors of the United Mine Workers, to a man, favor a strike, excepting President John Mitchell. He succeeded Mike Ratchford of Massillon, Ohio, as President. Ratchford is holding a political position through the aid of Senator Mark Hanna. Mitchell also hopes to gravitate into office. Ratchford still has a strong hold on Mitchell, and is holding him in check.

Hanna holds a large share of stock in the bituminous coal

districts, and is very close to the officers of the mine workers in Ohio and Pittsburg. He will influence them to advise against a strike, but the rank and file demand recognition of their union now that conditions are such as to make coal mining profitable, and it is believed the question will be threshed out by a strike.[14]

Mitchell still hoped for arbitration, and at his insistence the Executive Committee submitted on May 8 two alternative proposals to President Baer and the principal anthracite operators.

The first was that the Industrial Branch of the National Civic Federation select a committee of five persons to arbitrate and decide àll the questions in dispute, the award to be binding for one year. If this proposal was not acceptable, a second offered that a committee of three, composed of Archbishop Ireland, Bishop Potter, and another chosen by these two, investigate the controversy and make recommendations to be complied with by both sides. President Baer answered:

Anthracite mining is a business, and not a religious, sentimental, or academic proposition. The laws organizing the companies I represent in express terms impose the business management on the president and directors. I could not if I would delegate this business management to even so highly a respectable body as the Civic Federation, nor can I call to my aid as experts in the mixed problem of business and philanthropy the eminent prelates you have named.[15]

Again Mitchell's proffer of arbitration was rejected, though the operators did express themselves as ready to continue the existing wage rates until April, 1903. The union could not postpone the question of recognition, for fear the members would desert it as ineffectual. The operators seemed not unwilling to engage in the decisive conflict.

3. *The strike is called*

Faced with the refusal of the operators to arbitrate, the Executive Committee of the three anthracite districts on May 9 invoked the authority given it by the Shamokin convention to call a strike if necessary, and ordered all workers in the collieries, strippings, washeries, and breakers to stop work. Only those men who were required to preserve the mine properties—the engineers, firemen, and pump runners—were to remain at work. Whether or not the strike was to be made permanent was to be decided by a delegate convention on May 14 at Hazleton. In accordance with the strike order, nearly all the mine workers, numbering 144,000, quit work, removed their tools from the collieries, and waited for the decision of the convention. At the convention which opened on May 14 Mitchell urged peace and would very likely have obtained it if he could have announced the slightest concession from the operators. The first day Mitchell was able to stall a final vote, but on May 15, despite his opposition, the convention voted 461¼ to 349¾ for a strike, the majority being 111½. The newspapers displayed great surprise at the strike vote, for it had been expected that the resentment of the miners would subside and the existing conditions continue. There was even hope expressed for some last-minute arbitration, but that hope was quickly crushed when President Truesdale of the Delaware, Lackawanna, and Western Railroad declared that "No concession would be made and none was intended, no matter how long the strike would last." [16] The companies brought up the mules out of the mines and put them to pasture in preparation for a long shutdown.

The first week of the strike passed peacefully, with rumors in the press that conferences would soon bring arbitration and settlement. These rumors were supported by the sudden and mysterious trips of Ralph M. Easely, secretary of the National Civic Federation, between Wilkes-Barre, where Mitchell had set up strike headquarters, and Washington, where Senator Hanna was. Since there were still expectations of an immediate settlement, the price of coal advanced only $1 a ton. The operators, however, continued their preparations for a protracted struggle. Clerks and other employees were laid off, as were train crews and telegraph operators on the coal-carrying railroads. Moreover, the wholesale houses throughout the anthracite region closed their credit systems and insisted on cash payments, so that the retailers would be forced to demand cash in turn from the strikers in order to preserve their businesses. A number of independent operators were ready to yield to the strikers' demands, but they were forced to remain firm by the refusal of the railroads to carry their coal. The strikers settled down for a bitter siege.

To oppose the preparations of the operators, the strikers awaited two actions by Mitchell and the Executive Committee. The first was to be the call for a special convention of the United Mine Workers with the purpose of ordering a general strike in both bituminous and anthracite coal fields that would involve 449,000 mine workers. Before Mitchell could issue a call for a special convention, he needed the requests of five districts. By May 21 the Michigan district had joined the three anthracite districts in the request, and it was expected that the West Virginia district would soon make the fifth. The second action was to be the ordering out of the engineers, firemen, and pump runners to allow the mines to become flooded and thus prevent the introduction of non-union workers. This action was left by the Hazleton convention to the discretion of the national and district officers. Accordingly, the Executive Committee of the three anthracite districts met on May 21 at Wilkes-Barre and voted that all engineers, firemen, and pumpmen, unless they were granted an eight-hour day with no decrease in wages, were to stop work on June 2. When this ultimatum was not complied with, the engineers, firemen, and pumpmen left their posts as ordered; from 70 to 80 per cent of the 5,700 employed in the anthracite districts responded on the first day, nearly all of those who remained at work being engineers. At once the pumps and stationary engines were manned by superintendents, foremen, assistant foremen, clerks, and imported maintenance men. A few mines were shut down and flooded.

Every colliery was now a fortified camp surrounded by stockades and barbed-wire fences. Armed deputies guarded the shafts, breakers, and washeries. By June 2 there were 3,000 Coal and Iron Police and 1,000 secret operatives on duty in the anthracite field. Deadlines were established around the mine properties, and the guards were armed not only with guns, but also with flashlights and cameras to secure pictures of strike leaders for later blacklisting. Employees of the Lehigh Valley Coal Company were notified to vacate company houses unless they returned to work. Accommodations were prepared at the mines for non-union workers. The operators were resolved to stamp out the organization of the miners, and thus free themselves from future labor disturbances.

The miners retaliated against the importation of the Coal and Iron Police by organizing a boycott. They abstained from all intercourse not only with scabs and Coal and Iron Police, but also with all persons who continued to serve them. "Unfair lists" of those who refused to join the strike were posted. Any business place which supplied the wants of those on the "unfair lists" was deserted by the strikers. Even a secondary boycott was in force against the families of the scabs. Children of strikers in some of the Wilkes-Barre schools left the classrooms because of the presence of children of non-strikers. At the Wilkesbarre Lace Mill 1,100 girls walked out to demand the discharge of five girls whose fathers or brothers still worked in the mines. The boycotts were both spontaneous and effective; for the strikers, who with their families and sympathizers made up the vast majority of the population, regarded the boycott as their one weapon against the non-union workers who were undermining their attempt to improve their working conditions.

To combat the boycotts, a Citizens' Alliance was formed at Wilkes-Barre, and it offered rewards aggregating $5,000 for the arrest and conviction of persons engaged in boycotting or intimidation. The Alliance, furthermore, issued a protest:

When butchers and bakers may not supply meat and bread, when the doctor may not attend the sick, the druggist may not dole out medicine and the priest may not minister, either to those in health or to those at death's door; when public officers may not perform public duties, when teachers in the school may not teach or be appointed except by the consent of strikers or their sympathizers, then, indeed, the last vestige of personal liberty has gone and society must be rebuilt upon a basis of submission to the tyranny, not necessarily of majorities, but rather of a band of men who will not hesitate to employ every means of intimidation as a lawful instrument of control.[17]

Nevertheless, the boycott continued in full force. The strike was further strengthened by the calling out on June 16 of the fire bosses. Although they were not members of the United Mine Workers, about 30 per cent of them quit work. The collieries were now endangered by cave-ins and explosions.

Meanwhile the West Virginia district had sent in its request for a special national convention; however, Mitchell was reluctant to act, since he feared that a general sympathetic strike would be declared. He preferred therefore to pocket the requests for two or three weeks. Only on June 18 did Mitchell issue the call for a special national convention at Indianapolis, and he set the date one month distant, July 17. With a month's warning given them, the operators began a drive to open the collieries before the convention was to convene. Action was demanded of them by the *New York Times:*

The facts being as we find them, and there being no advantage apparent from arbitration, the duty of the operators is to begin mining coal without further delay. Their interests demand this. Nothing in the way of a policy could be more suicidal than to delay taking the initiative until the representatives from Pennsylvania can go into the Indianapolis convention and demand the recognition of their cause on the ground that they have maintained an absolute tie-up for three months, during which time not a pound of coal has been mined. Such a demonstration of their strength would entitle them to dominate the convention, and would be well calculated to rally to their support the miners of Illinois, Iowa, Indiana, and Western Pennsylvania, who, even in the absence of a grievance, might be glad of an opportunity to compel further concessions from employers.[18]

Notices were distributed by the operators among the miners urging them to return to work. The Coal and Iron Police became daily more provocative; and on July 1 the first loss of life in the strike occurred, when Antonio Giusuepe, a striker, was shot fatally by a Coal and Iron policeman from behind the stockade of a colliery. Arrests for "inciting to riot" became more frequent: on July 2 four pickets at Hazleton were held for $500 bail each on charges of "rioting and intimidation"; on July 7 at Williamstown 10 strikers were arrested for "inciting to riot." Adopting a different tactic, the Philadelphia and Reading Coal and Iron Company announced a 10 per cent increase in wages for all men who had remained at work during the strike. There was, nevertheless, no break in the strikers' ranks, and the operators could not procure the miners necessary to open the collieries. On July 11 about 25 bituminous companies met in New York at the offices of the Empire Coal Mining Company to form a combination in preparation for the Indianapolis convention.

As the day for the convention drew near, the anthracite operators made a last attempt to open certain selected collieries by concentrating in them all the non-union miners in the anthracite region. The attempt proved unsuccessful for want of sufficient labor, and the anthracite delegates were able to go victoriously to the national convention at Tomlinson Hall in Indianapolis. There were present 768 anthracite and 1,416 bituminous delegates. The debate opened on July 17. On the one side stood the anthracite delegates and many of the bituminous, who pointed out that the attack on the anthracite miners, if successful, would lead to a concerted drive to disrupt the entire United Mine Workers; that if the organization of the anthracite workers were broken, the bituminous would follow. On the other side stood a number of the bituminous delegates and Mitchell, who held for the sanctity of the contracts between the bituminous miners and the operators, which were not to terminate until April, 1903. Mitchell declared to the convention: "I am firm in my conviction that the strike in the anthracite fields can and will be won without repudiating our solemn contracts with the bituminous operators, provided the bituminous miners will rise to the occasion and do their full duty by their struggling fellow-workers. . . ." [19] Furthermore, he asserted that unless the bituminous miners were working and were able to contribute money to support the anthracite miners, the strike would fail. He won his point, and the convention voted not to call a general sympathetic strike, but instead did adopt certain recommendations suggested by Mitchell. Fifty thousands dollars from the funds of the national treasury was placed at the disposal of the three anthracite districts. A weekly assessment of either $1 or 10 per cent of the earnings was levied on all working members of the bituminous districts. National, district, and sub-district officers earning $60 per month or more were to subscribe 25 per cent of their salaries. With the promise of this support the anthracite delegates returned to their homes.

The refusal of the special convention to call a general sympathetic strike was a disappointment to the strikers. What aggravated the disappointment was the delay of a month in the financial aid voted at Indianapolis. The bituminous miners received their wages semi-monthly, and the money they earned during the last half of July was not paid to them until August 15; the result was that a full month passed before the strike assessments were turned into the anthracite districts. So despondent were the strikers after the Indianapolis convention that, according to Mitchell, the operators might have crushed them by inviting them to return to work:

During the first week of August a crisis was reached. The agents of the companies, taking advantage of the opportunity temporarily afforded them by this loss of confidence, circulated rumors among the strikers to the effect that the money contributed by the bituminous miners was being withheld, if not actually misappropriated. I am fully convinced that the strike would have collapsed, had the operators at this time opened their mines and invited the strikers to return to work. It was the crucial moment, the only time during the long, stubbornly fought contest in which there was

*any sign of wavering. The operators, evidently, did not real-
ize the extent of the disaffection in the ranks of the strikers
and failed to take advantage of the opportunity open to
them.*[20]

The early part of August was a dark period for the
strikers. Without the support they had asked for, they faced
defeat. At the end of the tenth week their strike seemed lost
and they had sacrificed $12,700,000 in wages.[21] Nearly 18,-
000 strikers had left the field to seek work elsewhere.[22] Moreover, the *New York Times* and the rest of the press assailed
the operators in daily editorials for their lack of aggressiveness, and the operators redoubled their efforts to open the
mines. They succeeded in introducing the militia after an
evening of fighting at Shenandoah on July 30 precipitated
by the deliberate firing of Deputy Sheriff Thomas Beddal
into a crowd of strikers.[23] The following day saw 1,200 state
troops under Brigadier-General P. H. Gobin encamped on
the hill overlooking Shenandoah.

With the assistance of the military, the operators made
every effort to open the collieries. Arrests, court action,
rumors, and sermons were used to break the spirit of the
strikers. On August 5 two strikers wounded at Shenandoah
in the shooting by Deputy Sheriff Beddal were taken into
custody and held on $2,000 bail each. An injunction, issued
by Judge W. B. Patton, restrained the Monongahela and
Carnegie brass bands of the United Mine Workers from
parading in the streets of Leechburg. Stories of violence and
rioting were spread by the press, and the Citizens' Alliance
of Wilkes-Barre charged publicly that the United Mine
Workers encouraged lawlessness. Many churchmen, from
their pulpits, advocated the return of the strikers to the collieries. On Sunday, August 3, Father O'Reilly preached in
the Church of the Annunciation at Shenandoah:

You should have the manhood to go back to work and defy this organization known as the United Mine Workers. It is a blood-stained organization, and it will be blood-stained until it ceases to exist. It was formed to promote crime and protect criminals. Every one was happy and contented here until Mitchell and Fahy came and organized unions. These men are not workingmen; they are not respectable, and I wouldn't give 2 cents for the opinion of either of them.[24]

To counteract these attacks, Mitchell opened a series of strikers' mass meetings in which he urged the miners to refrain from breaking the law and to keep the strike unimpaired. Notwithstanding the presence of the militia and of the Coal and Iron Police, the collieries stood idle.

When it became clear that the strikers would not surrender, the press began to speak once more of arbitration. The return of J. P. Morgan from Europe in August generated the hope that he would interfere to end the struggle. A Wilkes-Barre photographer, named W. F. Clark, wrote a letter to President Baer of the Philadelphia and Reading Company, appealing to him as a Christian to grant the strikers a slight concession, end the strike, and thus earn the blessing of God and the thanks of the nation. Baer replied:

I see you are evidently biased in your religious views in favor of the right of the working man to control a business in which he has no other interest than to secure fair wages for the work he does. I beg of you not to be discouraged. The rights and interests of the laboring man will be protected and cared for, not by the labor agitators, but by the Christian men to whom God in His infinite wisdom has given control of the property interests of the country. Pray earnestly that the right may triumph, always remembering that the Lord God Omnipotent still reigns and that His reign is one of law and order, and not of violence and crime.[25]

Any hope that remained for conciliation was quickly killed by a conference of anthracite operators on August 27 which reiterated that there would be no arbitration. The middle of September arrived. For four months no coal had been mined in the anthracite basins. Some coal—the operators said 13,000 tons daily—was reclaimed from the culm banks through the washeries, but this, at the most, amounted to no more than 5 per cent of the tonnage previous to the strike.

The people of the eastern and seaboard states began to suffer hardships. As the supply of coal dwindled and as profiteers appeared, the price of anthracite leaped upward, from $6 to $10 to $20 a ton; and the poor, who were compelled to purchase coal by the pail or bushel, paid as much as $30 a ton. The smoke ordinances of New York and other eastern cities were openly violated. There was fear of coal riots. Both operators and strikers, however, remained obdurate. Wherever the operators called for the militia, it was sent. On September 24 there were in the field four full regiments, two companies of another regiment, and two troops of cavalry—at Olyphant, Wilkes-Barre, Shenandoah, Lebanon, and Panther Creek Valley. But troops could not mine coal, and even though the pulpit and the press spoke heatedly of the rights and duties of non-union labor, miners could not be found.

Mitchell and the strikers were condemned by the press as obstinate and recalcitrant. In an editorial, "The Dissolving Strike," the *New York Times* said:

Two essential elements of greatness in leadership are the power to recognize defeat and the courage to retreat when nothing is to be gained by further resistance. Mitchell seems to lack both. Perhaps this is due to inexperience in adversity, and he will be much wiser after the anthracite strike is over than he was when he began it.[26]

The *Nation* in an editorial, "The Strike Unveiled," expressed itself similarly:

We have always wished that the operators could have seen their way to refer the controversy to a competent and impartial arbitration; but if none such was suggested, and if, as would appear to be the case, the chief thing in dispute was the demand of a heterogeneous labor union, not able to control its own men and confessedly wasteful and inefficient, to be allowed further to take the management of the coal business out of the hands of the operators, and make the consuming public foot the bill—we do not see how arbitration could well apply. A foolish strike can be settled only by the foolish strikers going back to work. We look to see that result greatly hastened by the revelation to the public of the indefensible nature of the position taken by the miners.[27]

Notwithstanding these insinuations that the strike was at the point of collapse, the ranks of the strikers became more solidified. The financial support from the bituminous miners and outside unions was now steady. Whatever the allegations of the press and the operators, winter was approaching and the collieries still remained closed.

4. Theodore Roosevelt, Arbitrator

Late in August, President Theodore Roosevelt began to devise some means of entering the stubborn conflict. He appointed Carroll D. Wright, Commissioner of Labor, to conduct an investigation into the matters in dispute, and in the early part of September a report was issued by Wright. It recommended that a nine-hour day be instituted for an experimental period of six months and that a joint committee be appointed for the purpose of conciliation. To these suggestions President Baer, as spokesman for the operators, replied that since the wages paid were sufficient, since no union would be permitted to determine who could and who could not be employed in the mines, and since it was impossible to adopt a uniform wage scale throughout the anthracite region and each grievance had to be considered and treated separately, there was no question involved which was subject to arbitration. After four months there was still no change in the position of the operators. Governor Stone of Pennsylvania likewise made an effort to secure arbitration and went to New York to confer with Morgan, who, according to the *New York Times*, said: "Tell the miners to go back to work. Then, and not till then, will we agree to talk about concessions." [28]

As the passage of each day brought winter closer, the threat of a coal famine grew more and more serious. Gas, wood, and imported Welsh coal were inadequate to replace the customary anthracite. Even if the strike were brought to an end, it would require months to restore the former supply, for many of the mines were filled with water and had to be pumped out before work could begin once more. Both the mayor of New York and the Governor of Massachusetts warned Roosevelt of the forthcoming misery and of the probability of fuel riots. On September 30 Roosevelt called together Attorney-General Knox, Secretary of the Navy Moody, Postmaster-General Payne, and Governor Crane of Massachusetts to discuss plans for ending the strike. The following day he dispatched telegrams to Mitchell and to several of the operators, including Baer, in which he requested them to meet at the White House on October 3 in order to talk over the strike. When both sides were assembled in accordance with his request, Roosevelt urged them as a matter of patriotism and public decency to end their warfare and settle their differences. At this Mitchell announced that the miners were ready to return to work immediately and leave all the differences either to Roosevelt or to a commission for arbitration.

The operators, however, refused Mitchell's proposal outright and insisted instead that the United Mine Workers be prosecuted under the Sherman Anti-Trust and the Interstate Commerce Acts. Two of the operators, in fact, Baer and John Markle, reminded Roosevelt of the action taken by President Cleveland during the Pullman strike of 1894 and demanded that federal troops be put in the anthracite field. Roosevelt was forced to pronounce the meeting a failure, and he wrote in a letter to Senator Hanna: "Well, I have tried and failed. I feel downhearted over the result, both because of the great misery made for the mass of our people, and because the attitude of the operators will beyond a doubt double the burden on us while standing between them and socialistic action." [29]

Although the public was unaware of the fact, Roosevelt entertained the demand of the operators that he station federal troops in the anthracite field. He even elaborated a secret plan: Senator Quay of Pennsylvania was to persuade Governor Stone to make a formal request for federal troops, and Major-General Schofield was to be sent to take command of the collieries, which were to be opened and kept open despite any protests from the strikers. In the meantime, a commission headed by ex-President Cleveland was to investigate conditions and report recommendations. The plan, however, was not employed, and it remained a secret until several years later, when Roosevelt disclosed it in his *Autobiography*.[30] In place of the plan to send federal troops, Roosevelt proposed on October 6 that the strikers return to work immediately, while a commission appointed by him was to make findings which he would "do all within his power" to get the operators to accept. A vote quickly showed Mitchell that the strikers were unanimously opposed to this proposition; and he replied in a letter rejecting the President's proposal and pointing out that there was no genuine assurance of even the slightest concessions for the strikers:

Having in mind our experience with the coal operators in the past, we have no reason to feel any degree of confidence in their willingness to do us justice in the future, and inasmuch as they have refused to accept the decision of a tribunal selected by you, and inasmuch as there is no law through which you could enforce the findings of the commission you suggest, we respectfully decline to advise our people to return to work simply upon the hope that the coal operators might be induced or forced to comply with the recommendations of your commission.[31]

When this reply by Mitchell was published, the operators offered to submit individual cases of dispute between employers and employees to the Courts of Common Pleas in the districts involved, but this offer was refused by the mine workers as a mark of the defeat of their strike. The conflict was still deadlocked.

The operators continued to raise the complaint that only the fear of violence at the hands of a few of the strikers deterred the majority of the strikers from returning to work. On October 6, therefore, Governor Stone ordered out the entire National Guard of 9,000 men for duty in the anthracite fields. It was to be a test of the operators' assertion that, given enough military protection, they could open the collieries. The strikers, for the most part, welcomed the showdown, and at meetings called by Mitchell they voted to remain on strike and to keep from violence. The militia marched into the anthracite fields, the operators were allowed every opportunity to make good their contention, but no one could be found to mine coal. Henry Demarest Lloyd, in a letter to his wife, described the demonstration of solidarity made by the strikers:

The finest episode of the strike has been the answer the miners have made, to-day, to Gov. Stone's calling out of the whole State guard. They have held meetings all over the anthracite country, and unanimously decided not to go back to work. The meetings were public, non-union men were invited as well as union men, Mitchell and the other heads did not go near the meetings, which were all under the control of the local forces, and yet so far as heard from to-night not one man voted to go back to work. What can troops do with men who will neither work nor riot? [32]

The pulpit opened up a new barrage of contumely against the strikers. The preachers not only attacked the strikers, but also praised the strike-breaker as the upholder of the constitutional right to labor. On Sunday, October 12, the Rev. Dr. David James Burrell said at the Marble Collegiate Church in New York:

The time has come to say frankly that they [the labor unions] are not fighting for the rights of labor, for the freedom of the workingmen. There are many men in the ranks of the union to-day who are unable to do it. They are the cowards of the situation. They are afraid to cut loose and declare their rights. They are not indeed led as mercenaries to "crimson glory and undying fame"—they are merely slaves who cannot call their souls their own. They fighting for the rights of labor? No! a thousand times, no! They are, in fact, arrayed against the fundamental rights of honest toil.

. . . the seventeen thousand independents to-day are working behind barricades maintaining the rights guaranteed in the preamble to the Declaration of Independence, the right

to life, liberty, and the pursuit of happiness. I sing the
praises of that heroic 17,000, who stand to-day as brave vin-
dicators of the right of labor. . . .[33]

But the strikers kept their peace; the *New York Times* reported on October 13: "Strike disorder is now almost wholly
wanting." It was obvious that the operators were completely
unsuccessful in their attempts to open the collieries, and that
the eastern states faced a winter without sufficient fuel.

On October 13 J. Pierpont Morgan and a partner, Robert
S. Bacon, traveled to Washington and conferred with Roosevelt about the coal strike. On behalf of the anthracite companies Morgan submitted a proposal for arbitration by a
commission to be chosen by the President. The miners were
to return to work at once, and the award of the commission
was to be binding for three years. The commission was to
be composed, according to the limitations set by the operators, of an officer of the engineer corps of either the army or
the navy service of the United States; a mining engineer,
experienced in the mining of coal, but not connected with
coal mining properties; one of the federal judges in eastern
Pennsylvania; a prominent sociologist; and one man actively
engaged in the mining and selling of coal. A dispute arose
over the composition of the commission, for it included no
representative of labor. Mitchell urged Roosevelt to add a
Catholic priest to the commission, since most of the strikers
were Catholic and they might be induced thus to accept a
commission which "represented the propertied classes."
Roosevelt was able to effect an agreement whereby he added
Bishop John L. Spalding of Illinois to the commission and
appointed E. E. Clark, Chief of the Order of Railway Conductors, as the eminent sociologist. On October 16 the Executive Committee of the three anthracite districts agreed to
recommend the acceptance of the commission and of the

arbitration proposal to a delegate convention of the strikers.

But when the delegates met at Wilkes-Barre on October 20, Mitchell found a deep opposition to the arbitration proposal. In the first place, there was still no representative of labor on the commission, for the miners regarded E. E. Clark, with his record of strike-breaking, especially during the Pullman strike, as a renegade. In the second place, there was no provision made for the 5,000 striking engineers, firemen, and pumpmen, many of whom were now locked out because their places had been filled with non-union men. Mitchell urged the convention to accept the proposal on the grounds that the "principle of arbitration" ought not to be rejected; as for the lockout of the engineers, firemen, and pumpmen, he declared that ". . . it may be true that some will be sacrificed, and, much as we shall regret that, I desire to say that no battle was ever fought, no victory was ever won, that did not carry with it some victims." [34] After two days of pleading Mitchell brought the convention to accept the proposal and declare the strike at an end. The miners returned to work on October 23, and on the following day the Anthracite Coal Strike Commission opened its investigation.

From the first hearings before the Commission it became apparent that the operators would fight against any recognition of the United Mine Workers, when Baer declared for them: "So far as he [Mitchell] appears here to represent any of the miners in the anthracite region that are in our employ, we have no objection, and we raise no question about it; but we do not want him to appear on the record as president of the United Mine Workers, because we have distinctly stated in the paper from which you have derived your authority to the President that we will not deal with that organization." [35] Mitchell submitted, and agreed to appear only as "the representative of the anthracite coal mine workers."

The Commission, after conducting hearings in Scranton

and Philadelphia and examining 558 witnesses, made its awards on March 18, 1903. The awards called for: (1) an increase of 10 per cent in the rates paid contract miners, retroactive to November 1, 1902; (2) an eight-hour day for engineers, firemen, and pumpmen, and a nine-hour day to replace the 10-hour day of "company men"; (3) a sliding scale for wages, with a 1 per cent increase for each 5-cent advance in the selling price of coal at New York over $4.50 per ton f.o.b. The miners were granted the right to hire check-weighmen and check docking bosses. During the life of the award, that is, until March 31, 1906, all difficulties and disputes that arose were to be settled by an arbitration board, which was to consist of six persons, three to be appointed by the operators, and one to be chosen by a majority vote of the miners in each of the three anthracite districts. If the board failed to arrive at an agreement, an umpire was to be appointed by a judge in the third circuit of the U. S. courts. The Commission made no change in the system of weighing or measuring coal in force at the various collieries. As for the demand of the strikers for the recognition of the United Mine Workers, the Commission decided that it had no jurisdiction over that question, since the United Mine Workers was not a party to the arbitration, and since Mitchell appeared to represent merely the striking anthracite miners.

The miners were dissatisfied with the award, chiefly because of the failure of the Commission to grant formal recognition of their union. One provision, in fact, which prohibited any discrimination for either membership or non-membership in any labor organization, gave sanction to the open shop, with the result that the non-union workers were to receive the same gains that the strikers had fought for. Furthermore, while strikes and lockouts were prohibited during the three-year period of the award, the employer did not lose his right to discharge workmen without reference to the board of conciliation. There was thus no guarantee that actually mine workers would not be discharged for entering a labor organization. Another demand of the strikers was ignored; there was no change in the system requiring 2,800- and 3,100-pound tons and excessive topping on the cars. After a five-month struggle, in which they had sacrificed $25,000,000 in wages and had suffered great privations, the miners found that only two of their demands had been considered in the award of the Commission, and these had been only partially satisfied. They had been betrayed, they believed, by the "principle of arbitration," and they looked forward to 1906, when they could demand once more the recognition of their union, a recognition which they won only after 13 more years of struggle.

VI. THE LAWRENCE STRIKE

1. A few loaves of bread

One of the extremely few strikes in the United States that resulted in an undeniable victory for labor was that conducted in the early months of 1912 by the textile workers at Lawrence, Massachusetts. It was a significant struggle, furthermore, in that the radical Industrial Workers of the World took active part and succeeded in welding together some 20,000 unskilled workers of a score of nationalities—Russian, Syrian, Italian, German, Polish, Belgian, Armenian, English, Irish, Portuguese, Austrian, Jewish, French-Canadian, Lithuanian—and holding them together for nearly 10 weeks, despite differences in language and custom. The adversary was the "Woolen Trust," represented principally by the American Woolen Company, which, protected by the benign Schedule K of the Payne-Aldrich tariff act, operated 34 mills, most of them in New England, four of them in Lawrence.

The outburst of the textile workers which brought a riot call from the bells of the Lawrence City Hall on the morning of January 12 seemed to outsiders to be a spontaneous protest against a minor grievance. A law passed by the Massachusetts legislature, which had become effective January 1, 1912, had cut the working hours per week for women and for children under 18 years of age from 56 to 54. Since more than half of the employees were women and children, the mill operators extended the new law to the men also. On the first pay day under the shorter week the workers found

171

that a corresponding reduction had been made in their earnings. The reduction appeared slight—about $3\frac{1}{2}$ per cent in weekly earnings, equivalent to a sum of 25 or 30 cents, merely a "few loaves of bread." To the low-paid textile workers, however, it was serious.

Approximately 60,000 of the 86,000 people living in Lawrence were directly dependent upon the earnings of the 25,000 employees in the textile mills. The full-time earnings of most adult employees were inadequate to support a family. For one week in November, 1911, when the mills were running full time, the average wage was $8.76; in this week one-third of the workers received less than $7 and only 17.5 per cent received $12 or more.[1] Even these small earnings were further cut through the time lost during slack seasons. As a result of the low earnings, the textile industry became a family industry. "The normal family of five, unless the father is employed in one of the comparatively few better-paying occupations, is compelled to supply two wage earners in order to secure the necessaries of life."[2] Many wives were forced into the mills and their small children had to be left all day with some other family. While a state law prohibited the employment of children under 14, half of the children in Lawrence between the ages of 14 and 18 worked in the textile mills.[3] With men, women, and children at work merely to support the family, a $3\frac{1}{2}$ per cent reduction in wages was no light matter.

Given long hours of labor and insufficient wages, unhappiness, suffering, and dissatisfaction were bound to arise among the textile workers. It is true that Judge W. E. Rowell, before whose court many of the Lawrence strikers were brought, maintained the opposite:

I shall make an assertion that I realize will meet with the scorn of all the gentlemen and ladies from abroad who have

*so kindly interested themselves in our affairs of late, namely,
that the foreign working people in Lawrence have been before this strike, and will be after it is over, decidedly prosper-
ous, happy, though perhaps not quite contented, and standing before a door of opportunity, wide open to them, such
as is to be found nowhere else in the world but in American
cities of which Lawrence is a good example.*[4]

Nevertheless, the report prepared for the U. S. Senate by
Commissioner of Labor Neill found malnutrition and premature death common in Lawrence. Fresh milk at 7 cents a
quart was too expensive, and most families depended entirely
upon condensed or evaporated milk. Little butter was used;
instead butterine, leaf lard, and beef suet were substituted.
The main meat eaten was cheap beef stew. Under such a
diet children, especially, suffered, and rickets were prevalent.
The infant mortality in Lawrence, too, was abnormally
high: out of every 1,000 births in 1909 there were 172 deaths
of infants under one year of age. A comparison with 34 other
cities made by the U. S. Census Office showed that only six
cities had higher infant death rates than Lawrence, and of
these, four were distinctly textile cities.[5]

These hardships were coupled with congested and dangerous housing. Practically all the textile workers in Lawrence
lived in wooden tenement buildings, usually three or four
stories in height. Tenements in the more thickly populated
portions of the city occupied both front and rear lots, and
the rear house was ordinarily reached by an alley or by a
narrow passageway, three and one-half to five feet in width,
between two front buildings. A three- or four-story wooden
tenement situated on a rear lot became a dangerous fire trap.
Moreover, the supply of light and air was decidedly inadequate. The courts separating front and rear buildings were
at times less than four feet wide; even when they were as

much as 10 to 15 feet wide, the entrance of light and air was impeded by porches, clothes hung out to dry, and ash chutes. Stairways in the older tenements were dark. Frequently the kitchens, used also as living rooms, were so dark that even on the brightest days artificial light was necessary. "Some of the rooms supposed to be used for bedrooms were too dark and damp for any use. Practically all the rooms had outside windows, but an outside window which opens into a space only 15 to 20 inches in width between three-story houses is of very little practical use so far as the admission of light is concerned." [6] The over-crowding was heightened, particularly among the more recent immigrants, by the necessity for taking in lodgers and boarders. Of the 188 households visited by agents of the Bureau of Labor 109 or 58 per cent kept lodgers or boarders; and 1,309 persons lived in the 188 households, more than one-fourth of them lodgers or boarders. The average number of persons per room was 1.52.[7] One household had 17 persons in five rooms, another 16.

When the workers left their homes and entered the mills, they endured the nervous and physical strain of the speed-up system. A premium plan, admittedly designed by the mill owners to increase the output of the individual worker, rewarded the employees each month for extra production, provided that not more than one day had been lost from work. If an operative worked under high pressure for three weeks and then, through illness or some other unavoidable cause, was absent two days, he lost his bonus. Toward the end of the premium month, therefore, the worker worried lest illness, bad luck with his machine, or some other trouble lose for him the benefit of his close application during the early part of the month. Women, in particular, suffered hardship during menstruation because they continued to work under pressure in order not to lose the month's premium. The speed-up was accentuated by the fact that the premium of the loom fixers and the assistant overseers was dependent upon the premium of the weavers under them. Favoritism and driving were in this way encouraged; the assistant overseers tended to drive the weavers in their rooms so as to increase the premium, and the loom fixers were apt to neglect the looms of weavers behind schedule and to arrange first the looms of weavers ahead of schedule.

The premium system was defended by the employers on the grounds that it attracted the steadiest and most efficient workers. It helped also to minimize the fixed capital charge on the machinery: since the capital invested in the machinery set up a fixed charge, each idle day and any reduced output for a machine created a loss which had to be assessed against the production of the other machines. With the standard wage rate in force, the employers maintained, there was no injustice in the additional reward for regular attendance and efficient work. The worker was free to earn the bonus or not as he pleased. The workers, however, objected that actually no such freedom existed, for workers who failed to earn the premiums and therefore failed to increase the earnings of the loom fixers and assistant overseers could not remain long in a weaving room. Furthermore, under the speed-up accidents became more frequent.[8] Whether the objections of the workers to the speed-up were valid or not, it is true that, because of poor living conditions, inferior housing, and the nervous strain of the mills, the general death rate in Lawrence was exceeded by that of only six cities out of the 34 with which it was compared.[9]

With such conditions existing in the textile industry, the press had no reason to be surprised at the sudden strike. It happened that the resentment broke through first at Lawrence. Nor was the press correct in speaking of the strike as spontaneous. Almost two weeks before the beginning of the strike, committees of the workers tried to confer with the mill officials about what effect the reduction of hours would have on the earnings. On January 2 the Lawrence English branch of the Industrial Workers of the World appointed a committee to wait on the mill officials, but the committee was referred to the main office of the American Woolen Company at Boston. The letter it sent to Boston was never answered. The Italian, Polish, and Lithuanian workers, made uneasy by the deaf ear turned toward their anxiety about wage reductions, gathered at Ford Hall on January 10 and 11 and determined to strike if their pay envelopes showed any reduction.

The general walkout began at the Everett cotton mill on Thursday afternoon, January 11, when the pay envelopes were distributed and it was seen that the mill owners, without any previous warning, had cut the wages. The weavers, nearly all Polish women, stopped their looms. Officials attempted to explain the reduction in pay, but the women replied, "Not enough money," and left the mill. The next morning at the Washington mill, employing 5,078, the workers also began to leave when their pay envelopes showed reductions. They congregated outside the mill and marched several blocks to the Wood mill of the American Woolen Company, where they rushed the gates, shut off the power for the looms, and called out the workers. A mass meeting was held that afternoon at the Franco-Belgian Hall and a telegram was sent to request Joseph J. Ettor, a member of the General Executive Board of the I.W.W., to come to Lawrence and assist in conducting the strike. By Friday evening about 10,000 had joined the walkout.

Ettor arrived from New York in time to address a mass meeting of the strikers at the City Hall on Saturday afternoon. An organization was set up for the strike. Two or three members were sent by each nationality to form the Strike Committee. This committee, numbering about 50 and representing the rank and file of the strikers, was to have absolute command of the strike. It met every morning to hear reports, investigate complaints, and formulate plans. The organizers sent by the I.W.W. assisted and furnished advice, while the Strike Committee made all the decisions, which were then passed on to strikers' meetings for a final vote. Substitute committee members were also chosen in order to fill vacancies caused by arrests. At a meeting of the strikers at the Franco-Belgian Hall on Sunday afternoon, January 14, Ettor was elected as chairman of the Strike Committee, Gilbert Smith of Lawrence as secretary, and Joseph Bedard as financial secretary. Four demands were drawn up: (1) a 15 per cent increase in wages on the 54-hour basis; (2) double pay for overtime work; (3) the abolition of the premium system; (4) the return of all strikers to work without discrimination. The demands were circulated through printed notices and the press. That evening Mayor Scanlon ordered a company of the local militia to spend the night at the armory. On Monday morning 250 militiamen patrolled the mill district.

2. The struggle for leadership

Before the strike began, there was no strong labor organization at Lawrence. The United Textile Workers of America, affiliated with the American Federation of Labor, had organized a small number of the skilled workers into craft unions, but had shown no interest in the unskilled and semi-skilled who constituted the bulk of textile labor. Several other craft unions in Lawrence, not members of the United Textile Workers, had joined the Central Labor Union of the American Federation of Labor. At most the membership of the craft unions was 2,500. The great mass of unskilled workers had remained unorganized, except for approximately 1,000 who were members of the I.W.W.; of this number fewer than 300 were paid up. When John Golden, president of the

United Textile Workers, came to Lawrence on the day after the opening of the strike, he found no response; for the strikers had turned to the I.W.W., which invited the unskilled workers to join together in an industrial union, irrespective of occupational divisions. Because of the differences in language, branches of the I.W.W. were formed mainly according to nationality. All were united in the Strike Committee, which, although not an I.W.W. committee, was closely advised by the I.W.W.

From the beginning of the strike a sharp division, which increased steadily in hostility and bitterness, developed between the craft unions represented by the Central Labor Union and the unskilled workers represented by the Strike Committee under the guidance of the I.W.W. The enmity arose from the very nature of the two groups. The craft unions of the American Federation of Labor were concerned with compromise and reform, with maintaining contracts and agreements, rather than with the overthrow of capitalism and the establishment of a new industrial order. The I.W.W., on the other hand, regarded all its activities as directed ultimately to the capture of the means of production. The preamble to its constitution declared:

The working class and the employing class have nothing in common. There can be no peace so long as hunger and want are found among millions of working people, and the few, who make up the employing class, have all the good things of life.

Between the two classes a struggle must go on until the workers of the world organize as a class, take possession of the earth and the machinery of production and abolish the wage system. . . .

Instead of the conservative motto, "A fair day's wages for a fair day's work," we must inscribe on our banner the revolutionary watchword, "Abolition of the wage system."

It is the historic mission of the working class to do away with capitalism. The army of production must be organized, not only for the everyday struggle with capitalists, but also to carry on production when capitalism shall have been overthrown. By organizing industrially we are forming the structure of the new society within the shell of the old.[10]

The revolutionary spirit was here opposed to those who wished to conserve.

In principle the I.W.W. resembled the "Chicago idea" anarchists of 1886, but had advanced beyond them to syndicalism. Resting, as it did, on the fundamental thesis that there existed an irreconcilable struggle between capital and labor, the I.W.W. rejected all political and parliamentary action as palliative, opportunistic, and enfeebling. The solidarity and consciousness of the working class were, on the contrary, to be encouraged and developed by partial strikes, constant agitation, protest meetings and parades, and every other form of direct mass action. Never was the ultimate aim —the seizure of the means of production by the working class—to be lost sight of. Thus far the I.W.W. followed the "Chicago idea" of 1886, but in advocating the use of the general strike and sabotage it approached the syndicalist principles of the *Confédération Générale du Travail* in France. The general strike, in its final stages the lever for the overthrow of capitalism, was to replace the craft strike during the preliminary struggles in order to prevent the "official scabbing" by one section of labor against another. If the strike failed, then sabotage (literally the throwing of *sabots* or wooden shoes into machinery) was to follow.

While John Golden refused to participate in the strike and kept the craft unions at work, the Strike Committee and the I.W.W. went ahead to call out the rest of the workers.

During the first week the strike assumed the customary complexion of picketing and arrests. On Monday morning, January 15, crowds of strikers gathered at Canal Street and marched in a body to the Atlantic and the Upper and Lower Pacific mills. As they approached the gates, streams of water from fire hose on the adjoining roofs drenched them. When the strikers retaliated by throwing pieces of ice, the police and local militia were summoned to disperse them. Thirty-six were arrested and, without opportunity to defend themselves, were quickly disposed of by Judge Mahoney, who, with punitive rather than judicial severity, sentenced most of them to one year in prison. Mayor Scanlon asked for additional troops, and five more companies were sent, so that eight companies of militia now patrolled the mill district in Lawrence. The I.W.W. replied by holding mass meetings and parades. The strike began to spread, to Fall River and Haverhill. A Citizens' Committee, consisting of city officials and merchants, was formed. Immigration Inspector F. G. R. Gordon was sent to investigate alleged illegal immigration into Lawrence. The Governor ordered out the state police and another four companies of militia. Nevertheless, the strike still continued to spread. By Saturday, January 20, the end of the first week, there were at least 14,000 out. Moreover, as the weavers and unskilled workers walked out, the loom fixers, mule spinners, and other skilled laborers had to stop also for lack of anything to do.

In the meantime an exchange of statements took place between President Wood of the American Woolen Company and the Strike Committee. President Wood, on January 19, wrote to his striking employees:

Last Friday many of you left our mills and have since remained away. This action was wholly a surprise to me. You sent no notice of what you were intending to do and you stated no grievances and made no demand. I learn from the newspapers that the reason for your staying away is that the company paid you for only 54 hours' work; but you know your wages are paid by the hour or by the piece, and as you work only 54 hours you could be paid only for 54 hours' work. . . . I have consulted long and anxiously with the directors and those associated with me in the management. Reluctantly and regretfully we have come to the conclusion that it is impossible, with a proper regard for the interests of the company, to grant at this time any increase in wages.[11]

The Strike Committee replied to President Wood's alleged ignorance of the opening of the strike:

Thursday morning, January 3, 1912, a committee called upon the agents of the Ayer, Wood, and Washington mills [all of the American Woolen Company] and endeavored to hold a conference with those gentlemen, and so come to a peaceful understanding concerning the demands of the workers. Two of the agents refused to have dealings with the committee, while the other advised the committee to write to or consult with you at your Boston office. As a result of the above advice, the committee sent a letter to your address containing the demands of the workers, but for some reason or other the letter was not answered. . . .[12]

The Strike Committee closed its statement by informing President Wood of the existence of the strike and listing the four demands of the strikers.

The interest in Wood's statement was suddenly replaced by the excitement of scare-heads in the newspapers reporting the discovery of dynamite in various sections of Lawrence. On Saturday afternoon, January 20, police and detectives found dynamite in a tenement house on Oak Street in the Syrian quarter of the city. Five men and two women living in the house were arrested. Dynamite was found also in an empty lot off Barker Street and in a cobbler's shop on Lawrence Street, next door to Colombo's printing shop, where Ettor got his mail. No time was lost by the police and the press in attributing the planting of the dynamite to the strikers, notwithstanding the absence of evidence. The *New York Times*, for instance, in its first editorial on the Lawrence strike, spoke with immediate certainty that the strikers were guilty of dynamite plots:

The Lawrence strikers, like the McNamara brothers, and in spite of the similarity of their methods, find reverend defenders. That gentlemen of the cloth should have more sympathy for the poor and suffering than the worldly wise is natural and commendable, and yet the conditions are such as to challenge attention. Clergymen are citizens as well as teachers of religion, and it would seem that they take up the cause of the users of dynamite and fighters of the militia too easily in times like these. . . . How can moral teachers defend such bad citizenship without neglecting an even greater duty to defend those suffering equally and without fault? When a striker goes on picket duty with a revolver in his pocket there is murder in his heart. When strikers use or prepare to use dynamite they display a fiendish lack of humanity which ought to place them beyond the comfort of religion until they have repented.[13]

As soon as the dynamite was discovered, Canal Street, passing near many of the mills, was closed off by the militia.

The strikers protested in vain that the dynamite had been planted to discredit them. Those arrested were dismissed in the Lawrence police court as patently not guilty. On January 29 the charges by the strikers that the dynamite planting was an attempt to discredit them were shown to have foundation, when John C. Breen, a local undertaker and a school committeeman, was arrested and charged with having planted the dynamite. When he came to trial on May 16, he was convicted of conspiracy to injure and was fined $500. Moreover, as will be shown later, he was acting for other persons closely connected with the mill owners.

The Strike Committee concerned itself little with the dynamite planting. It was too busy, faced as it was with an appalling problem of relief. There were at least 50,000 strikers and dependents in Lawrence, out of the total population of 86,-000, who had no source of income and required assistance. During the first days of the strike, the Strike Committee issued an appeal for funds; and an average of $1,000 a day was received for the duration of the strike from all parts of the country, from labor organizations, socialist groups, and private individuals. A general relief committee of 24 was promptly formed, in addition to special relief committees for the separate nationalities. A system of distributing stations and soup kitchens was organized. The distributing stations provided food or grocery orders to families and single women. The Franco-Belgian station alone furnished relief to 1,200 families, and the Italians had four stations, one of which cared for 1,000 families. Each family was allowed from $2 to $5.50 per week for food, according to the number it contained, $1.50 for fuel every second week, and orders for shoes. Two doctors gave medical assistance. The soup kitchens provided for men without families and for all strikers on the picket lines. The largest of these was the one at the Franco-Belgian Hall, which served 1,300 persons twice a day. Careful records were kept of all scabs, who were given no assistance whatsoever. The problem of relief was so efficiently handled by the Strike Committee that during the nine and one-half weeks there was no wavering in the strikers' ranks.

3. *Arrest of Ettor and Giovannitti*

From the outset of the strike, the Strike Committee remained unresponsive to offers of mediation made by city and state officials. At a conference as early as January 16 with the secretary to Governor Eugene N. Foss, who suggested that the State Board of Conciliation and Arbitration be invited to Lawrence, Ettor declared that the strikers were willing to discuss their grievances with the mill owners in the presence of the State Board, but were not willing to submit to arbitration. Again on Sunday afternoon, January 21, the Strike Committee attended a conference with members of the city council and several state officials, at which Colonel E. LeRoy Sweetser, the commanding officer of the militia at Lawrence, proposed that the employees at each mill meet their employers separately to arrive at some agreement. The strikers, however, were resolved on one settlement for all. Three days later, through the efforts of the State Board and city officials, a meeting of strikers and mill owners was held at the City Hall. In accordance with the I.W.W. policy of mass representation, the entire Strike Committee attended. Officials from the eight mills represented refused to meet the Strike Committee face to face and withdrew to another room, while the chairman of the State Board carried messages between the two bodies. The Strike Committee insisted on conferring directly with the mill officials and, after waiting one hour with no results, adjourned and left the City Hall.

In an open letter to mill workers and mill owners, dated January 25, Governor Foss urged both sides to agree to a 30-day truce so that a satisfactory settlement might be arranged:

The situation at Lawrence has become so serious that every possible effort should be made by all parties concerned to adjust matters, and I therefore request all workers to go back and resume their places in the mills for a period of 30 days, pending the efforts which I shall make to get all the differences adjusted; and, in view of the fact that no notice was given the mill operatives of a proposed reduction in wages when the change of hours went into effect, on January 1, I request all mill operators to give 56 hours' pay for 54 hours' work during that period without discrimination.[14]

While the mill operators appeared to favor the proposed truce, the Strike Committee declined to consider it. As another overture to arbitration, President Wood and other officials of the American Woolen Company at Boston consented to meet a committee of the strikers. Twice, on January 23 and 26, Ettor and five other members of the Strike Committee traveled to Boston and presented the strikers' demands, but returned when Wood did not grant them. Following the second trip a false report was somehow circulated that an agreement had been reached and that the strike was ended. In order to prevent any strikers from returning to work by misunderstanding, the Strike Committee decided to hold a parade at 6:30 A.M. on Monday, January 29.

As was expected, an attempt was made early Monday morning to open the mills and start work. The strikers countered with their parade, and the attempt failed. Militia and police attacked the paraders; there was rioting throughout the day. In the morning street cars were stopped and their windows smashed; the strikers maintained that this was the provocative work of 50 thugs hired by the mill operators and the city officials. That evening, during a clash between strikers and police, Anna Lo Pizzo, an Italian striker, was shot and killed. Thereupon the militia with fixed bayonets dispersed the crowd. The strikers present asserted that the bullet was fired by Police Officer Oscar Benoit, but the authorities arrested Joseph Ettor and Arturo Giovannitti, the two I.W.W. leaders at Lawrence, even though neither had been present at the scene of the shooting. They were held as accessories to the murder: the complaint declared that "before said murder was committed, as aforesaid, Joseph J. Ettor and Antonio[?] Giovannitti did incite, procure, and counsel or command the said person whose name is not known, as aforesaid, to commit the said murder in manner and form as aforesaid, against the peace of the Commonwealth. . . ."[15] On February 6 a petition for release on reasonable bail by a writ of habeas corpus was dismissed by a justice of the Massachusetts Supreme Court, and both men were held for trial. As soon as Ettor was jailed, his place as chairman of the Strike Committee was filled by William D. Haywood. Other national officers of the I.W.W.—William Yates, James P. Thompson, William E. Trautmann, Elizabeth Gurley Flynn—came to Lawrence to assist Haywood.

On the day following the shooting of Anna Lo Pizzo strict martial law was declared at Lawrence, and the rule of the city was turned over to Colonel Sweetser. At the request of Mayor Scanlon, 12 companies of infantry, two troops of cavalry, and 50 police officers from the Metropolitan Park Force were sent by Governor Foss. There were now 22 companies of militia patrolling the streets. Citizens were forbidden to form a group or to halt on the street to talk. The strikers who collected at the undertaking establishment in order to participate in the funeral of Anna Lo Pizzo were quickly scattered by cavalry. On Tuesday, January 30, John Ramy, a young Syrian striker, received a fatal bayonet wound. Arrests became more numerous; Mrs. Annie Welzenbach, for instance, and her two sisters, 15 and 18 years of age, were dragged from their beds at midnight to face charges of intimidation at the police court. Nevertheless, the ranks of the strikers swelled, and during the week ending February 3 the number still on the pay roll fell to the lowest point, 8,136. Even this number, since it included office employees and others not connected with the strike, may have been exaggerated; for, although the provocative clatter of the machinery issued from the mills, no one was at the looms. The *New York Times* reported:

A Times reporter visited the Washington Mill, at Canal and Mill Streets. In the spinning room every belt was in motion, the whirr of machinery resounded on every side, yet not a single operative was at work and not a single machine carried a spool of yarn. Outside the gates a large force of infantry kept the strikers away from the gates [16]

It was as Ettor had said: bayonets could not weave cloth.

The craft organizations of the American Federation of Labor had not as yet recognized the existence of the strike. It was early February, when the strike had been in progress for more than three weeks, before the skilled workers affiliated with the Central Labor Union officially declared a strike and submitted a list of grievances to the mill agents. Replies were promptly received, expressing the willingness of the mill operators to confer with committees of their own employees. The Strike Committee regarded the entry of the craft unions into the strike with suspicion. Could the United Textile Workers and John Golden, who had so often denounced the strike as a "revolution" led by those who "preached anarchy," be trusted as an ally? What was behind the strike endorsement of the Central Labor Union, which, together with the Boston Women's Trade Union League, had attempted to use their relief agencies to split the ranks of the strikers? Was it perhaps a plot with the mill owners to betray the strike?

The attitude of the strikers toward the craft unions was

rather mildly expressed by Mary K. O'Sullivan, who in 1892 had become the first woman organizer of the A. F. of L.:

Nothing was so conducive to organization by the Industrial Workers of the World as the methods used by the three branches of the American Federation of Labor. These were the Lawrence Central Labor Union, the Boston Women's Trade Union League, and the Textile Workers of America. Catholics, Jews, Protestants, and unbelievers—men and women of many races and languages,—were working together as human beings with a common cause. The American Federation of Labor alone refused to co-operate. As a consequence, the strikers came to look upon the federation as a force almost as dangerous to their success as the force of the employers themselves, and I violate no confidence in saying that the operatives represented in the strike committee have more respect for the mill owners than for the leaders of this antagonistic element within their own ranks. A striker who went to the federation for relief was looked upon as recreant to his cause and before the strike ended the American Federation of Labor organizations, by openly refusing to give help to anyone who refused to return to work, came to be looked upon as a trap designed in the interests of the mills to catch any workers who could be induced to desert their cause.[17]

The Strike Committee redoubled its watchfulness and aggressiveness. A new picketing plan was instituted on February 12: an endless chain of pickets, walking along the streets without halt so as to avoid arrest, surrounded the entire mill district. Most of the pickets, as many as 7,000 to 10,000 in the chain, wore a white ribbon or a white card reading "Don't be a scab." This strategy was employed until the end of the strike.

As though to confirm the suspicions of the Strike Committee, the first official step of the Massachusetts legislature to attempt a settlement coincided curiously with the strike declaration of the Central Labor Union and the remaining craft organizations. A joint committee of eight members from the Senate and the House tried to bring together the mill officials, the Central Labor Union, the United Textile Workers, and the Strike Committee. The Central Labor Union declared itself willing to have a committee from each mill make an agreement with the officials of that mill, but the Strike Committee remained adamant in its demand for one general settlement. According to the Strike Committee, the employers had forfeited all claims to arbitration by refusing to see the committees of the workers several days before the strike began. Furthermore, the Strike Committee maintained that the Central Labor Union and the United Textile Workers could not in any way speak for the strikers, since only a handful of skilled operatives were represented by them. The attempt of the legislative committee failed, and the mill officials saw the end of all possibility of turning out sample goods for the spring trade. The delivery, not only of woolens, but even of cottons and linens was uncertain. If the looms remained idle much longer, the strike would also cut into the fall business.

4. Exodus of the children

Notwithstanding the efficient relief system put into effect by the Strike Committee, the problem of providing for more than 50,000 men, women, and children was overwhelming. Partly to ease the burden of relief and partly to call the attention of the country to the struggle at Lawrence, the Italian Socialist Federation proposed, on February 5, that the children of the strikers be cared for during the strike by working class families and sympathizers in other cities. Such a plan had been often employed during strikes in Belgium, France, and Italy; this was, however, its first appearance in the United States. The publication of this project by the *New York Call*, the Socialist newspaper, brought 400 letters in three days from people who offered to care for one or more children. Action was taken quickly. The Socialist Women's Committee and an I.W.W. committee at New York investigated the homes of those who offered to care for children, while another committee at Lawrence gathered applications from parents who wished to send their children away, outfitted the children who were to leave Lawrence, and had a physician examine them. On February 10 the first batch of children, 119 of them, ranging from four to 14 years of age, was sent to New York under the supervision of four women, two of them trained nurses. When the train arrived at the Grand Central Station, crowds of working people and sympathizers greeted the Lawrence children with cheers and with the singing of the *Marseillaise* and the *Internationale*. After the children were established in their temporary homes, a committee of four women visited them regularly and sent reports to the parents at Lawrence, who received also letters from the children themselves. An impartial investigation revealed "rather remarkable standards" of physical care and personal interest shown by the temporary "foster-parents." [18] The plan was successful.

The Strike Committee at Lawrence, accordingly, made arrangements to send more children to temporary homes in other cities, always conducting examinations beforehand to make certain that the children would get proper care. Two groups of children were sent out on February 17, one of 103 to New York and another of 35 to Barre, Vermont. Further preparations were under way to send 200 children to Philadelphia and 40 to Manchester, New Hampshire. However, the authorities at Lawrence, disturbed at the sympathy aroused for the children and at the reflection upon the city, charged the Strike Committee with exploiting the children. The press, especially the *Boston American,* joined with the Lawrence authorities in protesting against the "exiling" of the children; the Strike Committee was accused of using the children for advertisement of the strike and of sending children away to questionable surroundings without

THE LAWRENCE WAY. A cartoon by Arthur Young. (*Collier's,* March 9, 1912)

their parents' consent. The Strike Committee replied that the parents' consent was always obtained through a regular consent form and identification card. Moreover, impartial inquiries showed that the children received far better food and treatment in their temporary homes than they had been accustomed to. As for exploitation, said the Strike Committee, what of the exploitation of the children in the mills? John Golden of the United Textile Workers was bitter in his denunciation of the Strike Committee for sending the children away "to keep up the agitation and further the propaganda of the Industrial Workers of the World." [19] On February 17 Colonel Sweetser informed the Strike Committee that he would not permit the sending away of any more children unless he was satisfied that the consent of the parents had been secured.

Sweetser's letter to the Strike Committee was followed on February 22 with an ominous statement by the marshal of Lawrence that no more children would be permitted to leave the city. This interference, as explained by C. C. Carstens, general secretary of the Massachusetts Society for the Prevention of Cruelty to Children, was based on a statute which held a child to be neglected by its parents if it "is growing up without education, without salutary control, without proper physical care or under circumstances exposing him to lead an idle and dissolute life." And later in court Judge Rowell declared that "the willingness of parents to send their children away without proper provision for their care might under some circumstances be sufficient evidence of the kind of neglect described in the statute." [20]

When, in the face of this arbitrary prohibition, the strikers of Lawrence attempted to send a group of 40 children to Philadelphia on February 24, they found the railroad station filled with police. As the children, accompanied by their parents, started to march to the train platform, they were attacked by the police and thrown into a waiting truck. Many women and children were beaten and clubbed. The Women's Committee of Philadelphia, which was to take care of the 40 children, testified before the House Committee on Rules:

The station itself was surrounded by police and militia, who, however, did not interfere with us while we were making preparations to leave. When the time approached to depart the children, arranged in a long line, two by two, in orderly procession, with their parents near at hand, were about to make their way to the train when the police, who had by that time stationed themselves along both sides of the door,

*closed in on us with their clubs, beating right and left, with
no thought of children, who were in the most desperate
danger of being trampled to death. The mothers and children
were thus hurled in a mass and bodily dragged to a military
truck, and even then clubbed, irrespective of the cries of the
panic-stricken women and children. We can scarcely find
words with which to describe this display of appalling brutality.*[21]

More than 30 arrests were made on charges of "congregation," and 14 children were committed by Judge Rowell's
juvenile court to the city farm. The news of this brutality
horrified the country. Protests poured in on the Lawrence
authorities. Congressmen received demands for a federal investigation. Victor Berger, who introduced a resolution in the
House of Representatives calling for an investigation, accused the Lawrence authorities and mill owners of attempting to establish at Lawrence a *reconcentrado* camp, such as
the Spanish had used in Cuba, and the English in South
Africa against the Boers, to drive women and children into
with the purpose of starving them and thus forcing the
men into submission.

So outraged was the country at the attack on the women
and children, and so alarming the protests, that the Lawrence
authorities made no further effort to prevent the sending out
of strikers' children; on March 8, for instance, a group of
40 left for Philadelphia without interference by the police.
Other police attacks, however, were suffered by the strikers,
particularly an assault on a group of women, one of whom
was pregnant and had to be taken to the hospital. In protest
against this savagery, the Strike Committee addressed an
open letter to Governor Foss, Mayor Scanlon, and other city
and state officials:

Peaceful women went to a meeting on March 1, on a Friday. Returning home, about 15 of them were suddenly surrounded by 50 or more Metropolitan police officers. There had been no provocation, no shouting, even, or any noise. These women were assaulted and clubbed, and an officer in blue, leaning out of a window of the city hall, instructed and commanded the Metropolitan police officers and urged them on in their fiendish, savage attacks. Breaking into two divisions, they would not allow the women to escape. The clubbing they received was shameful and atrocious. Not until one of the women, Bertha F. Crouse, 151 Elm Street, was beaten into insensibility did the thugs in uniform desist. The beaten woman was carried unconscious to a hospital, and pregnant with new life, this was blown into eternity by the fiendish beating and was born dead, murdered in a mother's womb by the clubs of hired murderers of the law that you have so recklessly overridden and abridged.[22]

Arrests of the strikers continued: 296 were arrested during the period of the strike, January 12 to March 13. Nevertheless, the strikers' ranks remained unbroken; indeed, the number on strike throughout February was the highest reached.

5. A victory for the strikers

The first sign of surrender by the mill owners appeared. The American Woolen Company posted notices that a new scale of wages would be put into effect on March 4 with increases amounting to at least 5 per cent over the existing rates. On the day the notices were posted, a sub-committee of nine from the Strike Committee, through the efforts of the State Board of Conciliation and Arbitration, met with President Wood. The offer of the American Woolen Company was explained and the strikers were urged to return to work. The Strike Committee, however, found the offer too indefinite and vague even to be submitted to the strikers for a vote. Notices posted by other mills were likewise found to be unsatisfactory. On March 4 some of the craft organizations affiliated with the Central Labor Union and the United Textile Workers voted to accept the new wage schedule and to return to work, with the hope that other grievances would be later adjusted. The Strike Committee in a circular warned the strikers against "the scab-herding agency, the Central Labor Union, which does the work which even professional strike-breaking agencies refused to do. . . ." [23] In compliance with this warning the strikers remained firm, and the mills could not be opened with the few skilled operatives who responded to the call of the Central Labor Union to return to work.

Again on March 6 a sub-committee of the Strike Committee, at the request of the State Board, conferred with the officials of the American Woolen Company. A second offer was made to increase wages not less than 5 per cent, with an average increase of at least 7 per cent. The detailed adjustment of increases would take several days; in the meantime, the officials urged the strikers to return to the mills. When the sub-committee refused to call off the strike until a definite proposal was made to cover all classes of workers, the officials agreed to have a schedule completed within two or three days. The Strike Committee realized the danger of the confusion that might be generated among the strikers by rumors and newspaper reports of conferences and concessions; consequently, a mass meeting was held on March 7, at which a full report of the negotiations was delivered by the sub-committee. Furthermore, on the following day circulars were issued to the strikers bearing the heading: *"Textile workers, men and women! Nobody back to work until all go back together!"* [24] Although John Golden and the Central Labor Union fulminated against "anarchism," the Strike

Committee insisted on a clear and specific offer from the mill officials before submitting it to the strikers for consideration. A third offer, made to the Strike Committee on March 9 by the American Woolen Company, called for average increases of 5 to 11 per cent; but the Strike Committee persisted in its demand for a statement of the precise increase in each wage class. What was more, the American Woolen Company had failed to say anything about the other demands of the strikers concerning overtime, discrimination, and the premium system.

Finally the American Woolen Company officials called the sub-committee to a conference on March 12 and submitted the following offer:

> *Time and one-quarter for overtime.*
> *All people on job work, 5 per cent increase flat.*
> *All those receiving less than 9½ cents an hour, an increase of 2 cents per hour.*
> *All those receiving between 9½ and 10 cents an hour, an increase of 1¾ cents per hour.*
> *All those receiving between 10 and 11 cents per hour, an increase of 1½ cents per hour.*
> *All those receiving between 11 and 12 cents per hour, an increase of 1¼ cents per hour.*
> *All those receiving between 12 and 20 cents per hour, an increase of 1 cent per hour.*
> *No discrimination will be shown to anyone.*
> *The premium being already adjusted to the 54-hour basis, it will be readily seen that an increase of 5 per cent in the wage list is that much to the advantage of the weaver in more easily acquiring the premium. Premiums will be given out every two weeks instead of every four, as heretofore.*[25]

Similar offers were submitted by the Atlantic and Kunhardt mills. The Strike Committee called a mass meeting of the strikers for a vote. On Thursday afternoon, March 14, some 10,000 strikers gathered on the Lawrence Common and heard the recommendation of the Strike Committee that the offers be accepted. Haywood put the question, and the strike, after nine and one-half weeks, was called off in the four mills of the American Woolen Company and in the Atlantic and Kunhardt mills. At several small mills the strike continued.

The strikers returned to work, overjoyed at having achieved one of the most remarkable victories ever won by labor in the United States. All their demands had been granted in full or in part. There was to be no discrimination against any of them for participation in the strike. They were to be paid extra for overtime work. The premium system was modified so that it would be much less injurious, for the payment of the bonus at biweekly periods, instead of monthly, would eliminate much of the former nervous strain and anxiety. Even the wage increases were additionally satisfying, since the lowest paid workers, the unskilled who were the backbone of the strike, were to benefit the most. Boys and girls who had worked at 8 cents per hour were to get, according to the new schedule, a 25 per cent increase. The skilled workers, it is true, had to be content with a 5 per cent advance. But more important, the strikers had won a victory for textile labor throughout New England: the American Woolen Company and other mill owners, apprehensive of strikes in other New England mills, were forced to grant the same wage increases to between 175,000 and 250,000 textile workers. It was not strange that the I.W.W., which had advised the Strike Committee all through the struggle, acquired a membership of 14,000 in Lawrence by the close of the strike.

What alarmed the press and the authorities was the fact that so sweeping a victory should have been won by labor under I.W.W. leadership. The effect might be to turn the workers from the conservative trade-unions to the avowedly revolutionary I.W.W. Robert A. Woods, headworker at the South End House in Boston, who had observed the strike closely, issued a warning:

> As suggesting the danger of the situation, let it be remembered that to-day in old New England some 250,000 people, largely newcomers, with their families, look with gratitude from the heart to William D. Haywood, who though classed among Socialists is really an avowed and unrestrained Anarchist, to whom nothing in the common law of civilized nations, nothing in legislative enactment or judicial decision, nothing in any part of that moral law which is the result of untold ages of human experience, not one single joint in the recently and toilsomely reared structure of labor organization—is worthy of an instant's consideration as against his purpose. His associates in the Industrial Workers of the World are pledged to the same creed; and it is the essence of this creed to despise words. It is far from sufficient to say— what is true enough—that these men were not essential to the Lawrence strike, that the situation would have developed in much the same way without imported leadership. The fact that these leaders should have held the center of the stage of action for the whole of New England for weeks, and are carrying away such prestige for themselves and their cause with them, represents an amount of harm which only years of aggressive educational effort can overcome. . . .[26]

In the midst of this widespread alarm the Strike Committee went out of existence on March 24, to be replaced by Local 20, National Industrial Textile Workers' Union of the I.W.W. Before it adjourned, the Strike Committee issued a statement that it regarded the Lawrence victory as only a "preliminary skirmish," and that "the battles will cease, the class struggle will end only when the working class has overthrown the capitalist class and has secured undisputed possession of the earth and all that is in and on it." [27]

6. "Open the jail doors or we will close the mill gates"

Although the strikers returned to work, they regarded their victory as not yet complete. Their leaders, Ettor and Giovannitti, were still in jail awaiting trial as "accessories before the fact" to the shooting of Anna Lo Pizzo. The workers felt that, before the strike could be termed a victory, Ettor and Giovannitti would have to be freed. This feeling was manifested in the banner inscribed "Open the jail doors or we will close the mill gates," which was exhibited when the children who had been sent to other cities were welcomed back to Lawrence. The prosecution of Ettor and Giovannitti soon became a *cause célèbre*. In fact, it resembled in many aspects the case of the Haymarket anarchists. It was neccessary, for example, that the police find an actual perpetrator of the crime who might have been instigated to the deed by the speeches of the "accessories." Such a principal was found in Joseph Caruso, a Lawrence textile worker, who was arrested in April and indicted by the grand jury. The State contended that Caruso only assisted in the shooting, which was actually done by a mysterious "man in a brown overcoat," whose name was Salvatore Scuito and who was never found. According to Justus Ebert, who acted as director of publicity for the I.W.W. during the defense, the police attempted unsuccessfully to force Caruso to leave the city and thus be unavailable for court evidence, so that, as in the Haymarket trial, the "accessories before the fact" might be more easily convicted in the absence of the guilty principal.[28] The trial of Ettor, Giovannitti, and Caruso was first set for May 27, but was postponed at the request of the defense.

To aggravate the workers' sense of injustice, the contrast

offered by the dynamite planting, for which Breen had been so mildly punished, was revived through certain fortuitous circumstances. Ernest W. Pitman, president of the Pitman Construction Company, which had erected two of the large mills at Lawrence, indiscreetly confessed to District Attorney Pelletier that the dynamite planting had been plotted in the Boston office of a textile corporation. Pitman was served with summons to appear before the grand jury, but committed suicide before the date set for his examination. Nevertheless, Pelletier already had sufficient evidence to procure indictments by the grand jury on August 31 charging conspiracy to plant dynamite in Lawrence against Dennis J. Collins, a Cambridge dog fancier and friend of Breen; Fred E. Atteaux, president of the Atteaux Supply Company; and William M. Wood, president of the American Woolen Company. Much later, in June, 1913, Collins was found guilty, while Wood and Atteaux were exonerated. In the meantime, 3,000 persons signed a petition demanding the recall of Breen as school committeeman. The workers asked again why Breen, guilty of so serious a crime as planting dynamite, should be free after the trifling punishment of a $500 fine, while Ettor and Giovannitti should be in jail awaiting trial for an act they admittedly had not committed.

As soon as the strike was ended, the Lawrence workers and the I.W.W. took active steps to secure the freedom of the indicted men. An Ettor-Giovannitti Defense Committee of 12 was organized, with William D. Haywood as chairman. Legal, publicity, and financial departments were formed. The financial department collected and expended $60,000 during the course of the defense. The publicity department helped to form Ettor-Giovannitti Defense Conferences in New York, Brooklyn, Philadelphia, Chicago, Boston, San Francisco, Pittsburgh, Cleveland, and other large cities in the United States. Agitation, by means of protest parades, demonstrations, and meetings, mounted steadily. In New York a huge meeting was addressed on May 21 at Cooper Union by Morris Hillquit. At Boston there was a great demonstration, September 15, on the Common. The wave of agitation, as it swept higher each week, frightened the Lawrence and Massachusetts authorities. Charges of conspiracy to intimidate the workers in various textile mills were brought against Haywood, William Trautmann, William Yates, Ettor Giannini, Edmundo Rossoni, Guido Mazerreli, James P. Thompson, and Thomas Holliday, all of them, curiously enough, members of the Ettor-Giovannitti Defense Committee. Indictments were returned against them, and they were released on bail.

Toward the day of the opening of the trial, September 30, there began to spread among the textile workers a strong sentiment for a demonstration strike. Ettor and Giovannitti sent letters to a mass meeting at Lawrence on September 25, requesting that the idea be abandoned, since such a strike might prejudice public opinion and would certainly cost the workers much misery. Nevertheless, the workers were determined on this means of protest against what they regarded as a crying injustice, and Local 20 of the I.W.W. decided to support them. Accordingly, on September 30 about 15,-000 textile workers at Lawrence quit work in a 24-hour demonstration strike. Never before had so revolutionary a strike—in fact, a political strike—occurred in the United States.

Mayor Scanlon and the officials were both terrified and infuriated at the threat to the existing government. Police, detectives, and state police were called out. Strikers were brutally clubbed, 14 were arrested. Textile workers at Lowell, Lynn, Haverhill, and other Massachusetts cities voted to call a strike if the trial of Ettor and Giovannitti went wrong. In retaliation for the demonstration strike, the mill owners at

Lawrence discharged and blacklisted between 1,500 and 2,000 of the more active strikers. When Haywood and the I.W.W. officials, however, threatened an exodus of textile workers from Lawrence, the blacklist was abandoned and the strikers were reëmployed without discrimination. Mayor Scanlon opened a "God and Country" campaign to run the I.W.W. out of town. Citizens appeared with American flags in their lapels, a 30-day flag display began, and a parade was announced for Columbus Day, Saturday, October 12. The I.W.W. countered with a mass outing at Spring Valley on Columbus Day, in order to avoid any violence in the city. The flag display was quickly quenched by a threatened boycott by the workers against all "patriots."

Amid this tense atmosphere the trial opened at Salem, Massachusetts, in the Superior Court of Essex County under Judge Joseph F. Quinn. The prosecution was in the hands of District Attorney Atwill. The defense attorneys were W. Scott Peters, Joseph H. Sisk, John P. S. Mahoney, George E. Roewer, Jr., and Fred H. Moore. So widespread were convictions and prejudices concerning the case that the selection of jurymen became difficult. A panel of 350 veniremen was exhausted in three days, with only four jurors chosen. Another panel was called, and court reopened on October 14. Finally, after 600 veniremen had been examined, the jury was completed. Each day crowds of workers gathered outside the courthouse to cheer the prisoners as they were conducted to and from the trial room. Protests poured in on the court from every part of the country. In Sweden and France a boycott of American woolen goods was begun. In Italy the Social Union announced the candidacy of Arturo Giovannitti to represent Carpi in the Chamber of Deputies, and the *Corriere d'Italia* called upon the Italian government to make representations to prevent the United States "from committing a repugnant injustice." [29] The demonstration strike had focused the attention of the world on Salem.

The prosecution, in the 58 days of trial, attempted to prove that Ettor and Giovannitti had incited the strikers, and hence Caruso, to violence and murder; but both the evidence and witnesses presented were easily discredited. Much was made by District Attorney Atwill, for instance, of a declaration by two detectives from the Callahan Detective Agency that in an Italian speech Giovannitti had commanded his listeners to sleep in the daytime and to prowl around at night like wild animals. The two detectives were forced to admit, however, that they had destroyed the notes of the incriminating speech; nor was their character as witnesses above suspicion. Caruso produced a complete watertight alibi: three witnesses swore that he had been at home eating supper when Anna Lo Pizzo was shot. It was soon apparent that there was no evidence on which to convict.

Since the prosecution had often assailed their political and economic principles, Ettor and Giovannitti requested and received permission to deliver closing speeches to the jury. They made no attempt to conceal, euphemize, or soften their unalterable and fundamental opposition to the existing order of society. Giovannitti, indeed, declared:

Let me tell you that the first strike that breaks again in this Commonwealth or any other place in America where the work and the help and the intelligence of Joseph J. Ettor and Arturo Giovannitti will be needed and necessary, there we shall go again, regardless of any fear and of any threat. We shall return again to our humble efforts, obscure, unknown, misunderstood soldiers of this mighty army of the working class of the world, which, out of the shadows and the darkness of the past, is striving towards the destined goal, which is the emancipation of human kind, which is the establish-

ment of love and brotherhood and justice for every man and every woman on this earth.[30]

On Tuesday morning, November 26, the jury returned a verdict of not guilty. Ettor and Giovannitti, free once more after 10 months in jail, were cheered and embraced by crowds outside the courthouse. That afternoon they addressed a mass meeting at Lawrence, at which more than 10,000 workers hailed them and celebrated the completion of the Lawrence strike victory, the accomplishment of their display of solidarity.

VII. BLOODY LUDLOW

1. Feudalism in Colorado

When in September, 1913, some 9,000 miners with their families and belongings left the company camps, marched down the canyons of the southern Colorado coal fields, and established tent colonies, they began a 15-month strike against the mine operators that was not so much a struggle for higher wages or other tangible advantages as a revolt against a political, economic, and social despotism. The scene of the struggle, the region surrounding Trinidad, particularly Las Animas and Huerfano Counties, was geographically isolated from the social and industrial life of the rest of the state. The coal fields were located in the foothills to the east of the Rocky Mountains, and the camps, situated in the narrow gorges and valleys, were shut in so closely by hills that often only two or three rows of houses could be erected. The principal towns were 10 to 30 miles from the mining camps, and could be reached only by branch railways. In these isolated communities the Colorado Fuel & Iron Company, the Rocky Mountain Fuel Company, the Victor-American Fuel Company, and a number of smaller operators furnished subsistence for 30,000 people, most of them Greeks, Italians, Slavs, and Mexicans. Since the 1880's and 1890's, when the development of the coal industry in southern Colorado began, the companies had performed all the functions of civil government and had regulated all social activities. Strikes of the miners in 1883, 1893, and 1903 had been quickly suppressed by the use of armed guards, the expulsion of strikers, and the importation of strike-breakers. That the working and living conditions in these isolated mining camps were the cause of the repeated strikes is supported by the fact that the strike-breakers of 1903 became, in large part, the strikers of 1913.

Isolation was only one factor in the economic and political oppression, in places approaching serfdom, which the miners suffered. More important was the ownership of the mining camps by the companies. Many villages and towns were owned outright by the companies; the Colorado Fuel & Iron Company alone owned at least 12. No land and no building could be occupied without the permission of the company. Not only the miners' dwellings, but the school and the church were the property of the company, with the result that teachers and ministers were supervised, if not openly selected, by the company. The miner bought his food, clothing, and other supplies at the company store. There was ordinarily only one place of public entertainment, the company saloon, which was usually operated under a concession; at rare intervals there were brief visits by traveling evangelists or moving-picture shows. The houses, according to one observer, who served during part of the strike as a militiaman, were "shabby, ugly, and small." Most of them had only two or three rooms, although sheds constructed of boards and old sheet iron were added by the tenants. There were few provisions for sanitation: refuse was dumped without care in or near the camp, and the water supply was often pumped directly from the mines and used without filtration. As a result, diseases arose easily and spread rapidly.[1] The miner who protested lost simultaneously his job, his dwelling, and his right to remain in the community.

The economic and political domination of the companies was rendered absolute by the use of the summary discharge. A system of espionage detected employees who, by word or deed, challenged the behavior of the companies, and the blacklist punished them. The rights of free speech, free press, and free assembly were arbitrarily suppressed: periodicals were censored, public speakers were expelled, and even the freedom of speech in informal gatherings was curtailed through the fear of spies. The miners and their families were at the mercy of the camp marshals, of whom a federal grand jury at Pueblo reported in November, 1913:

Many camp marshals, whose appointment and salaries are controlled by local companies, have exercised a system of espionage and have resorted to arbitrary powers of police control, acting in the capacity of judge and jury and passing the sentence: "Down the canyon for you," meaning thereby that the miner so addressed was discharged and ordered to leave the camp, upon miners who had incurred the enmity of the superintendent or pit boss for having·complained of a real grievance or for other cause. These, taken with brutal assaults by camp marshals upon miners, have produced general dissatisfaction among the latter. Miners generally fear to complain of real grievances because of the danger of their discharge or of their being placed in unfavorable position in the mines.[2]

A small army of deputy sheriffs, maintained by the companies, coöperated with the spies, the superintendents, and the camp marshals.

Nor could the miners appeal for protection to the civil authorities, since they were almost without exception in the control of the companies. With company officials acting as election judges, with large sums of money expended to buy votes, and with the polling places often located on company property where entrance could be denied objectionable voters, the political power of the companies was unlimited. In particular, the political machines in Las Animas and Huerfano Counties, whose bosses were the sheriffs, exercised a peremptory and pervading rule. That the miner had little, if any, chance of asserting his civil rights against the wishes of the companies was admitted before the U. S. Commission on Industrial Relations by General Superintendent L. M. Bowers of the Colorado Fuel & Iron Company:

> *Commissioner O'Connell. In the counties where these coal companies operate, they have the judges and sheriffs, and through the sheriffs can select the jurors, as was testified to in the evidence before us of Sheriff Farr himself, and by others before us as to how the juries were selected; how the election commissioners were appointed and sometimes where they did not show up at a certain precinct, Sheriff Farr said: "You and you and you act as election commissioners to-day." Under these circumstances I ask you, Mr. Bowers, as a man of great affairs and dealing with big business and big financial affairs, if you think a poor, humble miner, without any great amount of money, without any property behind him, or any influence, has any chance of getting justice in a situation of that kind?*
>
> *Mr. Bowers. Why, no; no one need to ask me that. . . .*[3]

Even the state government, as shall be seen, was not untouched by the political influence of the companies.

This political sway was maintained by the coal companies not only to guarantee the appointment of subservient marshals, constables, deputy sheriffs, and sheriffs, but also "in order that they might ignore or defy state laws enacted to safeguard the interests of their employees, prevent legislation by state or county unfavorable to their interests and obtain such legislation as they wished, control coroners and judges and thus prevent injured employees from collecting damages; and flagrantly disregard the constitutional and statutory guarantees that otherwise would have prevented them from procuring the imprisonment, deportation or killing of union organizers and strikers." [4] The grip of the companies on the coroners and juries who judged personal injury cases, for instance, is shown by the nearly complete absence of personal injury suits against the companies, notwithstanding the fact that the death rate in coal mining for Colorado was twice that of the United States as a whole.[5] Injured miners and the survivors of those killed in mine accidents were forced to accept whatever compensation the companies saw fit to give them. Out of 90 verdicts, involving 109 deaths, rendered by coroners' juries in Huerfano County, only one held the mine management at fault, while 85 charged the victims with "negligence" or "carelessness." For the period between January 1, 1910, and March 1, 1913, the coroner's records at Trinidad gave the names of the jurors in 30 cases; 24 of these had the same man, a gambler and bartender by the name of J. C. Baldwin, as foreman of the jury.[6] The companies made themselves immune from the inconvenience and expense of personal injury suits by denying the miners ordinary justice.

In the conditions arising from this economic and political despotism lay the fundamental causes of the strike that began in September, 1913. In fact, in a Brief for the Striking Miners filed with the Congressional Committee on Mines and Mining, during its inquiry into the Colorado coal strike, the following underlying causes were set forth:

1. Ignorance of the owners of the great coal-producing properties concerning actual conditions under which their employees live and labor.

2. The lack of any proper sense of personal responsibility on the part of those owners, for what is wrong in those conditions.

3. The maintenance by the coal-mining operators of a

modern system of monopolistic feudalism, with many of the evil features of the old feudalism, but without many of those features which made it somewhat beneficent.

4. The insistence by the operators upon their right to conduct a vast coal-producing business,—a business in reality affected with a public interest,—regardless of how their conduct may affect society at large, and as if it were a small private business.

5. The unwillingness on the part of the operators to concede to their employees the right of effective organization, while themselves maintaining a complete combination and organization.[7]

Two principal grievances are to be found in this brief: first, the ignorance and lack of responsibility of the companies; and second, the denial by the companies of the miners' right to organize.

Evidence in plenty exists to support the charge against the companies of ignorance and irresponsibility. John D. Rockefeller, Jr., who through ownership of 40 per cent of the stocks and bonds controlled the Colorado Fuel & Iron Company, by far the largest coal-mining company in Colorado, had not for the ten years preceding the strike visited Colorado or attended a directors' meeting. He admitted before the U. S. Commission on Industrial Relations that he had "not the slightest idea" of the wages, rents, or living conditions of the miners, and that he had turned over the entire management to President Welborn and Superintendent Bowers. The Commission condemned his ignorance of conditions in his own mines: "Such details as wages, working conditions, and the political, social, and moral welfare of the 15,000 or 20,000 inhabitants of his coal camps, apparently held no interest for Mr. Rockefeller, for as late as April, 1914, he professed ignorance of these details. Yet he followed, step by step, the struggle of his executive officials to retain arbitrary power, and to prevent the installation of machinery for collective bargaining, by which abuses might automatically be corrected, and he supported and encouraged this struggle in every letter he wrote to his agents." [8] President Welborn and Superintendent Bowers, to whom were intrusted the management of the Colorado Fuel & Iron Company, had offices in Denver—as did many of the other companies—some 200 miles north of the coal fields. The actual operations were in charge of Manager Weitzel of the Fuel Department, whose offices were in Pueblo, 80 miles from the mines. He, in turn, received reports from assistant managers and superintendents.

Faced with such a system of absentee control and ownership, the miner found it impossible to penetrate beyond the pit boss or foreman to the more responsible, but remote, officials of the company. The other companies displayed the same lack of interest and responsibility concerning the living and working conditions of their employees. Given this situation, the question of their right to organize was of the greatest importance to the miners. In organization and collective bargaining, they felt, lay their only defense against the "modern system of monopolistic feudalism," against the open encroachments upon their standards of living and their civil liberties.

2. Coal companies and mining laws

The profound discontent among the coal miners of southern Colorado led the United Mine Workers, during the summer of 1913, to send organizers into the field. At this time the United Mine Workers was numerically one of the strongest unions in the country, with 400,000 dues-paying members. Vice-President Frank J. Hayes came to Colorado to direct the organizational activities; and he, together with

John McLennan, president of District no. 15, which included
Colorado and New Mexico; E. L. Doyle, secretary of Dis-
trict no. 15; and John Lawson, a member of the Executive
Board of the United Mine Workers, constituted a Policy
Committee for the miners. This committee requested Governor Ammons of Colorado to try to procure a conference with
the mine operators. When Governor Ammons, however, approached President Welborn of the Colorado Fuel & Iron
Company, President Osgood of the Victor-American Fuel
Company, and President Brown of the Rocky Mountain
Fuel Company, they refused outright to meet any union
representatives, lest recognition of the union might thereby
be implied.

Apprehensive of the possibility of a violent industrial
conflict, Governor Ammons sent Edwin V. Brake, Deputy
Labor Commissioner, to Trinidad in order to discover what
might be done to avert the impending strike. After an investigation extending from August 16 to 23, Brake reported
that the companies had filled the region with armed guards
and detectives, one of whom, George Belcher, a Baldwin-
Felts detective in the pay of the Colorado Fuel & Iron Company, had already shot and killed a union organizer, Gerald
Lippiatt, in the public street of Trinidad; and that an outbreak of the miners was imminent. Brake recommended that
Ammons, if bloodshed was to be avoided, command the sheriffs of Las Animas and Huerfano Counties to disarm every
man in the mining fields. This Ammons failed to do. Even the
federal government made an effort to check the development
of the strike: Secretary Wilson of the Department of Labor
sent Ethelbert Stewart to New York to get Rockefeller's
aid; and Stewart, unable to see Rockefeller, went on to
Colorado, but failed to achieve a conference because of the
obduracy of the operators.

The officials of the United Mine Workers seemed anxious

to prevent a strike. For one thing, they feared the blood-shed and suffering that would certainly result; for another, the national treasury, because of strikes in West Virginia and other regions, was not equal to another struggle. The Policy Committee, therefore, on August 26, 1913, sent letters to all the coal operators in southern Colorado, asking for a joint meeting to discuss the question of union recognition. No reply was received, except from two small operators. A second letter was sent out by the Policy Committee on September 8 to inform the operators that a convention of the miners was to be held on September 15 at Trinidad, and to invite them to attend. When again no reply was received, the miners proceeded to gather at Trinidad. At the convention seven demands were drawn up: (1) Recognition of the union. (2) A 10 per cent increase in tonnage rates and a day scale to correspond with the rates in Wyoming. (3) An eight-hour day for all labor in and around the coal lands and at the coke ovens. (4) Payment for all narrow and dead work, which included brushing, timbering, removing falls, handling impurities, etc. (5) The election of check-weigh-men by the miners without interference by company officials. (6) The right of the mine workers to trade at any store they pleased, and to choose their own boarding places and their own doctors. (7) The enforcement of the mining laws of the state, and the abolition of the company guard system. If the demands were not complied with by September 23, a strike was to be called. Even after the convention the mere grant-ing of a conference by the operators might have averted the strike; that they realized this is shown in a letter written on September 19 by Superintendent Bowers to Starr J. Mur-phy, personal attorney to Rockefeller: "The strike is called for the 23rd, but it is thought on the part of a good many operators that the officials, anticipating being whipped, will undertake to sneak out if they can secure even an interview with the operators, which so far they have been unable to do, thus boasting before the public that they have secured the principal point, namely, recognition of the union." [9]

In the meantime, apprised by local officials and spies of the growing unrest among the miners, the operators multiplied the number of marshals and armed guards in the mining camps. By September 1 in Huerfano County alone 326 men, many of them imported from other states, had been commissioned as deputy sheriffs by Sheriff Jefferson Farr, who admitted that for all he knew they might have been "redhanded murderers," and that they were employed, armed, and paid by the coal companies. [10] In spite of this intimidating atmosphere, about 9,000 miners, from 40 per cent to 100 per cent of the workers at the various camps, complied with the strike order of September 23 and marched down the canyons, together with their families and household belongings. On this day there was a heavy fall of snow and sleet, but since the companies owned every house and every foot of ground in the camps, the sudden migration was necessary. "No more eloquent proof could be given of the intense discontent of the miners and their families, and of their determination to endure any hardship rather than remain at work under existing conditions." [11] The strikers and their families were established in tent colonies which had been previously set up by the officials of the United Mine Workers on land leased for the purpose. A system of strike benefits, paid out of the resources of the national treasury, was instituted, and the Policy Committee took complete charge of the strike and brought order into the new community life.

The strikers maintained that five of their seven demands merely called for the enforcement of existing state mining laws which were steadily disregarded by the companies. For instance, the demand for the eight-hour day had actually been granted in November, 1902, as an amendment to the

state constitution by a popular vote of 72,980 against
26,266:

*Section 250. The General Assembly shall provide by law
and shall provide suitable penalties for the violation thereof,
for a period of employment not to exceed eight hours within
any twenty-four hours . . . for persons employed in underground mines.*[12]

Notwithstanding this command by the citizens of the state,
the large mining corporations time and again obstructed the
passage of the required legislation. Finally in 1913 the legislature enacted an eight-hour measure which went into effect
April 3, only, in the opinion of the U. S. Commission on
Industrial Relations, because the coal companies wanted to
forestall and defeat the spreading unionization of the
mines.[13] Likewise, the right to employ check-weighmen had
been given the miners by state law in 1897. Nevertheless, the
right had been denied them by the companies, with the result
that the miners were forced to rely entirely upon the honesty
of the operators, and felt that they were the victims of extensive and deliberate cheating. Only in April, 1912, after
Superintendent Bowers discovered that coal was being boot-
legged to the railroads through the dishonesty of company
weighmasters, did he post notices permitting the election of
check-weighmen by the miners. For this action, despite its
selfish motivation, Bowers incurred the anger of the other
operators.[14] And the miners, accustomed to the threat of discharge, feared to select check-weighmen. At the time of the
strike, then, neither the eight-hour day nor the free election
of check-weighmen was in force.

Although a law enacted in 1899 by the legislature prohibited "any arrangement by which any person may issue a
truck order or scrip by means of which the maker may
charge the amount to the employer to be deducted from the

wages of the employee" and moreover "any requirement or understanding, whatsoever, by the employer with the employee that does not permit the employee to purchase the necessaries of life where and of whom he likes, without interference, coercion, let or hindrance," the coal miners found it necessary to demand in 1913 the freedom to trade where they pleased.[15] Through subsidiary companies the mine owners operated company stores in the camps to great profit. President Welborn, for example, testified that the stores of the Colorado Fuel & Iron Company earned annually 20 per cent on a capital of $700,000.[16] Since these stores had no competition in at least half of the mining camps, except from peddlers, the miners had to resign themselves to whatever prices were charged. Scrip, while not used to pay wages, was in use at the stores until the time of the strike, and Superintendent Snodgrass of the Delagua mine of the Victor-American Fuel Company admitted that his company regarded an employee holding scrip as under contract to spend it at the company store.[17] Furthermore, because of the close association between store managers and local company officials, the miner who failed to trade at the company store frequently risked loss of his job; the Rev. Eugene S. Gaddis, director of the medical and sociological department of the Colorado Fuel & Iron Company throughout the strike, reported that the manager of the Fuel Department had instructed a superintendent to use his influence to have employees trade at the company store, and that one store manager had threatened a young woman with her husband's discharge if she failed to buy her groceries from him.[18] Directly or indirectly, therefore, both scrip and the company store were forced upon the miners.

Similarly the miners were required to employ doctors furnished by the companies. One dollar a month was arbitrarily deducted from the wages of the miner, for which he and his family received treatment from the company doctor and hospital service for bad injuries. If the doctor rendered special services (confinement, venereal diseases, fight bruises), the charges were deducted from the employee's pay check; if the services were in any way unsatisfactory, the miner had no recourse. In fact, the Rev. E. S. Gaddis reported:

Presumably for an object lesson for the whole camp, a bill for services was collected through the mine office by the company physician when the family had been so bold as to call in a doctor of their own choice, and the father was discharged for being unwilling to pay it. This case was reported to the Denver headquarters, and no redress was ever made.[19]

In the same way, since the companies owned all the property in the closed camps, the miner was usually bound to live in a company house, whether it was fit for habitation or not. And many of the houses, according to the testimony of the Rev. E. S. Gaddis before the U. S. Commission, were unfit for occupancy: "The C. F. & I. Co. now own and rent hovels, shacks, and dugouts that are unfit for the habitation of human beings and are little removed from the pigsty make of dwellings. And the people in them live on the very level of a pigsty."[20] He testified further that on June 18, 1914, the camp physician at Red Camp reported 47 houses unfit for occupancy; that at Segundo there were 73 one-room shacks and 2 two-room; that the camp physician at Sopris "had to remove a mother in labor from one part of the shack to another to keep dry"; and that in one year, 1912-13, there were 151 cases of typhoid in the Colorado Fuel & Iron Company camps.[21] Hence it was that the strikers demanded the right to choose their own houses and doctors.

Other demands were included in the seven made by the strikers—those calling for an increase in wages, the abolition of the guard system, and the enforcement of state mining laws, such as one requiring semi-monthly pay and another prohibiting the use of the blacklist—but the principal demand was that for the recognition of the union. It was over this demand that the conflict was actually fought. The operators were unalterably opposed to any dealings with the United Mine Workers. They contended that this organization was illegal and criminal, and cited as proof a decision rendered by Judge Dayton of the Federal Court of West Virginia (a decision that was later unanimously reversed by the Court of Appeals). Furthermore, the operators charged the union with violating its contracts, limiting the output of the mines, diminishing the efficiency of labor, and increasing the number of accidents. All these charges were denied by the United Mine Workers, which asserted that it had kept 90 per cent of its contracts, that there was no evidence of decreased efficiency and output in the unionized mines, and that the death rate in Colorado's non-union mines was double that of the rest of the country, where most of the miners were unionized. The U. S. Commission on Industrial Relations tended to agree with the United Mine Workers: "The charge that miners protected by the union limit output and work less efficiently, cannot be supported by evidence gathered by the Commission." [22]

The union, maintained the operators, was unnecessary for the protection of the miners' interests, since the companies granted concessions and improvements voluntarily. Of this claim the U. S. Commission said:

It is hard to believe that this contention is made in good faith. Letters from Mr. Bowers to Mr. Murphy show that concessions and improvements were granted in the mines of the Colorado Fuel & Iron Company, in order to remove the incentive of the miners to join the union, and were thus directly brought about by the existence of the union in other fields.[23]

The operators objected further that better conditions existed in non-union than in union mines and that the miners in southern Colorado did not want unionism. Again the U. S. Commission held the contrary:

The allegation of the operators that their employees did not desire to join the union or to go on strike is best answered by the fact that 8,000 miners, according to Mr. Bowers' own estimate, left their homes with their wives and children on September 23 and moved down the canyons through a snow storm to take up their residence in the tent colonies. That 8,000 miners could have been intimidated by a handful of union organizers into taking this step is unbelievable. In the case of the Colorado Fuel & Iron Company, President Welborn's own estimate is that 70 per cent of their miners struck.[24]

But above all, the operators insisted that the union infringed upon the personal liberty of the miner and invaded the owner's right to manage his own property.

Here lay the real basis of the operators' opposition to the United Mine Workers and the strikers. Superintendent Bowers regarded the union's demands as "numerous requirements that practically take away the mines from the control of the owners and operators and place them in the hands of these, in many cases, disreputable agitators, socialists, and anarchists." [25] The coal companies refused to yield the slightest concession in the principle of collective bargaining. Each miner was to bargain with the company as an individual, with the understanding that he was always free to leave the mining camp. According to John C. Osgood, president of the Victor-American Fuel Company, the free-

dom of the miner to quit his job and move with his family
to another state was sufficient protection against any
abuses.[26]

Predominant among the companies in this stand for the
open shop was the Colorado Fuel & Iron Company, which
alone produced nearly 40 per cent of the coal mined in Colorado. And Rockefeller, through his control of the Colorado
Fuel & Iron Company, in reality dictated the labor policies
of practically all the coal companies in southern Colorado.
There can be no doubt of Rockefeller's approval and encouragement of the stand taken by the Colorado Fuel &
Iron Company against any recognition whatsoever of the
organization of the miners. On October 6, 1913, shortly after
the strike began, he wrote to Bowers: "We feel that what
you have done is right and fair and that the position which
you have taken in regard to the unionizing of the mines is
in the interest of the employees of the company. Whatever
the outcome may be, we will stand by you to the end." [27]
And again on December 8, 1913: "You are fighting a good
fight, which is not only in the interest of your own company
but of the other companies in Colorado and of the business
interests of the entire country and of the laboring classes
quite as much." [28] Rockefeller's endorsements steadily braced
the operators in their refusal to meet representatives of the
strikers and upheld them in their measures for defeating the
strike.

Thus, underlying all the reasons given by the operators
for their opposition to recognition of the union was their unyielding adherence to the open-shop principle. For the sake
of this principle, the companies barred union organizers
from the mining camps, and persecuted and arrested them
in the "open" towns of the coal-mining counties. This principle was defended by Rockefeller when, after the strike had

been in progress for more than half a year, he was questioned by Chairman Foster of the House Committee on Mines and Mining during its inquiry into the Colorado strike:

Q.—But the killing of people and shooting of children has not been of enough importance to you to communicate with the other Directors and see if something might be done to end that sort of thing? A.—We believe the issue is not a local one in Colorado. It is a national issue whether workers shall be allowed to work under such conditions as they may choose. As part owners of the property our interest in the laboring men in this country is so immense, so deep, so profound that we stand ready to lose every cent we put in that company rather than see the men we have employed thrown out of work and have imposed upon them conditions which are not of their seeking and which neither they nor we can see are in our interest.

Q.—You are willing to let these killings take place rather than to go there and do something to settle conditions? A.— There is just one thing that can be done to settle this strike, and that is to unionize the camps, and our interest in labor is so profound and we believe so sincerely that that interest demands that the camps shall be open camps, that we expect to stand by the officers at any cost. It is not an accident that this is our position—

Q.—And you will do that if that costs all your property and kills all your employes? A.—It is a great principle.

Q.—And you would do that rather than recognize the right of men to collective bargaining? A.—No, Sir—rather than allow outside people to come in and interfere with employes who are thoroughly satisfied with their labor conditions. It was upon a similar principle that the War of the Revolution was carried on. It is a great national issue of the most vital kind.[29]

To sustain the open-shop principle, the coal operators were ready to employ all the economic, political, and social pressure they possessed.

3. The "Death Special"

At the first evidence of strike sentiment during the summer of 1913, the Colorado Fuel & Iron Company and the other coal companies imported armed men from Texas, New Mexico, and West Virginia; and these imported men were readily deputized by the sheriffs in southern Colorado without any inquiries into their former records.

That many guards deputized in this illegal fashion and paid by the Colorado Fuel & Iron Company were men of the lowest and most vicious character has been clearly established. That their function was to intimidate and harass the strikers had been demonstrated in the strike of 1903, 1904, and had been made apparent early in the present strike by the shooting to death of Gerald Lippiatt, a union organizer, in the streets of Trinidad immediately after the calling of the strike, by a Baldwin-Felts detective employed by the Colorado Fuel & Iron Company and its associates and deputized by the sheriff of Las Animas County. In fact it was to these deputies, then masquerading as national guardsmen, that national guard officers attempted to attribute the murder, looting and pillage that accompanied the destruction of the Ludlow tent colony of strikers later in the strike.[30]

The Baldwin-Felts Detective Agency, which had already acquired a reputation for brutality in the West Virginia strikes, was engaged by the Colorado Fuel & Iron Company to assist in recruiting armed guards, in protecting the mines, and in suppressing the strike in southern Colorado.

Under the direction of A. C. Felts and Detective Belcher, an armored automobile mounted with a machine gun was constructed in the Colorado Fuel & Iron Company shops at Pueblo. It was named the "Death Special" by the strikers. Rifle pits were dug in the hills adjacent to the mining properties, and were equipped with rifles, machine guns, and searchlights. It seemed as if the operators were preparing to defeat the strike by the same tactics that had succeeded in 1903-1904: the assault, terrorization, and forceful deportation of strikers, and the importation of strike-breakers.

Determined to withstand any armed attacks, the strikers provided themselves with revolvers, shotguns, and rifles. Moreover, when the union officials observed the large numbers of imported guards commissioned as deputy sheriffs— 326 in Huerfano County alone by September 1—they decided to furnish arms openly to the strikers. On September 12 agents of the union purchased arms from a Pueblo hardware dealer. The union officials found justification for their action in the constitution of Colorado: "The right of no person to keep and bear arms in defense of his home, person, and property, or in aid of the civil power when thereto legally summoned, shall be called in question." [31] Concerning the arming of the strikers, the judgment of the U. S. Commission on Industrial Relations was:

In all discussion and thought regarding violence in connection with the strike, the seeker after truth must remember that government existed in southern Colorado only as an instrument of tyranny and oppression in the hands of the operators; that, once having dared to oppose that tyranny in a strike, the miners' only protection for themselves and their families lay in the physical force which they could muster.[32]

With guards and strikers both armed and tense, violence was inevitable. On September 24, the day after the strike opened, Robert Lee, a marshal at the Segundo camp of the

Colorado Fuel & Iron Company, was shot from ambush and killed while attempting to arrest four strikers. Detectives exchanged gunfire with strikers from the Ludlow tent colony on October 7; two days later, after mine guards attacked the Ludlow colony and killed one striker, the Policy Committee of the union wrote to the operators to ask for coöperation to prevent any further attacks and battles, but received no reply. On October 17 mine guards drove in the "Death Special" to the Forbes tent colony and opened machine-gun fire; one striker was killed and a boy was shot nine times in the leg. A few days afterwards mine guards fired upon strikers in the streets of Walsenburg and killed three. The U. S. Commission concluded that "a deliberate attempt was made at this time to terrorize the strikers in order to prevent further desertions and to drive the men already on strike back to work." [33]

While these skirmishes took place, Governor Ammons continued his endeavors to effect some agreement and put an end to the serious situation; for not only did 10,000 to 15,000 strikers, wives, and children face a winter in the tent colonies, but also the entire state was in danger of a coal shortage. He met with the Policy Committee and President White of the United Mine Workers on October 26, and informed them that the operators were calling for the militia. Upon his request for assistance in effecting an "amicable settlement," the union officials declared themselves willing to waive the questions of union recognition and wage increase, provided that the operators granted them a conference. But Governor Ammons' report of this willingness brought from the operators only the reply that they would make no concession whatsoever. On the following day Ammons summoned to his office Welborn, Osgood, and Brown, as representing the operators, and persuaded them to draw up a statement that they would observe all the laws. Ammons then asked the union officials to accept this statement as a basis for settlement, but they rejected it as merely a vague promise that had been made before and broken.

In the meantime, Adjutant General John Chase of the Colorado National Guard had sent Lieutenant K. E. Linderfelt to Ludlow to determine whether the state troops were needed. Although Linderfelt had come as the impartial representative of General Chase to conduct an investigation, upon his arrival at Ludlow he accepted a commission as deputy sheriff and took command of a force of mine guards which escorted strike-breakers to and from the mines. A fight broke out at Ludlow between Linderfelt's force and strikers, in which one deputy was killed, and Linderfelt was forced to retreat to Berwind Canyon, where the guerrilla warfare continued. On October 28, after all negotiations had fallen through, Governor Ammons ordered General Chase and the militia to the strike district.

The instructions given by Ammons to General Chase were that the state troops were to protect the mining properties and any men who wished to return to work, but were not to assist in the installation of imported strike-breakers. Accordingly, on October 29, Lawson of the Policy Committee spoke to the strikers in the Ludlow colony and informed them that the militia were to be impartial and that both strikers and mine guards were to be disarmed. In spite of their distrust of the state troops, particularly in view of the conduct of Lieutenant Linderfelt, the strikers agreed to welcome the militia and to surrender their arms peaceably, though many of them hid their weapons instead. Even after the state troops arrived, there were a few clashes between guards and strikers, but, on the whole, the strike zone grew quiet. However, the operators were displeased with Ammons' instructions forbidding the use of the state troops to escort strike-breakers, and Ammons found himself subjected to strong coercion from various business and industrial interests in the state to reverse these instructions. In a letter to Rockefeller, November 18, 1913, Bowers reported that pressure was being exerted upon "our little cowboy Governor" by bankers, the Chamber of Commerce, the Real Estate Exchange of Denver, and the editors of the 14 largest newspapers in the state. "There probably has never been such pressure brought to bear upon any governor of this state by the strongest men in it as has been brought to bear upon Gov. Ammons." [34] If the operators could only get the protection of the militia, they could import strike-breakers sufficient to supply labor for the idle mines and the strike could be quashed.

The U. S. Commission felt that Ammons was wise in his original instructions:

If employers and strikebreaking agencies are to be permitted to operate in this fashion without let or hindrance, it means that entire communities of home-making and home-loving citizens can be displaced almost over night by an army of homeless vagabonds, drawn from the scum of the labor markets of widely scattered cities. This practice makes wanderers of hard-working and home-loving men whose only offense is that they have taken part in a strike. It fills strikers with hatred and leads inevitably to violence, and finally it has a disastrous effect on the community and the State by working a deterioration in the quality of the citizenship. [35]

Nevertheless, Governor Ammons allowed himself to be persuaded to reverse his command, not, however, before another attempt to effect a settlement had failed. In November, at Ammons' request, President Wilson sent Secretary Wilson of the Department of Labor to Denver to arrange conferences. Thereupon the operators agreed to confer with three striking miners, not union officials, in the presence of Secretary Wilson, with the understanding that the question of union recognition would not be raised. Agreement was reached on all differences, with the exception of the wage increase and the manner of settling future disputes. In accordance with this partial agreement, Ammons drew up a letter on November 27 calling for a settlement on the promise that the operators would obey the laws and would take back all strikers, unless their places had been filled or they had been guilty of violence. Since this proposed settlement failed to provide for any wage increase, any contract, or any machinery for the adjustment of disputes, the strikers rejected it unanimously at a mass meeting.

A second letter was drawn up by Secretary Wilson to include the adjustment of future disputes by a conciliation board composed of representatives of both sides, but was rejected by the operators. Concerning this plan, Bowers wrote to Rockefeller on November 28:

I can see no particular objection to the formation of an arbitration board as suggested by Secretary Wilson, providing the three miners are nonunion men who have remained in the employ of the coal operators during this strike, but to this I am sure that neither Secretary Wilson nor the labor leaders would consent. . . .[36]

And on December 4, after the negotiations had fallen through, Welborn wrote to J. H. McClement, a member of the Board of Directors:

We reached no direct understanding; in fact, we wanted none, as we were almost sure that had an understanding between the miners and ourselves been reached it would have received the stamp of approval of the officers of the organization and in that way been twisted into an arrangement between us and the organization.[37]

Notwithstanding their own unwillingness to come to any agreement, the operators pointed to the rejection of Ammons' letter of November 27 by the miners as the cause for the final rupture of negotiations.

It was not only the pressure exerted by the operators and the failure of the conference under the aegis of Secretary Wilson that caused Governor Ammons to rescind his instructions forbidding the troops to escort strike-breakers. Attorney-General Farrar of Colorado, on his own initiative, advised Ammons to abandon the original orders on the grounds that they were not justified by law, and, moreover, that they interfered with the operation of the mines and contributed to the coal shortage. Under this combined coercion, Ammons rescinded his original instructions on November 28 and gave General Chase absolute command of the strike district. General Chase instantly issued a general order which suspended civil law. Arrests became more numerous, and strikers were held without charge and kept in jail incommunicado. Virtual martial law existed. What was more, General Chase had already shown his bias during a strike nine years before in the metalliferous mines, when he had thrown strikers into "bull pens" and had refused to release them despite a habeas corpus writ from the District Court. In the strike territory the militia was quartered by the coal companies and supplied by company stores. Welborn testified before the U. S. Commission concerning the economic dependence of the state troops: the Colorado Fuel & Iron Company itself advanced to militiamen between $75,000 and $80,000 on certificates of indebtedness collectible from the state.[38] As the days passed and many militiamen who had business or salaried positions to attend to asked to be released from duty, company guards began to appear in the uniform of the National Guard. This steady infiltration of the state troops by the mine guards led the

Colorado State Federation of Labor, in a three-day convention that opened on December 16, to accuse the militia of serious abuses and to demand correction by Governor Ammons. In response to a suggestion by Ammons, the convention appointed a committee of five—headed by James H. Brewster, who for 14 years had been professor of law at the University of Michigan—to investigate the conduct of the militia and to make a report.

Armed with the official sanction of Governor Ammons, the committee began its inquiries on December 23 and continued them for three weeks; it examined 163 witnesses, one-third of whom had no connections with the union. It found that the militia coöperated with the company guards in every way. "The militia have tried to persuade strikers to go back to work, in some instances threatening and abusing them at the same time; a major offers to release an arrested union man if he will work in the mine; mine guards have given orders to militiamen as to the arrest and release of strikers. . . ." [39] Strike-breakers were not only escorted to the mines, but were then kept there by force; many who afterwards escaped and joined the strikers maintained that they had been imported from other states with no knowledge of the existence of a strike. The committee further reported:

The pretense that the leaders of the militia have been impartial is absurd. A villainous mine guard may walk the streets, with his hand ready on his half-concealed gun in his coat pocket, and assault a union boy at noonday—as one guard did on Sunday, January 4th, at Walsenburg, while this committee was there—without interference from the militia, whereas a union man will be arrested and compelled by militiamen to work on a coal company ditch two days for being drunk, when, as a fact, drunkenness among the militia is more common than it is among the strikers. . . ." [40]

Constitutional guarantees were arbitrarily nullified. The militia arrested strikers and held them for periods of five to 53 days without placing charges against them. Homes were broken into and searched. Furthermore, the committee charged the militia with deliberate and unjustified brutality. Strikers were attacked and provoked to fight; Lieutenant Linderfelt assaulted Louis Tikas, a leader of the strikers, and arrested him without cause. On another occasion Linderfelt was reported as having abused a young man and declared: "I am Jesus Christ, and my men on horses are Jesus Christs, and we must be obeyed." [41] Women and young girls frequently suffered insult and abuse from the militiamen:

Unprotected women have been roused from sleep by militiamen attempting to enter their homes at night. Young girls have been grossly insulted by militiamen on the public street, and their protesting father laughed at. . . . Restaurant waitresses are so insulted by militiamen that they will not wait upon them.[42]

Even robberies and holdups by the militiamen were reported.

After it had gathered its evidence, the committee reported to Governor Ammons and made the following recommendations: (1) that General Chase be asked to resign; (2) that Major Boughton, Major Townsend, and Lieutenant K. E. Linderfelt be discharged at once from the National Guard; (3) that all company mine guards and private detectives be discharged from the militia; (4) that the militia prohibit the importation of workmen ignorant of the existence of the strike in violation of a state law against such deception; and (5) that election of company officers by members of the company be discontinued. When Ammons paid no heed to this report, the Colorado Federation of Labor began to circulate petitions for a recall election.

Ammons charged the committee with unfairness in its investigation of the militia; yet the U. S. Commission judged the report an accurate one and discovered much testimony in corroboration. Captain Van Cise of the National Guard, for example, testified that while Company K, 1st Infantry, which was stationed at Ludlow, had been made up at first almost wholly of college graduates, its composition deteriorated so that on December 12, six weeks after it entered the field, five of its members were convicted of burglary. When these men were examined, only two were found to be Colorado men. Nevertheless, three of the five were merely fined and then returned to duty.[43] Testimony like this bore out two serious charges made by the committee—that militiamen were guilty of burglary, and that many of them were not citizens of Colorado. As the tent colonies, notwithstanding the incitement and violence of the mine guards and militia, held together firmly, violations of the constitutional guarantees grew more frequent, more open. When Mother Jones, then more than 80 years old, attempted to enter Trinidad on January 4, she was immediately deported to Denver by the militia. Two further attempts by her to enter Trinidad resulted in her being held incommunicado, once for nine weeks at San Rafael Hospital, again for 26 days in an "insanitary and rat-infested cell." Congressman Keating of Colorado introduced a resolution in the House of Representatives for an investigation because "the constitutional rights of citizens have been trampled upon," and on January 27 the resolution was adopted.

4. The massacre at Ludlow

During February and March, although the enmity between strikers and militiamen remained bitter, the strike area grew comparatively quiet. Governor Ammons, therefore, recalled the militia, with the exception of Company B, which was left near Ludlow, the largest of the tent colonies, housing 900 to 1,200 men, women, and children. Company B, under the command of Major Hamrock and Lieutenant Linderfelt, was composed of 35 men, mainly mine guards. In addition, during the week preceding April 20, 1914, a troop of cavalry, Troop A, was organized by officers of the National Guard with the assistance of the mine operators, and was put in charge of Captain Edwin Carson. Troop A consisted of 100 men, "not more than thirty" of them mine guards, as Captain Carson admitted to an investigator for the U. S. Commission, while the rest were "pit bosses, mine superintendents, mine clerks and the like." [44] These men continued in the employ and pay of the operators, but held themselves ready for duty at call. Bowers wrote to Rockefeller of Troop A on April 18:

Another favorable feature is the organization of a military company of 100 volunteers at Trinidad the present week. They are to be armed by the State and drilled by military officials. Another squad is being organized at Walsenburg. These independent militiamen will be subject to orders of the sheriff of the county. As these volunteers will draw no pay from the State, this movement has the support of the governor and other men in authority.[45]

The U. S. Commission commented: "Thus, by April 20th the Colorado National Guard no longer offered even a pretense of fairness or impartiality, and its units in the field had degenerated into a force of professional gunmen and adventurers who were economically dependent on and subservient to the will of the coal operators." [46] The combined force of Company B and Troop A was centered on Ludlow, which was strategically situated near the station of the Colorado Southern Railroad, the point of arrival for strikebreakers for several important mines.

Because of widespread rumors that Ludlow was to be

SUCCESS. A cartoon by O. E. Cesare. (*Harper's Weekly*, May 23, 1914)

wiped out, the colonists grew apprehensive of the presence of Linderfelt and Company B. When, therefore, on Monday morning, April 20, the militiamen occupied a hill overlooking the tents, mounted a machine gun, and exploded two dynamite bombs, the strikers, remembering what had happened to the Forbes tent colony and determined to resist a similar attack, seized their rifles and took up a position in the arroyos nearby. The militiamen later maintained that the explosion of the two bombs had been merely a signal for Troop A. Whatever may have been the actual reason for the occupation of the hill, and whoever may have been guilty of firing the first shot, a rain of rifle and machine-gun fire fell on Ludlow. Hundreds of women and children ran from the tents to seek shelter in the hills and at ranch houses. However, scores, failing to escape, hid in pits and cellars underneath the tents to protect themselves from the bullets. The gunfire continued for 12 hours and resulted in the deaths of one boy and three men, one of them a militiaman.

On orders from their officers, the militiamen poured coal oil on the tents and set them afire, while the women and children who had huddled in their pits ran in terror from their shelters. "During the firing of the tents, the militiamen became an uncontrolled mob and looted the tents of everything that appealed to their fancy or cupidity." [47] In one pit 11 children and two women of the colony were discovered suffocated or burned to death after the tents had been set on fire. The militia took three strikers prisoner and shot them while they were unarmed and under guard. One of the three was Louis Tikas, a leader of the colony and "a man of high intelligence who had done his utmost that morning to maintain peace and prevent the attack and who had remained in or near the tent colony throughout the day to look after the women and children." [48] Tikas, wholly defenseless, was brought before Linderfelt, who broke a rifle stock over his head; the prostrate man was then shot and killed by militiamen. All that night men, women, and children wandered through the hills, in momentary danger of being shot by the militia.

As the story of the Ludlow massacre spread, strikers in the surrounding districts armed themselves and marched to avenge the slaughter. E. L. Doyle, secretary-treasurer of District no. 15 of the United Mine Workers, dispatched a telegram to President Wilson, Colorado's Senators and Representatives, and the House Committee on Mines and Mining at Washington:

Striking miners and families shot and burned to death at Ludlow, Col. Mine guards, with machine guns, riddled tents of striking miners and set fire to tent colony. Four men, three women, and seven[?] children murdered. State not only fails to protest [protect?], but uses uniforms and ammunition of the commonwealth to destroy the lives of the workers and their families. We shall be compelled to call on volunteers in the name of humanity to defend these helpless persons unless something is done. Tent colony burned to the ground.[49]

By Wednesday, April 22, the strikers were in possession of the field between Ludlow and Trinidad, an area 18 miles by four or five. It was open warfare against the civil authorities, the militia, the mine guards, and the operators. The armed strikers attacked mine after mine—Southwestern, Hastings, Delagua, Empire, Green Canyon, Royal, Broadhead—and set fire to the buildings. On Thursday General Chase left Denver with 362 militiamen, and, reinforced the next day to a total of 650, he occupied the territory from Walsenburg to Ludlow, but did not advance farther south.

Meanwhile, union officials at Trinidad organized companies of strikers and furnished them with arms and ammunition. Throughout the state, workingmen, incensed by the attack upon Ludlow, volunteered to arm themselves and join the strikers against the enemy forces. Horace N. Hawkins, attorney for the United Mine Workers, received offers from various unions to raise 10,000 volunteers. For 10 days the rebellion continued, with from 700 to 1,000 armed strikers engaged. The fighting spread to the northern coal fields in the Louisville district, some 250 miles north of Trinidad. A truce arranged by Hawkins and General Chase was violated; the miners refused to trust themselves again to the authority of the state. Finally, Governor Ammons wired President Wilson for federal troops, and on April 30 six troops of cavalry arrived and the fighting ended. At least 30 persons had been killed, aside from the 21 who died in the Ludlow attack.

The news of the annihilation of the Ludlow tent colony, the death of the women and children, the murder of Tikas, and the subsequent civil warfare horrified the nation. By cartoon and editorial the press denounced the unjustifiable attack and slaughter. A good deal of both liberal and conservative opinion laid the blame on the coal operators and the state authorities; the *Survey*, for instance, declared:

The employers who have disobeyed the laws, the state which has not enforced them; the employers who hired mine guards to assault and intimidate, the state which took those mine guards in company pay into its militia, made some of them officers and then turned them on the strikers; the employers who had machine guns shipped in from West Virginia, the state which took those machine guns and turned them on the tented camps where dwelt the families of the strikers—what answer have they to the question of responsibility for war? [50]

Some conservative opinion, on the other hand, blamed the state officials for stupidly playing into the hands of union advocates and giving new fuel to the demands of labor; thus the *New York Times*, in an editorial, "The Ludlow Camp Horror," wrote:

Hitherto the labor interests have not been ashamed nor afraid to introduce laws preventing railways from transporting "strike-breakers." They were solicitous, often bold in their demands. Solicitude and boldness will now change to defiance and insistence. Pointing to Ludlow, they will justify the legalizing of any act of usurpation. Their doctrine is to deny the right of any man to work for whom he pleases, and they have sought to undermine the law that protects every citizen in rights equal for all. They are now nerved to take this citadel by storm. The right to work becomes in their eyes the right to prevent others from working. In defense of that right they have used bombs, firearms, even artillery, and against sleeping enemies of any sex or age. But when a sovereign State employs such horrible means, what may not be expected from the anarchy that ensues.[51]

Of course, Rockefeller, as the actual owner of the most powerful of the coal companies in Colorado, and as the supporter of their anti-union policies, became the principal target of caricature, editorial accusation, and mass indignation. Upton Sinclair and four women picketed the office of Rockefeller in New York, and when they were arrested, others took their place in the line of "mourners." Efforts of the police to break up the picketing resulted in the formation of a Free Silence League. Demonstrations were held before Pocantico Hills, Rockefeller's home at Tarrytown. To the suppression of the right of public assembly by the Tarrytown authorities, the I.W.W. responded with a free-speech fight, during which more than a score were arrested. Sinclair called upon the Socialist Party to join in a nation-wide picket movement against all the Rockefeller properties, but Morris Hillquit declined in the name of the Party. Mass meetings were addressed by Judge Lindsey and others.

Aroused by the widespread protest and accusation, Rockefeller issued a statement declaring that the Colorado Fuel & Iron Company had already granted of its own will the concessions demanded by the strikers and that the obstinacy of the strikers had produced the violence, only to have the press point out that the concessions granted by the company had for years been required by the laws of Colorado. In consternation Starr J. Murphy, personal attorney to Rockefeller, wrote to Bowers on May 7:

In the statement which Mr. John D. Rockefeller, jr., gave out to the press, he said that the eight-hour day, semi-monthly pay, right to use checkweighmen, freedom to deal at the company stores or not, and the increase of wages, were all made by the company voluntarily. The statement is now made by some of his critics that all these points, except the increase in wages, were covered by law, and that the company did not make the concessions until statutes were passed requiring them. He asks me on his behalf to find out what are the facts in this connection, and would be obliged if you could inform us when the statutes went into effect, and when the various matters above mentioned were granted to our workmen, and what, if any, are the relations between the granting of them and the statutes.[52]

To counteract the unfavorable publicity generated by the Ludlow massacre, Rockefeller instituted a "union educational campaign" to persuade the nation that not the mine guards and militia, but the "well-paid agitators" sent out by the union were responsible for the lawlessness and bloodshed. For this purpose, Ivy L. Lee, publicity agent for the Pennsylvania Railroad, was borrowed by Rockefeller, and by June 1 the "education" of the people was well under way.

From Lee's offices in Philadelphia the country was deluged with pamphlets, articles, and bulletins whose authorship was kept secret. Most effective was a series of bulletins entitled *Facts concerning the Struggle in Colorado for Industrial Freedom*, sent from June to September at intervals of four to seven days to a carefully prepared mailing list of public officials, editors, ministers, teachers, and prominent professional and business men. Misrepresentations were frequent. Bulletin no. 14, for example, deliberately falsified the salaries of union officials: Frank J. Hayes was reported as receiving $4,052.92 for nine weeks' salary, in addition to $1,667.20 for nine weeks' expenses, or a total of $5,720.12. "Frank J. Hayes was thus paid over $90 a day, or at the rate of over $32,000 a year." Actually Hayes, according to the report of Secretary-Treasurer Green of the United Mine Workers for November 30, 1913, had received for the preceding *year*, not nine weeks, a salary of $2,395.72 and $1,667.20 for expenses. Not content with falsifying the time for which the money was paid, Bulletin no. 14 combined salary and expenses to get $4,052.92 as salary, and then added $1,667.20 a second time as expenses. Figures of similar reliability were given for other union officials.[53] Although J. A. Fitch of the *Survey* called attention to the falsification, no correction was made until later, December, 1914, after a hearing before the U. S. Commission at Denver.

While Ivy Lee was circulating his attacks on trade-unionism and the strikers, the authorities in southern Colorado began legal prosecution of those who had engaged in warfare against the militia. At Trinidad in August, 1914, a grand jury, instead of being drawn, as usual, from a panel supplied by the county commissioners, was appointed by Sheriff

J. S. Grisham of Las Animas County. Among the jurors thus selected were:

J. S. Caldwell, proprietor of a shoe store. Formerly with the Colorado Supply Company, the company store department of the Colorado Fuel and Iron Company.

James Roberts, public trustee. Secretary to F. R. Wood, president of Temple Fuel Company.

Charles Rapp, assistant cashier Trinidad National Bank, of which W. J. Murray, general manager of the Victor-American Fuel Company is stockholder and director. Formerly with Colorado Supply Company.

Henry C. Cossam, rancher. Deputy sheriff since April 25, 1914. Participated in one of the so-called battles.

J. H. Wilson, real estate and insurance agent. Deputy sheriff since September 30, 1909. In charge of the deputies who attacked the Forbes tent colony October 17, 1913.

William C. Riggs, rancher, whose son, W. E. Riggs, has been a deputy sheriff since January 20, 1911, and was in some of the battles in the fall of 1913.[54]

Yet Attorney-General Farrar testified before the U. S. Commission concerning this jury: "I desire to say here that, regardless of the reports which have been made, I have never seen a more fair-minded body of men gathered together under conditions such as prevailed there than were the 12 men who constituted that grand jury. And the charges which have been made that they were absolutely one-sided and partisan were absolutely without foundation whatever."[55]

The attorneys for the United Mine Workers refused to appear before a jury of such composition. Nevertheless, under Farrar's direction the grand jury returned 163 indictments, most of them involving charges of murder, against 124 strikers and union officials, including the leaders of the United Mine Workers in Colorado. No indictments were found against any deputy sheriffs. At the same time, the militia officers who took part in the Ludlow massacre were brought before court martial of their fellow officers and were all acquitted, with the exception of Lieutenant Linderfelt, who, although found guilty of the brutal beating of Tikas with a rifle stock, perhaps even of murder, was punished by a "trifling demotion in rank." In this way, as Major E. J. Boughton, judge-advocate of the Colorado National Guard, admitted to J. A. Fitch, Linderfelt and the other officers were saved from prosecution in the civil courts.[56]

5. Birth of the company union

President Wilson was particularly disturbed by the civil strife in southern Colorado, inasmuch as the United States was then engaged in war with Mexico and was further suffering economic disorder because of the war that had broken out in Europe. When as a result, therefore, of the Ludlow attack public opinion was sufficiently aroused to demand governmental interference, President Wilson requested Secretary of Labor Wilson to attempt again to make some settlement. A commission of two—Hywell Davies of Kentucky, a coal operator, and W. R. Fairley of Alabama, a former official of the United Mine Workers—was appointed by Secretary Wilson to investigate the stubborn struggle and formulate some plan for mediation. In August the commission completed its report, which was used by President Wilson as the basis for a plan of settlement; and on September 7, almost one year after the outbreak of the strike, he proposed publicly that both operators and strikers accept it.

The plan called for a three-year truce, in which period there were to be (1) enforcement of the Colorado mining and labor laws; (2) reëmployment of all strikers not guilty of violence; (3) prohibition of any intimidation of either

union or non-union men; (4) posting of the current wages
and regulations at each mine; and (5) proscription of contractual relations. Moreover, during the truce, grievances,
if they could not be adjusted by local grievance committees,
were to be submitted to a commission of three—made up of
a representative from each side and one impartial member—
to be chosen by President Wilson; and while the arbitration
commission deliberated, there were to be no suspension of
work and no picketing by the miners, with the result that, in
practice, strikes were to be outlawed for the three-year
period. Many labor sympathizers protested that in the inter-
dictment of contractual relations and strikes lay the danger
of "a gradual undermining of the power of the union, a
nibbling of the advantages slowly gained, a reversion eventually to the individual bargain (which is no bargain at all),
and a sacrifice of industrial liberty and industrial representation to the desire for an immediate peace." [57] Nevertheless,
the Policy Committee accepted the plan without reservation
on September 15, and it was ratified by a special convention
of strikers at Trinidad.

With the pressure of public sentiment behind President
Wilson's plan, the operators realized that outright rejection
might be dangerous. Starr J. Murphy, in behalf of Rockefeller, wrote on September 8 to warn President Welborn of
the necessity for a carefully considered reply:

*The fact that the President of the United States has sug-
gested a plan of settlement and has given it out to the public produces a delicate situation which we have no doubt you
gentlemen in the West will handle in the same careful and
diplomatic way in which you have handled the whole situation thus far, avoiding on the one hand any entanglement
with the labor union, and, on the other, an attitude which
would arouse a hostile public opinion. . . .*[58]

With the assistance and advice of Ivy Lee, who made a special trip to Denver for the purpose, President Welborn wrote a letter of rejection which left the impression that a better plan was being formulated by the Colorado Fuel & Iron Company:

We are now developing an even more comprehensive plan, embodying the results of our practical experience, which will, we feel confident, result in a closer understanding between ourselves and our men. This plan contemplates not only provision for the redress of grievances, but for a continuous effort to promote the welfare and the good will of our employees.[59]

Forty-eight other coal companies in Colorado, representing 82 per cent of the coal mined aside from that mined by the Colorado Fuel & Iron Company, likewise rejected President Wilson's proposal.

Many reasons were given by the operators for their uncompromising stand. They felt, for one thing, that a permanent conciliation commission, as set forth in the President's plan, would interfere with their right to manage their business as they saw fit. For another, the setting up of local grievance committees would give the United Mine Workers an opportunity to foment trouble constantly. Again, while the companies could be penalized effectively by the commission, there was no guarantee that irresponsible workmen could be similarly penalized. But, above all, the operators objected to the provision for the reëmployment of all strikers not guilty of violence: it would be necessary to discharge workers and strike-breakers who had remained loyal throughout the troubles, in order to make room for men who had engaged in active hostilities against their employers. "It would be manifestly unfair to our workmen to ask any of them to give up their places in order that work might be furnished to strikers, and it would seem quite as unfair to the operators that they should be required to make concessions to those who have incited and directed the lawlessness, for the purpose of inducing them to make a promise of keeping the peace." [60]

In hinting at a "more comprehensive plan" in his letter of rejection, President Welborn referred to a project undertaken by Rockefeller earlier in the summer. Alarmed by the aftermath of the Ludlow massacre, Rockefeller engaged W. L. Mackenzie King, formerly Minister of Labor for Canada, to conduct through the Rockefeller Foundation an inquiry into the means of developing closer personal contact and more friendly coöperation between capital and labor; in the opinion of the U. S. Commission, however, Mackenzie King was to assist in devising "specious substitutes for trade unions that will deceive, mollify and soothe public opinion while bulwarking the employers' arbitrary control." [61] Mackenzie King suggested tentatively the establishment of boards "in a spirit of fair play" with both employer and employees represented; but Bowers, in a letter on August 16, declared: "To form such a board now would discount every utterance we have made and insisted upon, that there were no differences whatever and the strike was not forced because of any grievances or differences." [62] And Welborn, in a letter to Rockefeller on August 20, objected that the formation of such boards would be a public admission that "a weakness, the existence of which we had previously denied, was being corrected." [63]

However, after President Wilson made his settlement proposal, Welborn perceived that a substitute plan might be useful, and on September 19 he wrote to Starr J. Murphy:

I appreciate your very thoughtful letter of the 16th instant, with suggestions for consideration in the event of its being necessary to propose some plan to take the place of that presented to us by the President.[64]

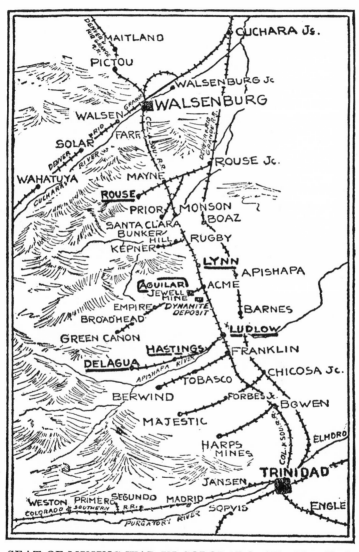

SEAT OF MINING WAR IN COLORADO. (The *New York Times*, April 25, 1914)

When Murphy next suggested the formation of committees representing both miners and operators "charged with the duty of enforcing the statutes of the State and also the regulations of the company looking to the safety and comfort of the miners and the protection of the company's property," Welborn was more amenable.[65] And although he still objected to granting at that time "the appointment of a committee, as that would come too near one of the demands of the miners' organization, which has been frequently made and is expressed through their so-called truce proposal presented by the President," he was willing to have the manager of each mine select a committee of miners who would "in every sense of the word be safe," in order to foster regularity in work, efficiency, observance of regulations, watchfulness against accidents, loyalty to the company's interests, and cleanliness in the homes.[66] Here were the embryonic foreshadowings of employee representation, or the company union.

While these various schemes were being considered privately by the operators, the strike was being steadily crushed. Even though President Wilson had prohibited the importation of strike-breakers from other states during the occupation of the coal fields by the federal troops, the operators were gradually able to obtain sufficient labor within the state which could enter the mines under the protection of the military. The prosecution of strikers and union officials continued relentlessly in the courts, and was assured of continuance by the election in the fall of 1914 of a "law and order" ticket headed by Governor Carlson and also by the reëlection of Attorney-General Farrar. Bowers testified later before the U. S. Commission that the Colorado Fuel & Iron Company sent out 150 men on election day to work for prohibition and the "law and order" ticket:

*Chairman Walsh. Didn't you use the prohibition senti-
ment that was strong in the State to get support for what
you called the law and order platform that was for the Colorado Fuel & Iron Co. and the others to aid in the ruthless
prosecution of the strikers and the union officers and a relentless policy of suppressing those men?*

Mr. Bowers. It was all interlocked together.[67]

On November 19 the Policy Committee of the strikers called
on President Wilson at Washington to learn what action he
would take, since the operators had not accepted his peace
plan. Wilson, in reply, appointed the conciliation commission of three in accordance with his plan, but it was not
recognized by the operators. The Policy Committee then
understood that it was defeated and called a convention
of the United Mine Workers at Denver, which voted on
December 10, after 15 months of struggle, to terminate the
strike.

Only after the strike was unquestionably defeated did the
officials of the Colorado Fuel & Iron Company set about to
elaborate the plan of friendly coöperation which they had
so often hinted at. On December 17 President Welborn announced publicly that he had assigned to David Griffiths the
duty of promoting the general welfare of the employees and
fostering better relations between them and the higher officers of the company. The appointment of Griffiths as inter-
mediary was followed shortly by an invitation to the employees to elect representatives for a joint meeting with the
officers of the company to be held at Denver on January 19.
At this conference was born an early form of the Rockefeller
Industrial Representation Plan, which was to serve as the
model for workers' councils, shop committees, employee
representation plans, and other variations of the company
union during and after the World War. As a result, Rocke-

feller was able to say before the U. S. Commission on January 25:

Thus, it will be seen that the Company has already taken steps to initiate a plan of representation of its employes. It is my hope and belief that from this will develop some permanent machinery which will insure to the employes of the Company, through representatives of their own selection, quick and easy access to the officers, with reference to any grievances, real or assumed, or with reference to wages or other conditions of employment.[68]

During the spring and summer of 1915 W. L. Mackenzie King visited Colorado and constructed the machinery for the plan. Rockefeller himself came to Colorado for the inauguration of the Industrial Representation Plan at a joint meeting of miners' representatives and company officials held at Pueblo on October 2, 1915. The plan was submitted to a general vote of the miners; and it was passed by 2,404 against 442, although only 2,846 voted out of a total of 4,411.[69] The plan promulgated the right of the miner to appeal grievances from local officials and committees to Joint Committees on Industrial Coöperation and Conciliation composed of representatives of the company and of the employees. The originators of the plan wished to make one large family of the company and the miners, in which coöperation was to supplant the essential antagonism between capital and labor intentionally fostered, so they maintained, by the union. The plan "brings men and managers together, it facilitates the study of their common problems, and it should promote an understanding of their mutual interests." [70] It was to be the missing link between capital and labor.

From the beginning the United Mine Workers was hostile to the Industrial Representation Plan. It felt that only a powerful and widespread organization of workers in an industry can meet successfully the powerful combinations of capital. It is impossible, the union said, for workers to be justly represented by a fellow worker who depends on the company for his right to labor and earn a living. Besides, the plan was financed by the company and hence was controlled by the company. Vice-President Hayes called the plan "pure paternalism" and "benevolent feudalism." [71] The U. S. Commission condemned the plan, while it was being drafted, even more harshly, declaring that it "embodies none of the principles of effectual collective bargaining and instead is a hypocritical pretense of granting what is in reality withheld," and that it was "conceived and carried out, not for the purpose of aiding the Company's employees in Colorado, but for the purpose of ameliorating or removing the unfavorable criticism of Mr. Rockefeller which had arisen throughout the country following his rejection of President Wilson's plan of settlement. . . ." [72] And again: "The effectiveness of such a plan lies wholly in its tendency to deceive the public and lull criticism, while permitting the Company to maintain its absolute power." [73]

Several years later, from 1919 to 1921, Ben M. Selekman and Mary Van Kleeck conducted for the Russell Sage Foundation an investigation into the workings of the Industrial Representation Plan of the Colorado Fuel & Iron Company. They found that although there had been many beneficial results—improvement in housing conditions and community life, absence of compulsory buying at the company stores, the end of interference by the company in county and state politics, better schooling—there were still many serious shortcomings. The workers, having had no voice in the actual drafting of the plan, were indifferent to it and still regarded the United Mine Workers as their sole protection; wages, for example, followed those in the union fields, except once when they were lower. Workers were afraid to appeal grievances, and felt that there was for them no true representation, since their representatives were fellow workers entirely dependent upon the benevolence and good will of the company. "It did indeed seem to us that many of the miners' representatives were timid, untrained, and ill-prepared to present and argue the grievances of the miners, and that their experience as representatives was not developing initiative or leadership in them." [74] Yet this plan, a form of the company union, was the only fruit won by the coal miners of southern Colorado after their long and bloody struggle.

VIII. STEEL, 1919

1. Labor policy in the steel industry

After the disastrous defeat suffered in the Homestead lockout of 1892, the Amalgamated Association of Iron, Steel and Tin Workers found its influence in the steel industry greatly reduced. Even this restricted influence was further cut when approximately half the steel industry pooled its financial resources in 1901 to form the United States Steel Corporation, with its avowed hostility toward labor organizations. Unions did not make for "tractable" labor. At a meeting on June 17, 1901, the Executive Committee of the Steel Corporation laid down its anti-union policy in the following resolution:

That we are unalterably opposed to any extension of union labor, and advise subsidiary companies to take firm position when these questions come up and say they are not going to recognize it, that is, any extension of unions in mills where they do not now exist; that great care should be used to prevent trouble, and that they promptly report and confer with this corporation.[1]

Twice, in 1901 and 1909, the Amalgamated Association made vain efforts to come to some agreement with the Steel Corporation and both times carried on losing strikes. The struggle in 1909 resulted in the complete elimination of the Amalgamated Association; thereafter the Steel Corporation and most of the independent companies refused to deal with any union.

For the decade following 1909, since its employees had no
means of representation, the Steel Corporation arbitrarily
determined hours, wages, and working conditions. In 1919,
whereas in unionized industries the coal miners worked 52
or 53 hours per week, the railroad men 48, and the building trades 44, half the employees in the iron and steel plants
worked the 12-hour day, or the 72-hour week, and fewer than
one-fourth worked under 60 hours per week.[2] Chairman El-
bert H. Gary of the Steel Corporation admitted before the
Senate Committee on Education and Labor, when it was investigating the steel strike of 1919, that 69,000 out of the
191,000 employees in the Corporation's manufacturing
plants, or 36 per cent, were subject to the 12-hour day. This
number did not, however, include the men who worked 10 or
11 hours on the day shift, but 13 or 14 hours on the night
shift on alternate weeks. Superintendent Oursler of the
Homestead works testified that 21.2 per cent of his workmen
were on the eight-hour day, 25.9 per cent on the 10, 16.4 per
cent on the 11, and 36 per cent on the 12. Since the 16.4 per
cent on the 11-hour day worked 13 hours on alternate weeks,
there were actually 52.4 per cent at Homestead on the 12-
hour day. The president of the Carnegie Steel Company estimated in November, 1919, before the Commission of Inquiry
of the Interchurch World Movement that 60 per cent of his
55,000 employees worked the 12-hour day.[3] The 12-hour day
was accompanied often by a long turn of 18 to 24 hours every
second week; moreover, in such continuous departments as
the blast furnace and the open hearth the seven-day week, although its presence could not be accurately calculated, was
not unknown. The Senate Committee, like the Interchurch
Commission, found that the large majority of the men in the
steel mills worked 10 or 12 hours per day, and concluded
"That the laborers in the steel mills had a just complaint
relative to the long hours of service on the part of some of

them and the right to have that complaint heard by the company." [4]

Three-fourths of the 400,000 and more employees in the steel plants were thus affected by the long hours of labor. Most of these were the immigrant workmen from southern and eastern Europe who constituted the bulk of common and semi-skilled labor. The officials of the steel companies regarded the long hours as a useful lesson in hard work and close application, as good "experience" for a young man, especially a foreigner, before promotion. The workmen felt otherwise. They found tending the furnaces, hearths, ovens, and converters to be extremely exhausting work carried on under great heat, with the dangers increased through the fatigue of long hours. Gary, on the other hand, felt that the reports of hard labor in the steel mills were exaggerated, and declared before the Senate Committee on Education and Labor:

Nowadays none of these men, with very few exceptions, perform manual labor as I used to perform it, on the farm, neither in hours, nor in actual physical exertion. It is practically all done everywhere by machinery and the boy who opens the door I think touches a button and opens the door. And this work of adjusting the heavy iron ingots is done by the pulling of a lever. It is largely machinery, almost altogether machinery. That is not saying there is no work in that, because of course there is, and I would not belittle it, of course. It is hard work to work hard whatever one does, and to the extent one does work hard he, of course, is doing hard work. [5]

The officials maintained, furthermore, that the work on many of the 12-hour turns came in spells and that frequently workers had as much as three or four hours in the turn for rest or sleep.

Nevertheless, the Senate Committee concluded: "The policy of working men 10 and 12 hours per day in the steel mills is, it seems to the committee, an unwise and un-American policy. . . . These non-English-speaking aliens must be Americanized and must learn our language, so the question of a reasonable working day is involved in the question of Americanization. Men can not work 10 and 12 hours per day and attend classes at night school." [6] Indeed, the long hours left neither time nor energy for education, recreation, family or community life.

To public criticism of its 12-hour day, the steel industry replied that, because of the nature of the processes involved, it was necessary to keep most of the apparatus in steady and continuous operation. Actually, however, in only one department out of the 14, the blast furnace, was there a "metallurgical necessity" for uninterrupted operation day and night. Here, it is true, a reduction in hours would have required three shifts at eight hours instead of two at 12. The other departments employed the 10- and 12-hour day only because of the desire for additional output. That the 12-hour day was not a necessity was shown by its absence in English steel mills and in several independent American plants, such as the Pueblo plant of the Colorado Fuel & Iron Company, where the eight-hour shift was in force.

Besides the plea of necessity, the Steel Corporation offered two explanations for retaining the 12-hour day. First, there was a shortage of labor, and sufficient workmen could not be obtained for a third shift. Second, the workmen themselves preferred the longer day with the accompanying opportunity for increased earnings; in fact, the Corporation insisted that it would lose its men to independent steel companies if it instituted the eight-hour day, and that at times when it tried allowing one day of rest in seven the men sneaked off to another plant to work the seventh. Both of these excuses were impugned by the Senate Committee on Education and Labor: "It is the general consensus of opinion of the best economic writers and thinkers that the establishment of 8-hour-day systems does not diminish production. Nor do we think the claim made that an 8-hour day is impossible because the workmen can not be secured for three shifts is tenable." And again: "It is true some of the workers testified that they wanted to work longer in order to get the increased compensation, but most of them seemed anxious for an 8-hour day with a living wage." [7] The long hours were closely intertwined with the question of wages, for the common and low-skilled laborers could not have withstood a cut in wages to correspond with a cut in hours.

However, wages were not popularly regarded as a source of labor unrest in the steel industry; and the Senate Committee felt that the workmen were satisfied with the wages they received. The impression was widespread that steel workers were among the highest paid in the country. Reports of extravagant wages were current: in an editorial, "Speaking of the 'Poor' Steel Workers Who Get from $4 to $70 a Day," *Current Opinion* listed average daily wages as $28.16 for steel rollers, $21.12 for sheet heaters, $11.92 for roughers, and even discovered wages as high as $65 and $70 per day.[8] Aside from the fiction of $65 and $70 as daily wages, what *Current Opinion* and other commentators failed to point out was that the high wages listed were earned only by the most highly skilled, less than 1 per cent of all the employees. The wages of the bulk of steel labor were based not on a high rate per hour, but on an average rate for many hours. While the steady worker, skilled and semi-skilled, had the opportunity of earning good wages (it must be remembered that the cost of living was proportionately high in the period immediately following the World War), these wages were found to be merely average when reduced to a 44-hour basis.[9] As for common and low-skilled labor in steel, unless it endured the 12-hour day, it was unable to earn more than a subsistence wage.

The Commission of Inquiry of the Interchurch World Movement, after an extensive study of the relation between steel wages and the cost of living, pronounced inadequate the earnings of common and low-skilled labor. (The specific accuracy of these calculations has been questioned by Marshal Olds in his *Analysis of the Interchurch World Movement Report on the Steel Strike*.) It first set up budgets for families of five according to two standards of living: (1) the "minimum of subsistence level," which furnished simple animal well-being, and (2) the "minimum comfort level," which provided for comfortable clothing, insurance, and some recreation, in addition to animal existence. It then estimated the average earnings for the skilled, semi-skilled, and unskilled classes of steel labor, and compared them with the two budgets. The results are indicated in the following table:

	1918	1919
Average annual earnings of skilled labor	$2,373	$2,749
Budget for minimum of comfort	1,760	2,024
Average annual earnings of semi-skilled	1,683	1,952
Budget for minimum of subsistence	1,386	1,575
Average annual earnings of unskilled	1,265	1,466 [10]

Both the semi-skilled and the unskilled, who together constituted 72 per cent of the workers in the steel industry, fell below the level of minimum comfort; and the unskilled, who alone made up 38 per cent of the workers, failed to achieve even the level of minimum subsistence.[11] Some support for the conclusion of the Commission is found in the case of a Polish steel worker, with a family of eight children, who applied to the Home Service Division of the Pittsburgh Red Cross for

relief. The minimum budget set up by the Home Service
Division for this family was $180.75 per month; yet the
earnings of the family in normal times, with three members
employed, were only $143.[12] The Interchurch Commission
charged the Steel Corporation with underpaying the bulk
of its labor at a time when its profits, because of war-time
production, were enormous. Gary himself testified that the
net profits of the Corporation were $107,832,016 for 1915;
$303,449,476 for 1916; $253,608,200 for 1917; and $167,-
562,280 for 1918.[13] Whether the Interchurch Commission
was just or not in its conclusions concerning steel wages, the
dependence of the alleged high wages upon long hours was
undoubted.

When charges of long hours and inadequate wages were
brought against it, the Steel Corporation asked consideration of its record in welfare work, for which it had spent
more than $65,000,000 from 1912 to July, 1919. The
Senate Committee commended the Corporation on its welfare policy—on its stock subscription plan for employees,
its measures for accident prevention, its care for the injured,
its sanitary precautions, its recreational facilities, its housing. The Corporation was particularly proud of the 25,965
dwellings and boarding houses which it leased to employees
at low rentals. Most of these, however, had been erected for
the coal miners of the Steel Corporation, and fewer than
10,000 were available for steel labor, occupied for the most
part by the skilled workers. One hundred and eighty-one
thousand of the 191,000 steel workers in the Corporation,
therefore, received no benefit from the low-rental housing.[14]
The housing of these steel workers was extremely poor and
crowded, especially in the Pittsburgh district. Marian D.
Savage, who conducted an investigation into housing for the
Interchurch Commission, reported:

The first thing which strikes the attention of one who visits the homes of the strikers is the shocking overcrowding. The majority of [41] families which I have seen live in only two rooms, and only four of them have more than three rooms. As the families are composed of from four to eight people, this means that the air space necessary for hygienic living is wholly lacking, and the right kind of home life is made impossible. It means that frequently a bed must stand in the kitchen all the time, taking up space greatly needed for other things. . . . In many cases the apartments have no water in them and several families are forced to use a single pump in the court yard. In still a larger number of cases there are no toilet arrangements except dilapidated water closet sheds in the yard. In a few places there are open unsanitary drains in the court yard, around which the wooden houses are built. Many of the strikers live in alleys which are very dirty and cluttered with rubbish collected by the authorities at infrequent intervals. In one place in Homestead I found what appeared to be drainage water flowing down the middle of the alley. In a good many cases families live in rear houses which can only be reached by narrow dark passageways or ramshackle wooden staircases leading in from the street.[15]

The Steel Corporation was far ahead of most of the independent steel companies in provision for safety devices and safety committees. Other aspects of its welfare policy—such as stock participation, pensions, and bonuses—benefited principally the managerial and skilled forces, but failed to reach the great mass of semi-skilled and unskilled.

The welfare policy of the Corporation was part of the method for keeping the workers contented and unprotesting. Each phase of the welfare activity served to intensify the arbitrary control of the Corporation. Stock subscriptions were a premium for "loyal service." Pensions could be discontinued at any moment because of "misconduct." Employees could be evicted from company houses during a strike, or, if they owned the house, could be forced by means of the blacklist to move from the community. And recreational facilities, like gymnasiums, athletic fields, swimming pools, and libraries were of little use to men subjected to the 12-hour day.

As far back as 1910, J. A. Fitch, in his findings for the Pittsburgh Survey, wrote of the welfare activities of the steel companies:

These in no wise affect or limit the underlying labor policy in both Corporation and independent mills. That is a determination to control, in pursuance of which object the employers inflexibly exclude the men from any voice in the conditions of their employment. Consistent with this policy, repressive measures have been introduced designed to enable the companies to retain the advantages which they gained for themselves when they eliminated the unions. These measures are doubtless intended to preserve industrial efficiency, but they have resulted in a thorough-going and far-reaching censorship that curtails free speech and the free activity of citizens. The effect of these measures is seen in every department of community life wherever, in Allegheny County, steel is made.[16]

The welfare activities were part of a labor policy: together with high wages, they bound the highly skilled workers, so essential in the industry, to the managerial force. Meanwhile, the hope of promotion acted to subdue any discontent among the semi-skilled. Only the unskilled could see no relief from long hours, inadequate earnings, and the absolutism of foremen, except in organization. The National War Labor Board, it is true, had laid down as one of its principles:

Right to organize. The right of workers to organize in trade unions and to bargain collectively through chosen representatives is recognized and affirmed. This right shall not be denied, abridged, or interfered with by the employers in any manner whatsoever.[17]

Notwithstanding this ruling, the Steel Corporation throughout the war years denied its employees the right of collective bargaining, and the men, in the absence of representation, felt that they were without effective means of redressing their grievances.

2. New tactics: the federation of unions

Partly because of the discontent and unrest prevalent in the steel industry, partly because of the ever-dangerous gap left in the ranks of organized labor by the vast body of non-unionized steel workers, and partly because of the opportunity afforded by the scarcity of labor during the war, the feeling began to spread through the American Federation of Labor in 1917 and 1918 that the time was ripe for the organization of steel labor. If the workers in this basic industry at the very heart of America's industrial life could be unionized, then the strength and influence of the A. F. of L. would be markedly multiplied. The main impetus for this feeling came from the Chicago Federation of Labor, whose president, John Fitzpatrick, with William Z. Foster, general organizer for the Brotherhood of Railway Carmen, had succeeded in unionizing the packing industry in Chicago. Foster was sent by the Chicago Federation to the St. Paul convention of the A. F. of L. in June, 1918, with instructions to introduce the following resolution:

Whereas, the organization of the vast armies of wage-earners employed in the steel industries is vitally necessary

*to the further spread of industrial democracy in America,
and*

*Whereas, Organized Labor can accomplish this great task
only by putting forth a tremendous effort; therefore, be it*

*Resolved, that the executive officers of the A. F. of L.
stand instructed to call a conference during this convention
of delegates of all international unions whose interests are
involved in the steel industries, and of all the State Federa-
tions and City Central bodies in the steel districts, for the
purpose of uniting all these organizations into one mighty
drive to organize the steel·plants of America.*[18]

It was Foster's idea to achieve the results of industrial unionism without sacrificing the craft unionism of the A. F. of L.
He hoped to avoid the ancient dispute in the A. F. of L. between industrial and craft unionism by a temporary federation of all the national and international craft unions in any
way associated with the steel industry for the purpose of
joint action in the organization of the steel workers, negotia-
tion, and, if necessary, strike. Such a federation, he believed,
when the occasion demanded, could tie up the entire steel
industry at once, not merely one department, one craft, one
plant, or one district.

The essence of Foster's plan was surprise and speed. "The
idea was to make a hurricane drive simultaneously in all the
steel centers that would catch the workers' imagination and
sweep them into the unions *en masse* despite all opposition,
and thus to put Mr. Gary and his associates into such a predicament that they would have to grant the just demands of
their men." [19] Foster expected the federated unions to dispatch organizers immediately to all steel centers; according
to his plan, simultaneous mass meetings were to be held
throughout the steel districts, committees were to be elected
to present grievances, and, with the assistance of the pres-

sure put on the industry by the government's war needs, the steel companies were to be forced to yield. However, he failed to consider the inefficiency and inertia of the A. F. of L.; and although his resolution was adopted unanimously, the convention instructed President Gompers to call a conference of the unions involved not instantly, as Foster wished, but 30 days later.

When representatives from 15 international unions met at Chicago on August 1, 1918, a National Committee for Organizing Iron and Steel Workers was set up, to be composed of representatives of the 15 (later 24) participating national and international unions. Fitzpatrick was elected chairman, and Foster, secretary-treasurer. The representatives agreed to undertake a concerted campaign for organization, to adopt a uniform application blank, and to set the initiation fee at $3, of which $1 was to go to the National Committee and $2 to the union to which the applicant was assigned. Elements of delay, ultra-conservatism, and timidity appeared. Instead of raising a fund of $250,000, which Foster believed necessary for an effective organization campaign, each of the 24 unions contributed only $100, or a total of $2,400. Nor did the unions furnish a sufficient number of organizers. Moreover, it was decided to restrict the opening campaign to the Chicago district, rather than attempt a nation-wide drive. Foster's plan had to be revamped to fit the limits imposed by the conference of representatives. The first mass meetings were held during September in South Chicago, Gary, Hammond, and Joliet. The drive was on.

As soon as the Steel Corporation saw the early successes of the drive in the Chicago district, it instituted what it termed the "basic 8-hour day." This, however, affected wages, not working hours. It granted the workers time-and-a-half pay for all hours beyond eight, but required them to continue with the 10- or 12-hour day as before. This concession forced

the National Committee for Organizing Iron and Steel
Workers to quicken and broaden its organizing activities.
Recognizing the difficulty of invading the Pittsburgh district, the very center of the steel industry, the National
Committee determined first to encircle it with organized districts. At Youngstown, Cleveland, Buffalo, Sharon, Johnstown, and Wheeling, organizers appeared, meetings were
held, steel workers were enrolled. To solidify and centralize
the federated action of the 24 unions, Iron and Steel Workers' Councils were formed in each district. Notwithstanding
the lack of funds, the failure of the constituting unions to
coöperate harmoniously and honestly, and the difficulties involved in the presence of 40 and more nationalities among
the steel workers, the organizing campaign progressed so
encouragingly that the National Committee decided early in
1919 to attack the Pittsburgh district itself.

Here the first step was to establish the rights of free
speech and free assemblage, for the authorities of Monessen,
Braddock, Duquesne, McKeesport, Homestead, and the
other towns of the district refused to permit meetings of
steel workers; at Duquesne, in fact, a speaker sent in February by the Committee on Public Information, a federal
agency, to lecture on Abraham Lincoln was arrested and
jailed for three days.[20] A special crew of about 10 organizers,
known as the Flying Squadron, headed the free-speech fight.
It invaded town after town, and held public meetings in the
streets in defiance of the local authorities. Arrests were frequent and meetings were broken up, but steel workers were
organized. In the spring a call was issued for rank-and-file
delegates from all the steel centers to convene at Pittsburgh
on May 25. At the same time the Amalgamated Association
of Iron, Steel and Tin Workers, one of the 24 federated
unions, held a congress at Louisville, and on May 15 M. F.
Tighe, president of the Amalgamated Association, wrote to

Gary to ask for a separate conference—an action regarded by the other 23 unions as sheer desertion and treachery. Gary refused Tighe's request.

On May 25 there gathered at Pittsburgh 583 delegates representing some 80,000 newly organized steel workers in 80 steel centers, from points as distant as Pueblo, Colorado, and Birmingham, Alabama. Reports were delivered of discharge suffered for membership in the unions, of the blacklist, of intimidation and espionage. The sentiment of the congress was for immediate action, and the National Committee had difficulty in preventing a premature call for a strike. The congress called upon the A. F. of L. officials to lend open support to the free-speech fight in western Pennsylvania by holding test meetings, urged the 24 federated unions to furnish more organizers for the steel drive, and instructed the National Committee to begin negotiations with the steel companies. The National Committee, however, waited for further support from the A. F. of L. before opening negotiations.

When Fitzpatrick reported at the Atlantic City convention of the A. F. of L. in June, 1919, that the number of organized steel workers had leaped to 100,000, President Gompers was instructed to write to Chairman Gary of the U. S. Steel Corporation to request a conference. Accordingly, on June 20 Gompers sent a letter in which he expressed the attitude of organized labor in the A. F. of L.:

We believe in the effort of employer and employees to sit down around a table and, meeting thus, face to face, and having a better understanding of each other's position in regard to conditions of labor, to hours, standards, etc., and after reaching an amicable understanding to enter into an agreement for collective bargaining that is to cover wages, hours of labor, conditions of employment, etc.[21]

In this letter Gompers named a conference committee of five, which included Fitzpatrick and Foster, to represent the organized steel workers. While Gompers waited for a reply to his letter, pressure from the rank and file for action increased daily. The steel companies were resorting to wholesale discharge of workers who joined the unions. Although Gary denied later before the Senate Committee that men were discharged for unionism, President Buffington of the Illinois Steel Company remarked: "We don't discharge a man for belonging to a union, but of course we discharge men for agitating in the mills." [22] Ordinarily the practice of the companies was to make examples of the most active unionists and thus intimidate any others from joining; the investigators for the Interchurch Commission found in the "labor file" of a plant at Monessen the list of officers elected at the local union with a cross through the five chief officers, who were thus selected for discharge, and found further that in Johnstown "literally thousands of men were summarily discharged." [23]

When Gary failed to reply to Gompers' letter, the National Committee assembled at Pittsburgh and ordered the taking of a strike vote among the 100,000 organized workers in the steel industry. It took a month for the balloting to be completed. The tabulation showed a 98 per cent vote for a strike. Thereupon the National Committee drew up 12 demands to be the basis for discussion with the steel officials, provided that a conference was granted: (1) right of collective bargaining; (2) reinstatement of all men discharged for union activities, with pay for time lost; (3) eight-hour day; (4) one day's rest in seven; (5) abolition of 24-hour shifts; (6) increase in wages sufficient to guarantee an American standard of living; (7) standard scale of wages for all crafts and classifications of workers; (8) double pay for all overtime work, and for work on Sundays and holidays; (9)

check-off for collecting union dues and assessments; (10) principle of seniority in maintaining, reducing, and increasing the working force; (11) abolition of company unions; and (12) abolition of the physical examination of applicants for employment. Two of these demands were further explained: the check-off was to apply only to the United Mine Workers, which was one of the 24 federated unions; and the last demand resulted from objections that the physical examination, when conducted by company physicians, served as an instrument for blacklisting men active in the unions.

The committee of five appointed by Gompers was charged with the duty of trying to arrange a conference within 10 days. If the steel companies refused to agree, then it was to set a strike date. The committee called at the offices of Gary in New York on August 26, but he declined to meet it and asked that a statement be sent in writing. Such a statement was sent the same day. Gary replied:

As heretofore publicly stated and repeated, our corporation and subsidiaries, although they do not combat labor unions as such, decline to discuss business with them. The corporation and subsidiaries are opposed to the closed shop. They stand for the "open shop," which permits one to engage in any line of employment whether one does or does not belong to a labor union. This best promotes the welfare of both employes and employers. In view of the well-known attitude, as above expressed, the officers of the corporation respectfully decline to discuss with you, as representatives of a labor union, any matters relating to employes. In doing so no personal discourtesy is intended.[24]

Another letter by the committee brought no answer.

The conference committee still hesitated to set the date for a strike that was certain to bring privation and suffering to the workers, and yet it feared lest further delay would produce sporadic unauthorized strikes throughout the country which would be quickly crushed. It journeyed to Washington to consult with the Executive Committee of the A. F. of L. There Gompers was instructed to ask President Wilson to try to arrange a conference. At the same time a meeting of the presidents of the 24 federated unions was called for September 9 at Washington. President Wilson's reply to Gompers' request contained no assurance of a conference. Pressure from the rank and file mounted. A strike broke out at the Standard Steel Car Company at Hammond, and on September 9 three strikers were killed and many others wounded by police fire. The 24 presidents, convened at Washington, decided to send a last telegram to President Wilson. When the President's answer still gave no definite assurance of a conference and suggested no alternative, the 24 presidents, by unanimous vote, set the strike date for September 22, and the National Committee was informed of the decision. However, unexpectedly and suddenly, after the strike date had been set, Gompers received a telegram from President Wilson's secretary, requesting that the strike be postponed until after the meeting of an Industrial Conference which had been called for October 6 at Washington:

In view of the difficulty of arranging any present satisfactory mediation with regard to the steel situation, the President desires to urge upon the steel men, through you, the wisdom and desirability of postponing action of any kind until after the forthcoming industrial conference at Washington. J. P. Tumulty.[25]

Gompers forwarded the telegram to Fitzpatrick and the National Committee at Pittsburgh with the hope that it would be possible to conform with the President's wish.

The National Committee was placed in an awkward dilemma. If it acceded to President Wilson's wish and post-

poned the strike, the rank and file threatened to break out
of control and the great organization of more than 100,000
steel workers, the result of a year's effort, would be dissipated
in scattered and futile strikes. If it did not accede to the
President's wish, then it faced the production of a hostile
public opinion. For several days the National Committee
deliberated. It was flooded with protests from organizers and
local unions against the postponement of the strike. In the
meantime, at McKeesport, Mayor Lysle swore in 2,000 to
3,000 special deputies and prohibited all meetings. In the
Pittsburgh district stockades were erected around the mills.
Workers were being discharged steadily by the companies
for membership in the unions. Under these circumstances,
further delay would discredit the A. F. of L. Foster explained the predicament of the National Committee:

*In the face of this situation it would have been folly to
have the steel workers abandon their strike preparations,
even if it could have been done. It was like asking one bel-
ligerent to ground arms in the face of its onrushing antag-
onist. The employers gave not the slightest sign of a truce.
Long before anything could be hoped for from the Industrial conference, they would have cut the unions to pieces,
had the workers been foolish enough to give them the opportunity.*[26]

Finally on September 18 the National Committee voted
down the proposal to postpone the strike and reaffirmed
September 22 as the opening date. For this action it was
afterwards condemned by the Senate Committee on Education and Labor:

*It would seem that the request of the President of the
United States, backed up to a large degree by the request
of the president of the American Federation of Labor to*

*postpone the strike, should have been complied with. It is
hardly sufficient answer to say that Judge Gary likewise
declined to accede to the request of the President of the
United States that he confer with the claimed representatives of the laborers of the United States Steel Co. with relation to the strike. Both parties, it seems to us, are at fault
in refusing to heed the request of the President, and evi-
dences[?] upon both sides a lack of that consideration for
that great third party, the public, which is always the greatest sufferer in a strike of this character. The refusal of the
labor leaders who seem to have been the guiding spirits of
this strike to accede to the request of the President, even
when backed to a certain degree by the president of the
American Federation of Labor, lends weight to the idea that
radical leadership, instead of conservative leadership, was
taking possession of and guiding this particular strike. We
regret that Mr. Gompers did not take a firmer position as to
postponement.*[27]

The National Committee sent a long letter to President Wilson in explanation of its position, and then circulated 200,-
000 copies of the strike call.

3. 100 per cent Americanism

Even though only 100,000 steel workers had joined the
unions, approximately 275,000 obeyed the strike call of the
National Committee and quit work at midnight of September
21—an indication that many had been prevented from unionizing through fear or intimidation. By the end of the month
the number on strike had increased to between 300,000 and
350,000, the highest point reached. Foster estimated that the
strike at this time was 90 per cent effective.[28] The Chicago
district, Youngstown, Cleveland, Johnstown, and Wheeling
were completely paralyzed, as was also Pueblo, Colorado,

despite the existence there of the Rockefeller Industrial Representation Plan. In the Pittsburgh district the strike was 75 per cent to 85 per cent effective, though some towns, like Duquesne, were only 50 per cent shut down. A few large plants, such as those at Birmingham, Lorain, and Duluth, where organizational activities had been inadequate, were little affected by the strike.

Most of the men who remained at work were the highly skilled Americans, hesitant to jeopardize the well-paying positions they had achieved after many years of effort. The mass of unskilled and semi-skilled labor, for the greatest part recent immigrants from eastern and southern Europe, walked out almost solidly in protest against its chronic grievances. The response to the strike call by the immigrants, the "hunkies," customarily so submissive to the steel management and so ignorant of trade-union principles and practice, lent itself easily to the propagation of the idea that the strike was "alien" rather than "American"; for the public was victim to the after-war hysteria against everything alien. With strikes among the railroad workers only recently smothered, with the strikes of the Boston police in September, 1919, and of the bituminous coal miners in November, with a Labor government threatening in England and Bolshevik rule actually existing in Russia, the popular mind was panicky and peculiarly receptive to any charges of "un-Americanism," "radicalism," or "revolution."

The steel officials and the press took advantage of the popular frame of mind to generate a nation-wide "red" scare. In news column, editorial, and cartoon the strike was denounced as "radical" and "alien," at a time when these terms were dangerously provocative. For example, widespread publicity was given to a sermon preached on Sunday, September 21, the day before the opening of the strike, by

the Rev. P. Molyneux, pastor of St. Brendan's Roman
Catholic Church at Braddock:

. . . *This strike is not being brought about by intelligent
or English-speaking workmen, but by men who have not interest in the community, are not an element of our community, and who do not have the welfare of our men at
heart. . . .*

*But—you can't reason with these people. Don't reason
with them. You can't, any more than you can with a cow or
a horse. . . . And that's the only way you can reason with
these people; knock them down!*

*We dare those outsiders to start a little gun music on our
streets, and they will quickly see how long we will stand
it. . . .*

*In case this strike should take place, and there is a riot, I
want to give you people a solemn warning; smother your
curiosity. Let the women keep off the streets with their children, and give the men a clear field, and we will show these
hoodlums what we are. I want all these men that have been
abroad to put themselves at once under the direction of the
men in authority who can use them. Show them that you
fought for liberty abroad, and will maintain liberty at
home!* [29]

When this sermon was disseminated in pamphlet form, Governor Sproul of Pennsylvania wrote in a letter of commenda-
tion to the Rev. P. Molyneux: "I wish to compliment you for
the very good judgment expressed . . ." and "I heartily
agree with your analysis of the present situation." [30]

While the press kept up its barrage of "agitation" and
"bomb plots" and "revolution," the steel companies opened
an advertising campaign; over 30 full-page advertisements
appeared in the various Pittsburgh papers alone between
September 27 and October 8. The advertisements, which re-

iterated continuously the note that it was un-American for the steel workers to be on strike, usually were written in English and four or five foreign languages. One such advertisement, a representative example, was headed THE STEEL STRIKE CAN'T WIN and listed 10 reasons "why the strike will fail," "why you and every other man who is loyal to America will go back to work":

1. There is no good American reason for the strike.

2. A very large majority of the workers did not want to strike.

3. The strike is not between workers and employers, but between revolutionists and America.

4. It is becoming more and more apparent that the strike is merely the diabolical attempt of a few Radicals to seize industry and plant Bolshevism in this country.

5. The strike is doomed to fail, just as all unpopular and unpatriotic movements have failed in this country.

6. Public sentiment is against the strike; Americans have great sympathy for genuine wrongs but they have neither sympathy nor tolerance for Radicals who seek to use organized labor as a tool in their nefarious campaign against industry and American liberty.

7. The strike is an economic failure and the loss will be felt by everyone including you.

8. America will never stand for the "red" rule of Bolshevism, I.W.W.ism or any other "ism" that seeks to tear down the Constitution. Radicalism must be put down.

9. There is a strong possibility that the Huns had a hand in fomenting the strike, hoping to retard industrial progress in America.

10. Keep America busy and prosperity will continue.[31]

The idea was even spread among the immigrants that the "U.S." in the name U. S. Steel Corporation signified that the Corporation was an official part of the federal government, and that a strike against it was a rebellion against the United States.

Of particular importance was the mysterious appearance during the week preceding the strike of a pamphlet on "Syndicalism," which had been written in 1911 by Foster and E. C. Ford, and had been long out of print. Copies were circulated everywhere by the steel companies, and were furnished to newspapers, preachers, and public officials. Long extracts were given front-page prominence by the press. It was of little use for Foster to assert that he had long since left the I.W.W. and had changed his ideas. He offered to resign his position as secretary-treasurer, if it was felt that his presence might injure the strike movement, but the National Committee refused to accept his resignation. The repeated charges of "radicalism" moved the U. S. Senate to send the Committee on Education and Labor to investigate the steel strike. During its inquiry this Committee placed heavy emphasis on the "Syndicalism" pamphlet and in its report quoted extensively from it. The conclusion of the Committee was "That behind this strike there is massed a considerable element of I.W.W.'s, anarchists, revolutionists, and Russian soviets, and that some radical men not in harmony with the conservative elements of the American Federation of Labor are attempting to use the strike as a means of elevating themselves to power within the ranks of organized labor." [32] Among its final recommendations the Committee advocated the deportation of alien strikers. Great publicity was given by the press to the findings of this Committee.

On the other hand, the Interchurch Commission of Inquiry accused the Senate Committee of being biased and misled in its conclusions concerning radicalism in the strike, and pointed out that of the 28-page Senate report many pages

(7½) were devoted to "Bolshevism," whereas only one page dealt with the numerous violations of the civil liberties of strikers in western Pennsylvania. Time and again the Interchurch Commission called upon Gary, President H. D. Williams of the Carnegie Steel Company, and President E. J. Buffington of the Illinois Steel Company for evidence of "Bolshevism" in the strike; it made 12 calls at the office of President Williams. No evidence whatsoever was produced. The Interchurch Commission commented: "Evidence on this interpretation of the strike as a Bolshevist plot failed entirely to substantiate it," and "Altogether, analysis of all data seems to make it more profitable to consider the steel strike of 1919 in the light of one hundred years' industrial history than in the glare of baseless excitement over Bolshevism." [33]

With the "un-Americanism" of the strikers and the possibilities of violence as their alleged reasons, the local public officials, particularly in Allegheny County and western Pennsylvania, forbade outright all public gatherings at the opening of the strike. Within a few days the rights of free speech and free assembly were practically abolished. Whenever strikers tried to gather for instructions and encouragement, their meetings were broken up and they were arrested, fined, and jailed. The authorities seemed to be coöperating openly with the steel companies to break the strikers' morale and crush the strike in the Pittsburgh district, the crucial point in the steel workers' struggle. In Pittsburgh itself Mayor Babcock prohibited all meetings on the South Side except at the Labor Temple. By the middle of October at Braddock strikers were forbidden to hold any meetings, and by the end of November at least 150 men had been arrested. At McKeesport not more than six strikers were permitted to congregate together at one time, outdoors or indoors. At New Castle, Sheriff Boyd arrested 300 strikers during October and November, but offered to release them immediately provided that they would return to work. Thousands of strikers at Sharon and Farrell had to march twice a week across the Ohio line to hold their meetings.

At Monessen spy Z-16, in the employ of a steel plant, complained in a secret report about the meetings allowed in a nearby town:

> *It is very difficult for me to understand why the local authorities permit these regular meetings to be held in Charleroi on every Tuesday, Friday and Sunday afternoon of each week. When the men attend a meeting like this and hear such inflammatory speeches their body and soul is with the strike organization. . . .*
>
> *Undoubtedly it occurs to me that our clients have considerable influence with the local authorities. No meetings are being held in Monessen territory, nor in any of the other nearby mill centers, and I cannot see why these meetings could not be suppressed in Charleroi also. It, undoubtedly, would be a boon for all steel interests in this particular section.*[34]

When the strikers were arrested and brought to court, they were frequently denied the right of counsel, and were either jailed or fined from $10 to $60, often with no charges preferred, or with such charges as "stopping men from going to work," "cursing," "abusing," "refusing to obey orders," "going out of his house before daylight," "laughing at the police," "throwing strike cards out on the street," and "smiling at the state police." [35] Both the Senate Committee and the Interchurch Commission condemned the civil and judicial authorities in western Pennsylvania, the latter declaring: "During the strike violations of personal rights and personal liberty were wholesale; men were arrested without warrants, imprisoned without charges, their homes invaded without legal process, magistrates' verdicts were rendered frankly on the basis of whether the striker would go back to work or not." [36]

The strikers and certain labor organizations in Pennsylvania attempted to call public attention to the abrogation of civil liberties, but met with the silence of the press and the indifference of public officials. At a special meeting on October 10 at the Labor Temple the Pittsburgh Central Labor Union charged Mayor Babcock and Sheriff W. S. Haddock of Allegheny County with assisting the steel companies in their efforts to break the strike, and petitioned the City Council to be permitted to place the evidence before it, but the petition was denied. On October 17 W. B. Rubin, attorney for the strikers, filed a petition before Judge Ford of the Common Pleas Court to restrain the city of Pittsburgh from interfering with strikers' meetings. Not only was this petition denied, but Sheriff Haddock addressed an open letter to Rubin:

All but a mere handful of Allegheny County's more than one million inhabitants welcome the day when Messrs. Rubin, Foster, Fitzpatrick and company conclude they have reaped their harvest here and move on. When the workingman thoroughly understands that out of the initiation fee $1 of every $3 it costs to join your anti-American movement belongs to Foster and those who are associated with him, and that they hope to accumulate not less than $500,000 in this manner, your self-assumed task will be at [an] end. . . .

There has never been a demand for your presence here, and the people of Allegheny County, I am sure, will be greatly relieved to learn that all non-resident agitators, syndicalists, and revolutionaries have left the community, thereby restoring peace and order throughout the county and lifting the ban on all meetings for both American or alien workingmen.[37]

A delegation of 18 persons, representing 150,000 organized workers in Pittsburgh and Allegheny County, went to Washington on October 28 to protest the denial of the rights of free speech and assembly to labor; the federal officials failed to act. As a matter of fact, two investigations into the state of civil liberties in western Pennsylvania—one by Ethelbert Stewart for the Secretary of Labor in 1919, and the other by George P. West for the War Labor Board—had already been made, but the reports, for some reason, had been suppressed. Finally on November 2 the Pennsylvania State Federation of Labor, in a special convention at Pittsburgh, voted to call a general strike unless Governor Sproul acted to restore civil liberties.

Besides the suppression of their civil liberties, the strikers suffered daily brutality and violence at the hands of police, deputy sheriffs, detectives, strike-breakers, and vigilantes. In Pennsylvania the State Constabulary, which had been sent to the steel districts before the strike began, rode into crowds at meetings and clubbed men and women alike with unwarranted brutality. Mill guards and detectives made unprovoked attacks upon strikers, often entering homes to do so. Strikers were murdered and hundreds wounded without cause. At Gary federal troops under the command of Major General Leonard Wood were called in and martial law was declared; likewise, state troops were sent to East Chicago and Indiana Harbor.

In addition to the regular company detectives and spies, the steel officials employed two large labor-detective agencies to assist in breaking the strike—the Corporations Auxiliary Company and Sherman Service, Inc. It was the function of some of the under-cover men from these agencies to spy secretly and engineer raids and arrests, of some to whisper among the strikers that the strike was failing and to spread rumors about union leaders, and of others to provoke vio-

lence and incite to riot. For example, Sherman Service, Inc.,
on October 2 instructed its operatives in South Chicago mills
as follows:

*We have talked to you and instructed you. We want you
to stir up as much bad feeling as you possibly can between
the Serbians and Italians. Spread data among the Serbians
that the Italians are going back to work. Call up every question you can in reference to racial hatred between these two
nationalities; make them realize to the fullest extent that far
better results would be accomplished if they will go back
to work. Urge them to go back to work or the Italians will
get their jobs.*[38]

In fact, so dangerous did the activities of Sherman Service,
Inc., become that the State's Attorney was constrained to
raid its Chicago offices; and, as a result, its advisory director,
R. V. Philips, was indicted for trying to incite to riot and
for "fraudulent and malicious intent to unlawfully, willfully
and with malice aforethought kill and murder divers large
numbers of persons." Although the grand jury of Cook
County found this indictment in November, 1919, one and
a half years later Philips had not yet been brought to trial.[39]
Racial hatreds were further inflamed by the importation of
thousands of Negroes from the South to act as strike-breakers, at a time when the country was swept by race riots.

The National Committee urged the strikers constantly,
despite all instigations to disorder and violence, to hold
firm and keep the peace. General Wood found during his
stay at Gary:

*The strikers themselves generally behaved particularly
well, the Americans especially. They adopted a resolution
standing for law and order. Many men from the ranks of the
strikers joined the police force to maintain law and order.*

John Fitzpatrick, the leader of the strike, and other leaders came to see me and said, "We stand for law and order." They were as much worried as anybody else about what was going on.[40]

In the meantime, on October 3 the Interchurch World Movement appointed its Commission of Inquiry to investigate the steel strike; and on October 6 the Industrial Conference, for which the National Committee had been requested by President Wilson to postpone the strike, opened at Washington. At this Industrial Conference were present representatives of capital, labor, and the public. Gompers again made a bid for arbitration by introducing a resolution "That each group comprising this conference select two of its number and these six so selected to constitute a committee to which shall be referred existing differences between the workers and employers in the steel industry for adjudication and settlement. Pending the findings of this committee, this conference requests the workers involved to return to work and the employers to re-instate them in their former positions." [41] But Gary, who was also present, opposed the resolution and it was not brought to a vote. There was to be no arbitration or compromise in the steel strike.

4. Signs of defection and failure

More effective in breaking the morale of the strikers than the charges of "radicalism" and "un-Americanism" and the denial of civil liberties was the continued propagation by the steel companies of the belief that the mills were resuming work and that the strike was unsuccessful. The press, particularly in Pittsburgh, was an important instrument in the spread of this belief. The *Pittsburgh Leader* carried on September 24, two days after the beginning of the strike, the front-page headline: PITTSBURGH MILLS RUNNING FULL;

UNION MEN MEET. And on the following day a headline on page 4 declared: WORKERS FLOCK BACK TO JOBS, BRADDOCK REPORTS THREE TIMES AS MANY WORKING TODAY AS YESTERDAY, MANY PLANTS OPEN. The *Pittsburgh Chronicle-Telegraph* carried on September 27 the headline: REPORT LABORERS GOING BACK ALL THROUGH DISTRICT. On October 1 a headline on page 1 read: STRIKE CRUMBLING, STEEL MEN SAY.[42] The *New York Times* on September 30, when the actual number out on strike had risen above 300,000, carried an editorial on "The Dying Steel Strike."

Assisting the press was the whispering campaign conducted by under-cover men, who lived with the strikers, mingled with them, and talked failure. Operatives X-199 and Z-16 of the Corporations Auxiliary Company worked steadily in Monessen to spread the belief of a waning strike; and Z-16 reported: "I trust, however, to become acquainted very rapidly with the different elements and factions here and believe I shall be able to influence a good many men to return to work." [43] Other means were employed by the steel companies to discourage the strikers. At Johnstown the Cambria Steel Company formed Back-to-Work organizations. At Gary Negro strike-breakers were paraded through the streets from plant to plant, so as to produce the belief that many plants were reopening. Many mills were kept running with skeleton forces merely for the impression created by the noise and smoke.

The strike leaders, on the other hand, were unable, for lack of means, to counteract effectually the belief of failure that was growing among the strikers. Meetings and picketing, which might have informed and heartened the strikers, were badly hampered—at many places entirely prevented—by the abrogation of civil liberties. To reach the strikers, the National Committee had only a weekly strike bulletin, printed in four or five languages. There was no reliable labor press in the Pittsburgh district to publish accounts of the progress of the strike and to strengthen the morale of the strikers: the three weekly "labor" papers there were privately owned, were indistinguishable in attitude from the daily papers, and were not endorsed by the Central Labor Union. Although many liberal papers and journals were sympathetic toward the strikers, they failed to reach the great mass of non-English-speaking immigrants. Moreover, because of their distrust of most of the press, the strike leaders did not prepare adequate statements of aims and facts for publication. And the press in Pittsburgh, while it gave wide publicity to "Bolshevism" and "violence" and "failure," either maintained silence about the denial of civil liberties and the actual grievances of the strikers, or misrepresented such material as it did print. The investigator for the Interchurch Commission reported: "Without a single exception worthy of note, the statements, demands, grievances and testimony from the side of the strikers were printed under headlines or in a context tending to give the impression that what the striking steel workers sought was something unwarranted and that their grievances were unfounded." [44] The same investigator pointed out further that at no time did the newspapers carry headlines such as "Half the Steel Workers Are on the 12-Hour Day" or "Workers Demand Right to Hold Union Meetings." [45] Throughout the struggle the strike leaders developed no antidote for the hostility of the press.

Although the campaign of "failure" did much to weaken the strike by the middle of November, the principal causes of collapse existed in the organization of the strike itself, in the pessimism, the lack of support, the discord, and the defections. Foster, who laid the main responsibility for the ultimate defeat of the strike upon organized labor, said: "Official pessimism, bred of thirty years of trade-union failure in the steel industry, hung like a mill-stone about the neck of the movement in all its stages." [46] Partly because of this pessimism, the organizing campaign from the beginning was handicapped by the lack of support, especially by the lack of sufficient funds. The 24 federated unions contributed very little; in fact, outside unions were much more generous with assistance, the International Ladies Garment Workers' Union, among others, donating $60,000 to the strike fund, and the Amalgamated Clothing Workers of America $100,000. During the course of the strike there was no money for the payment of benefits, and relief had to be restricted to destitute families. The National Committee met this problem by establishing 45 local commissaries throughout the strike districts, which distributed rations twice a week to all strikers in need, whether union members or not. The total expenditure of the commissariats from October 26, 1919, to January 31, 1920, three weeks after the strike ended, was only $348,509.42, approximately $1.40 per striker for the 15 weeks, or 9⅓ cents per week.[47] Moreover, not only was the supply of organizers inadequate, but the National Committee had little control over the small number that were furnished by the 24 federated unions, with the result that many important steel centers were either poorly campaigned or completely neglected.

Above all, however, was the discord and disunity among the 24 participating unions. Ancient jealousies and jurisdictional disputes aroused mutual distrust, which was further heightened by the existing racial antagonisms. The International Brotherhood of Steamshovel and Dredgemen and the International Union of Steam and Operating Engineers quarreled over the disposition of cranemen, as did the Amalgamated Association of Iron, Steel and Tin Workers and the International Hod Carriers', Building, and Common Laborers' Union of America over common laborers. The

Switchmen's Union of North America refused to call out its men in the Chicago district, since the Trainmen would have taken their places. Although the railway locals on the switching roads of the Pittsburgh district voted to strike, no support came from their Brotherhoods. One strike leader said: "This organization has as much cohesiveness as a load of furniture." [48] Throughout the preliminary campaign and the strike itself the National Committee found it necessary to expend valuable time and energy in trying to conciliate differences and achieve harmony.

Aside from the discord and the lukewarm support, there were open defections among the 24 federated unions. On the first day of the strike President Snellings and Secretary Comerford of the International Union of Steam and Operating Engineers urged their men not to quit work, but to wait for the Industrial Conference of October 6 at Washington. Only when Gompers on September 24 pledged the support of the A. F. of L. did Snellings and Comerford publicly approve of the strike. The main deserter was the Amalgamated Association of Iron, Steel and Tin Workers, which after a few weeks began to order its men back into several plants, on the grounds that certain groups of skilled workers had contracts. Thus in the Youngstown district President Tighe of the Amalgamated Association ordered his men back at the Trumbull Steel Company and the Sharon Steel Company; and in Cleveland when several local unions refused to obey a similar order to return to work, the Amalgamated Association took away their charters. Despite the accusation of desertion and treachery leveled at it by the other participating unions, the Amalgamated Association not only continued to order its men back, but also attempted to settle separately, as in a proposed agreement with the Bethlehem Steel Corporation at Sparrows' Point on November 19, which was, however, rejected.

It may be that some of the discord and defection was due to the activity of under-cover men within the unions. S. S. Dewson, manager of the Pittsburgh office of the Corporations Auxiliary Company, informed the investigator for the Interchurch Commission that several of the under-cover operatives were officers in the 24 federated unions and that a member of the National Committee was accepting money from the Corporations Auxiliary, and said further: "Take Akron, Ohio, for example; we control the situation there. There is no trouble in Akron. When the A. F. of L. organizer comes to Akron he reports to our man." [49] That this was not a vain boast was shown a year after the strike in the sensational exposé, with confessions, of several of the officers high in the Central Labor Union of Akron as under-cover men in the pay of private detective agencies. Nevertheless, the principal difficulty lay within the A. F. of L. itself, in its old cleavages and quarrels.

Toward the end of November the strike began to weaken seriously. The National Committee, in an effort to win whatever concessions it could for the strikers, looked about for some impartial body that might try to mediate between the strikers and the steel companies. Accordingly, Fitzpatrick and Foster wrote to the Interchurch Commission of Inquiry, which had been in the field since early October investigating the strike:

We all agreed that, because of the tremendous power and influence of the Publicity Bureau of the United States Steel Corporation over the newspapers of the country, the men in active charge of the strike have been thoroughly discredited, and it is impossible for them to be of service in bringing a reasonable, fair and just termination of the controversy. Realizing this, they searched around for some neutral interest sufficiently interested who might be able to exert their

*influence that a reasonable and fair conclusion of the strike
could be brought about and, inasmuch as the Commission
representing the Interchurch World Movement had come
into the situation for the purpose of investigation, etc., we
decided to ask the Commission to use their good offices in
bringing about an adjustment of this controversy.*[50]

Fitzpatrick, on November 27, personally laid the proposal
of the National Committee before the Commission. If the
Steel Corporation would accept any plan suggested by the
Interchurch Commission, the strike leaders agreed to order the strikers back to work and then step out of the
situation.

The Commission undertook the mediation; and on December 5 Bishop F. J. McConnell of the Methodist Episcopal
Church, Dr. D. A. Poling, and Dr. J. McDowell, as representatives of the Interchurch Commission of Inquiry, called
on Gary at his offices and held a two-hour interview with
him. Gary declined to listen to any plan for mediation. He
insisted that the strikers sought "the closed shop, Soviets
and the forcible distribution of property," and declared
finally: "There is absolutely no issue." [51] After this effort
at mediation failed, the National Committee met at Washington December 13 and 14 to see what should be done. Although it found that the number on strike had dropped to
109,300 and estimated that production was 50 per cent to
60 per cent normal, it decided that the strike was still strong
enough to be won.[52]

5. Victory for the Steel Corporation

Notwithstanding the efforts of the National Committee,
the number out on strike continued slowly to dwindle; and
while production in the mills was still greatly hampered,
there seemed little hope of victory. Consequently, on Janu-

ary 8 the National Committee called a meeting of the 24 federated unions at Pittsburgh. Here, although it was estimated that 100,000 men were yet on strike and that production was no more than 60 per cent or 70 per cent normal, the congress judged that it would be unwise to sacrifice the remaining strikers in a futile struggle, and decided to end the strike—a strike which had lasted three and one-half months, had spread over nine states, and at its inception had involved more than 300,000 men. The strikers—those who were not blacklisted—returned to work without having won a single concession. They had made a determined effort; they had suffered some 20 deaths and wage losses between $87,-000,000 and $112,000,000. But the Steel Corporation had proved too strong. It stood at the very heart of American industrial and financial life; its ramifications gave it control over the independent steel companies, railroads, mines, shipping, and banks. "The United States Steel Corporation was too big to be beaten by 300,000 workingmen. It had too large a cash surplus, too many allies among other businesses, too much support from government officers, local and national, too strong influence with social institutions such as the press and the pulpit, it spread over too much of the earth—still retaining absolutely centralized control—to be defeated by widely scattered workers of many minds, many fears, varying states of pocketbook and under a comparatively improvised leadership. The 'independent' steel companies gave the Corporation solid speechless support; not a spokesman was heard but Mr. Gary." [53] Steel, the core of American industry, remained untouched by collective bargaining.

The Steel Corporation had defended with complete success its anti-union policy and its arbitrary control over labor. A few small independent plants, it is true, signed trade-union agreements; but, on the whole, the steel workers continued to have no voice in their working conditions. In an editorial, "Back to the 12-Hour Day," the *Survey* wrote:

Three hundred and seventy thousand steel workers, it is estimated, from various districts throughout the country left their jobs on September 22, 1919, after they had been refused a conference with Judge Gary to discuss the conditions of their work. Many of those who return go back to the twelve-hour day, the seven-day week, the twenty-four-hour shift. With no machinery by which they can protest against these conditions, and with an espionage system which effectively prevents them from letting their wants be known, it would seem to be a sweeping statement of Judge Gary that the men are "satisfied." [54]

The cost of the strike to the steel companies had been great. Production had practically ceased during the first month and had been badly crippled for the remaining two and one-half months. It had been necessary to maintain a large and costly force of guards, deputies, under-cover men, and strike-breakers. Moreover, through the blacklist or through voluntary decisions to seek other work, thousands of experienced workmen were lost and had to be replaced by untrained men. Besides, the morale and efficiency of those men who did return to work were lowered by disillusionment, disappointment, and despondency. Still, no matter how high the cost, the Steel Corporation believed that it had to crush embryonic labor organizations once every 10 or 15 years in order to retain its absolutism. That this absolutism was the main issue for the Steel Corporation is indicated in Gary's announcement on January 29, after the strike had been unquestionably defeated, of an increase of 10 per cent in the wages of common laborers; whatever concessions the Corporation made were to be of its own will.

While the labor movement lost prestige because of the

defeat in steel and while anti-union employers throughout the country were thus encouraged to attack organizations of their workmen, nevertheless certain valuable lessons were gained by organized labor. First, it learned the necessity for having its own press to communicate its aims to the public and keep its own ranks well informed. One of the results of the strikes of 1919 was the establishment of the first national news service owned by trade-unions, the Federated Press. Second, the A. F. of L. became aware of the seriousness of the Negro question. It saw that its traditional indifference, discrimination, and outright hostility toward Negro labor had proved a boomerang, for the Negro was forced into the rôle of strike-breaker. Foster warned organized labor of the dangers involved in its attitude toward the Negro: "The need for action looking towards better relations between whites and blacks in the industrial field should be instantly patent; for there can be no doubt but that the employing class, taking advantage of the bitter animosities of the two groups, are deliberately attempting to turn the negroes into a race of strike-breakers, with whom to hold the white workers in check. . . . Should they succeed to any degree it would make our industrial disputes take on more and more the character of race wars, a consummation that would be highly injurious to the white workers and eventually ruinous to the blacks." [55] And the National Committee advised Gompers to confer with prominent Negro leaders concerning means of fostering better relations between white and Negro labor. Third, the immigrants from southern and eastern Europe, long regarded as unorganizable and as potential strike-breaking material, manifested undeniable trade-union discipline, courage, and loyalty despite the trying difficulties of the struggle. Finally, and probably most important, organized labor was shown unmistakably that defeat was inevitable unless it overcame its internal disputes, discord, and disunity. Solidarity and harmony were essential if the next struggle was to be won. On the whole, the leaders of the strike felt that they had achieved significant gains, not only in the comprehension of problems, but also in the actual organization of 150,000 steel workers and in a new confidence that the Steel Corporation might not always be invincible.

After the strike was concluded, the Interchurch World Movement hoped that, by disclosing the underlying conditions in the steel industry and by arousing public opinion, it might bring about the reforms which it thought necessary. The report by the Commission of Inquiry which was adopted unanimously on June 28, 1920, by the Executive Committee of the Interchurch World Movement, was sent to President Wilson and made public the following month. To the steel companies it recommended the introduction of the eight- or 10-hour day with a minimum comfort wage, the creation of more and better housing for workers, and the recognition of the right of collective bargaining; to the trade-unions, the repudiation of the closed-shop principle and the democratization of organized labor; to the federal government, an investigation into under-cover men and labor-detective agencies and the establishment of a permanent commission of conciliation in the steel industry.

The report was given wide publicity, both because of the wide difference between the actual findings and popular belief concerning conditions in steel, and because of the influence and reputation of the Interchurch World Movement. While most editorial opinion approved of the report and its recommendations, some of the more conservative press accused the Interchurch Commission of partiality and radicalism. Thus the *New York Times* declared:

*The gravity of certain facts revealed in the Interchurch
World Report on the steel strike should not be permitted to
obscure the partisan bias of the report as a whole. It is
doubtless true that something over a third of the steel workers are subject to the twelve-hour day, and that a similar
number are subject to the seven-day week. It is doubtless
true that the Steel Corporation made a highly questionable
use of spies and detectives to gather evidence against employés with a tendency to unionism. Such conditions call
for the most serious consideration. On the face of the facts
adduced, moreover, Judge Gary was either sadly ignorant of
conditions in the works or he willfully misrepresented them
in his testimony before the Senate committee. Yet the value
of these revelations, and especially the value of the conclusions
drawn from them, is impaired by evidence recurring throughout the report that it is written out of strong preconceptions
and that it seriously warps the facts in the interest of radical
propaganda.*[56]

The attitude of the steel industry to the Interchurch report was decidedly hostile; for example, the Steel Corporation distributed 1,200,000 copies of an address by a New
England clergyman, which read in part:

*Somebody is responsible for an industrial heresy about
hours of work that may have poisoned the judgment of our
Interchurch Commission. It is the first principle of their
industrial creed and it advocates gradually and reasonably
reducing "the hours of labor to the lowest practicable point."
This is the hobo's doctrine. It glorifies leisure and denounces
toil. How could it ever be advocated by a confessed follower
of the ceaseless Toiler of Galilee who said in reply to his
critics that objected to his Sunday work, "My Father work-
eth hitherto and I work!" The extent to which this heresy
has spread amazes us. It was adopted by our last Congrega-*

*tional Council in its industrial platform and is published by
our social service department throughout the country. It
ought to bring the blush of shame to every one of us that be-
lieves in work as the greatest means of character building
and as the demonstrator of the highest manhood. How can
we advocate reducing work to its lowest practicable point if
we have left in us any of the spirit of him who said, "I must
work the works of him that sent me while it is day; for
the night cometh when no man can work."* [57]

Nevertheless, the light thrown upon working conditions in
the steel industry did make the Steel Corporation uneasy,
and, perhaps as a result of the Interchurch report, it announced on March 17, 1921, that the seven-day week and the
long turn at the change of shifts "have been entirely eliminated." Furthermore, one month later it said that it was "in
favor of abolishing the twelve-hour day" and declared its
intention "to decrease the working hours—we hope in the
comparatively near future." [58] It remained to be seen, however, whether working hours would actually be decreased and
what effect public opinion would have on other working conditions in the steel industry if labor itself was without effective means of protest.

IX. THE SOUTHERN TEXTILE
STRIKES AND GASTONIA

1. Textiles migrate to the South

The sporadic strikes that spread through Tennessee and the Carolinas in the spring and summer of 1929 and culminated in the murder of Chief of Police O. F. Aderholt and a striker at Gastonia and of six strikers at Marion, North Carolina, had their roots in the extensive migration of the textile industry from New England to the South during the 1920 decade. Whereas in 1921 the southern cotton-growing states produced 54 per cent of the nation's total yardage of woven cotton goods, in 1927 they produced 67 per cent; and the value in dollars of this production jumped from 44 per cent in 1921 to 56 per cent in 1927.[1] Southern towns encouraged this migration by advertising the lower cost of production in the South, which was attributable to cheaper power, a greater accessibility to raw material, reduced transportation rates, lower taxes, and, most important by far, an abundance of cheap labor with freedom from the restrictions of stringent labor legislation and of labor unions. Thus the cost of manufacture in a typical southern mill was 16.8 per cent less than in a typical Massachusetts mill, a difference amounting to $6.73 per spindle, of which $4.53 was due to a saving in labor costs.[2] There could be no doubt of what attracted northern capital to the South. "The real reason for the migration of the looms was plentiful, cheap, and unorganized labor. This was the main argument employed by southern chambers of commerce and booster organizations, the lure dangled before the noses of harassed New England mill owners." [3]

It was almost entirely at the expense of labor that the southward movement of textiles was accomplished. Wages in the southern mills were roughly one-third below those in New England mills. The 1927 Census of Manufactures gave the average annual earnings of cotton-mill workers in the four leading New England states as $966 for Massachusetts, $1,053 for Rhode Island, $1,029 for New Hampshire, and $1,040 for Connecticut; as against averages in the four leading southern states of $691 for North Carolina, $658 for South Carolina, $652 for Georgia, and $642 for Alabama. In this year the average weekly earnings were $19.16 in the four leading New England states and $12.83, or $6.33 lower, in the four leading southern states. [4] Although the textile manufacturers in the South maintained that a cheaper cost of living made the real wages of their workers as high as those in the North, there was no evidence to support such a claim. It is true that rents in the southern mill villages were low—about $1 a month per room; but food and clothing were as high as in the North. The National Industrial Conference Board found in January and February, 1920, that the average minimum cost of living for a family of five, including three children under 14, was $26.80 per week in Greenville, South Carolina; $26.43 in Pelzer, South Carolina; $27.66 in company houses at Charlotte, North Carolina; and $24.38 in Fall River, Massachusetts; and, while these figures were several years old, the Senate Committee on Manufactures, after conducting preliminary hearings on the textile industry in 1929, felt that "there is no reason to doubt them or to believe that the relative difference in the cost of living in the North and South has changed since then." [5]

The southern textile workers were able to subsist on their

earnings, not because their *cost* of living was low, but rather because their *standard* of living was low, and because, more than in the North, women and children, as well as men, entered the mills. "It usually takes three wage-earners in a family to piece out the sum necessary for subsistence and a small saving." [6] As a result, child labor was more prevalent in the southern than in the northern mills. "Preliminary investigation shows that child labor for children of 14 and over is almost universal in southern cotton mill villages because the wages paid the average adult will not support a family in decency without the children's wages." [7]

Not only were the wages of cotton-mill operatives lower in the South than in the North, but the working hours were longer. In contrast to the 48- and 54-hour week permitted in the New England states, South Carolina allowed a 55-hour week, North Carolina and Georgia had a 60-hour week, and Alabama set no legal limit whatever on the hours of labor. The longer hours were intensified by the greater prevalence of night work in the South, where both men and women alternated the 10- to 12-hour day shift with the 10- to 12-hour night shift. In New England, on the other hand, night work for women was prohibited. According to the southern mill owners, night work was necessary in order to reduce overhead expenses. Engineers, however, pointed out that the reduction in overhead was offset by such disadvantages as the production of a larger number of seconds in night work than in day work, the increase in industrial accidents, the poorer care of machinery, and the financial danger of excess capacity. At any rate, through night work and longer hours, the southern textile mills speeded up each spindle, with the result that in 1929, while they had 54.9 per cent of the nation's spindles, they had 68.8 per cent of the total spindle hours.[8]

Thus in the South women, like men—and also children 16

and over—were subjected to long hours and the night shift under working conditions that produced nervous tension and physical debility. "The grinding, noisy monotony amid whirring machinery, in a temperature nearer 85 than 75 degrees, produces a strain, and, when continued for ten hours, brings fatigue and lowered vitality, leaving the victim susceptible to almost any ill. . . . A ten-hour day in a spinning or spooling room—worse still in the deafening weave room, with the odor of oil filling every cranny, and the floor permeated with grease which scrubbing does not remove—seems to the outsider to spell life at its worst, unless it be compared with a ten-hour night or an eleven-hour night, as in some South Carolina yarn mills." [9] Through increased hours of work and decreased earnings the 300,000 southern textile workers sustained the economic advantage of the southern mills over the northern.

To any public protest against low wages and long hours, the southern textile manufacturers replied that they gave their workers "wage equivalents" worth more than the cash difference between wages in the North and South. These "wage equivalents" were to be found in the social agencies and welfare work of the company-owned mill villages in the South. Originally such mill villages had been a necessity in order to house the workers brought in from the surrounding hills and farmlands, but they easily lent themselves to the fostering of a paternalistic, yet absolute, control by the mill owner over his employees:

From the first, of course, the congregation of large numbers of untrained and unsocial ruralists, unused to the necessities of living in groups, created problems of social control; and it devolved upon the management to furnish the solution. In isolated communities, this resulted eventually in management-controlled policing, management-made laws and regu-

lations, management-devised codes of morals, management-influenced schools, management-maintained poor relief during periods of unemployment or in case of accident, sickness, or old age, and management-supported churches. With the inauguration of more extensive activities during the war, and with the development of the idea of the use of village government and welfare activities for the purpose of controlling the labor force (an idea that did not originate in the southern mill villages), these villages entered upon an era of greater industrial significance. What had been the incidental and unconscious effects of prewar mill village superintendence, now became, generally, the primary and deliberate effects of postwar control. . . .[10]

Whether the mill owners were conscious or not of the control given them by the mill village, the effect was there. The mill village, like all company-owned housing and company-directed welfare work, served to keep the workers docile and to prevent organization among them for a betterment of their conditions. "Once a local union has been exploded into a mill community, the employer can fall back upon his extraordinary powers as owner of the settlement. In a strike he can evict, arrest through deputies paid by himself, forbid trespass to organizers, prevent distribution of literature, close meeting halls, influence merchants to refuse credit, even array local mill-subsidized ministers against the union." [11]

Moreover, the "wage equivalents" were usually non-existent: even though a few model mill villages were constructed, like that of the Avondale mill near Sylacauga, Alabama, with comfortable houses, gardens, nurseries, playgrounds, etc., most of the villages were composed of ramshackle wooden houses practically bare of furniture, with the faucet and surface privy outside. Social agencies and welfare work were absent. Nor did the low earnings permit the worker to eat proper foods. A diet of corn meal, bread, greens, and fat back, with no fresh vegetables, no fruit, and little fresh meat or milk, produced a high rate of pellagra among the southern cotton-mill workers.

Besides the low labor costs, the southern textile manufacturers enjoyed—at least according to the enticements offered to northern capital—advantages both in the quantity and the quality of the labor supply. The cotton mills of the South were situated in the hills and rural districts, which contributed a steady stream of unskilled workers willing to sell their labor at extremely cheap wages, for even these low earnings seemed great in comparison with the earnings of tenant farming. This reservoir of untrained labor acted to depress wages still further and to enfeeble the bargaining power of those workers already in the industry: the cotton-mill employee was always in competition with the masses of poverty-stricken tenant farmers who were eager to exchange their semi-starvation existence for the comparatively better life in the mill villages. What was more, the exceptionally high birth rate in the southern textile states guaranteed the continued replenishment of the reserve of cheap labor; for example, in 1927 the excess of births over deaths in North Carolina was 18.3 per thousand for whites and 15.0 for Negroes, whereas in 1928 it was 7.7 for the United States as a whole.[12]

But even more emphasis was put by southern boosters on the quality of southern labor. It was widely advertised as individualistic and non-unionized, as native American, as docile and tractable. It was contrasted with the collective, unionized, and "volatile" immigrant labor of the New England textile mills. R. W. Edmonds, after making a survey of cotton-mill labor conditions for *Barrons*, reported:

The southern mill help is almost wholly native American; almost 100 per cent American-born, of American-born parents. They come originally almost wholly from the farms, and whether they be tenant farmers, as most of them were, or owners, as a good many of those in North Carolina were, they have the American idea of progress by individual effort. As a class they are not very ambitious. What can be expected of them? Except in North Carolina, where most of them come from the mountains, the great majority have come from the tenant-farmer class—the poorest, least thrifty, least energetic, least capable and ambitious, of the farming class as a whole. And most of them have come to the mills because they had failed at farming and had nowhere else to turn. They are the dregs of the farmer population. . . .

Ambition is rare, and the will to rise is rare. But where it exists, the natural thought seems to be to rise by individual effort rather than by organization and class effort. . . . The point is that the American idea of individual improvement and individual effort is innate in the southern mill people, and is being developed to the limit of the people's ambition by the mills.[13]

The immigrant mill workers of New England, on the other hand, were found to be subject to "a deep conviction of the insurmountability of the barrier that separates them from the upper classes. . . . The idea furnishes a fertile soil for the socialistic conceptions and for the suspicions implanted and vigorously cultivated by the professional labor agitators. . . . The European class idea is a heavy handicap to individual progress."[14] In this way the South was seen as a new industrial paradise, with a vast reservoir of tractable labor, untouched by the doctrines of unionism and willing to work long hours for low wages.

Notwithstanding the numerous advantages it enjoyed, the textile industry in the South was seriously depressed during the 1920 decade. After the World War the market for American cotton goods shrank. Foreign markets—China,

India, South America—were captured by Japan, and the home market was curtailed by new styles in women's dress which required less cloth and by the growing competition of rayon materials. Nevertheless, even though the market demand fell, the overproduction of cotton goods continued. Jealous competition among mill owners made it impossible for them, in the face of a glutted market, to agree on even the abolition of night work. The industry was further disrupted by poor merchandising methods, particularly by the commission system of selling, about which Ethelbert Stewart, U. S. Commissioner of Labor Statistics, said:

Goods are manufactured and turned over to a commission man for sale, and he gets a commission on that sale whether he sells it at a price below the cost of production or not. Very few manufacturers know what their cost of production is, and the commission man does not care. He gets his money from the sale. In other words, his object is sales, not profits to the manufacturer, and when he sells below the cost of manufacture of course the difference between the cost of manufacture and the price secured flows from the capital invested in the factory into the pockets of the commission man. Thus we find scores of mills throughout the South, and probably just as true in the North, owned by the commission men.[15]

Their industry crippled by a limited market, overproduction, excessive competition, and a ruinous merchandising system, the southern cotton-mill operators sought means to cut still further the cost of production.

They attempted to create new savings in the cost of labor. In 1927 the Loray mill at Gastonia, North Carolina, introduced the stretch-out and the other mills soon followed. The stretch-out gave the workers additional machines to operate without a commensurate increase in pay, often with no increase whatsoever, or even with an actual decrease. Weavers were stretched from 24 to 48 looms, and from 48 to 96. An investigating committee sent to the cotton mills in 1929 by the South Carolina House of Representatives found that in the card-room of one mill a force of five men at $23 each per week had been reduced to three men at $20.23 with no change in the total amount of production; at another mill a weaver who had operated 24 looms at $18.91 per week was stretched to 100 looms at $23.[16] For the workers the stretch-out meant harder labor, greater fatigue, and the displacement of part of the labor force from the industry. It remained to be seen how far the southern cotton-mill worker could be exploited without protest.

2. Revolt of the "lint-heads"

In the absence of unionization, the possibility of organized protest by the southern cotton-mill workers was small. Had there been a strong union in the field, the differentials in wages and hours between North and South might have been wiped out; but many powerful factors operated against the development of such a union. First, the "lint-heads," as the southern cotton-mill workers were called, received wages so low that they could not pay union dues and would have been unable to sustain a strike if it proved necessary. The financial support, therefore, would have to come almost entirely from the northern textile unions, who were themselves in dire need of money. Second, the southern mill owners were unalterably opposed to the unionization of their employees; in fact, many northern mills had moved to the South to escape union restrictions. Third, the existing textile unions in the North were not only weak, but also divided among themselves. In addition to the United Textile Workers of America, which was affiliated with the American Federation of Labor, there were the American Federation of Textile

Operatives and a number of small independent local craft unions. In 1927 the United Textile Workers had 20,000 members and the other unions together an equal number—in all, 40,000 organized workers out of a total of 600,000 in the nation's textile industry. These unions, furthermore, had no foothold in the South; although there had been a good-sized flurry in unionization among the southern textile workers during the World War, practically every trace had been stamped out in the two years following the war. Moreover, the workers in these unions were the highly skilled operatives; and little effort was made to organize the unskilled and semi-skilled until late in 1928 under the impetus of the newly-formed National Textile Workers' Union, initiated under Communist guidance to rival the conservative unions in the field.

Consequently, it was not union penetration that caused the sudden outbursts of southern textile workers in the spring of 1929; it was rather the slow accumulation of grievances against low wages, long hours, and the stretch-out. With one exception, the simultaneous strikes that broke out spontaneously in three widely separated areas—Elizabethton, Tennessee; Gaston County, North Carolina; and the Piedmont region of South Carolina—and involved 17,000 workers were not at first concerned with the right of collective bargaining.

The first of the strikes began at Happy Valley, near Elizabethton, Tennessee, where the American Glanzstoff Corporation, a German firm, had recently constructed two rayon plants, the Glanzstoff and the Bemberg. On March 12, 1929, some 500 girls in the inspection department at the Glanzstoff plant walked out in protest against full-time wages of $8.96 to $10.80 a week. The next day found the entire force of 3,000 on strike for an increase in pay to equal the higher pay at the Bemberg plant. The strikers called upon the

United Textile Workers for assistance, and Alfred Hoffman was sent to organize them. When President A. M. Mothwurf of the American Glanzstoff Corporation procured a writ of injunction which forbade outright all picketing, the Bemberg plant replied by a solid walkout in sympathy with the Glanzstoff strikers. On March 22 the strikers at both plants returned to work, after Mothwurf agreed to increase the wages at the Glanzstoff plant, to take back all the strikers without discrimination. and to meet grievance committees of the workers.

Notwithstanding this agreement, Mothwurf undertook to break the union—which included 4,653 members out of the 5,500 employees at the two plants—and complaints of discrimination against union members were numerous. As a result, President Green of the A. F. of L. sent Vice-President E. F. McGrady to investigate. McGrady reported that in one week more than 300 workers were discharged for unionism.[17] Discrimination and provocation against union members continued. On April 4 McGrady and Hoffman were kidnaped by groups of armed men, taken across the state line, and threatened with death if they returned. They returned the next day and filed charges against their kidnapers; five prominent business men of Elizabethton were arrested and indicted on charges of kidnaping and felonious assault, but were never brought to trial. When a grievance committee of the workers was discharged by Mothwurf and another committee sent to find out the cause was likewise discharged, the forces at both plants walked out a second time on April 15. Mothwurf called for troops; and even though there had been no violence, Governor Horton immediately dispatched two companies of the National Guard. G. F. Milton, editor of the *Chattanooga News*, concluded: "The truth seems to be that the Tennessee manufacturers were apprehensive of a labor success at Elizabethton; they looked upon it as an entering wedge for the unionization of the South. . . . There is every reason to believe that the troops went to Elizabethton to quiet this apprehension." [18]

In the meantime, on April 1 another strike broke out under widely different circumstances near Gastonia, North Carolina. Here at the Loray mill, owned by the Manville-Jenckes Company of Pawtucket, Rhode Island, Fred E. Beal of the National Textile Workers' Union had secretly organized the workers. As soon as the management discovered this secret union, it discharged five of its members. More than half of the force of 2,200 walked out in protest. A strikers' committee called upon Superintendent J. A. Baugh with a list of demands, including recognition of the union, a 40-hour week, a minimum weekly wage of $20, and the abolition of the stretch-out; but he replied by roping off the street leading to the mill and by keeping the looms going with a small force. A scuffle between pickets and deputies on April 2 brought out five companies of the National Guard.

From the outset of the strike the National Textile Workers' Union was attacked with more than usual vehemence; for it was not merely a union, it was not merely an importation from the North, it was also a Communist union which advocated equality of Negroes with whites and admitted both to membership. Across the front page of the *Gastonia Daily Gazette* was printed a picture of an American flag with a snake coiled at its base, and the inscription: "Communism in the South. Kill it!" Advertisements were published under such headlines as RED RUSSIANISM LIFTS ITS GORY HANDS RIGHT HERE IN GASTONIA. Handbills were distributed: "Bust up your Russian union and let's go back to work" and "Would you belong to a union which opposes White Supremacy?" [19] The issues of communism and race equality were drummed up until soon Gastonia was ripe for intimidation and violence. On April 18, despite the presence of the National Guard, a band of 100 masked men demolished the frame building that served as the local headquarters for the National Textile Workers' Union, and destroyed the relief groceries kept there. Although 14 arrests were made and 100 witnesses testified, the Gaston County grand jury refused to indict anyone. The strike, however, began to spread, and by the end of the month there were walkouts at the Gambril and Melville mills in Bessemer City, the Chadwick-Hoskins mill in Pineville, the Wenonah mill in Lexington, and the Osage and American mills in Gastonia.

Coincident with the strikes at Gastonia and Elizabethton, yet not immediately related to them, there sprang up a series of scattered strikes in the South Carolina textile mills. The main objective of these strikes was the abolition of the stretch-out. Beginning late in March with the walkout of 800 workers at the Ware Shoals Manufacturing Company, Ware Shoals, and of 1,250 at the New England Southern plant, Pelzer, the strike spread very quickly until within three weeks over 8,000 had walked out at 15 mills in the Piedmont area of South Carolina. P. Blanshard reported that these strikers would have nothing to do with "imported" labor organizers and opened their strike meetings with prayer. "Many of them, when the strikes began, shook hands with their superintendents and managers as they filed out of the mills to 'make certain that there was no hard feelin's.' " [20] At Ware Shoals and Pelzer the mill managements agreed to abandon the stretch-out, and the strikers returned to work. Other mills followed, and before the end of April all but four of the strikes were won.

The most stubborn strikes in South Carolina involved the 1,750 employees of three plants of the Brandon Corporation —the Brandon and Poinsett mills at Greenville, and the Woodruff mill at Woodruff. Affidavits of the strikers showed that here too the stretch-out was the principal grievance:

three weavers, who had been paid $25 a week for 24 looms, received only $23.40 for 28 looms; a section man, who had been paid $20.90 a week for 40 frames, received the same for 50 frames; and a sweeper on warp received no increase on his $9.60 per week, although he was stretched from 36 to 72 frames.[21] It was May 19 before these three strikes were settled, with the granting of the strikers' demands for the adjustment of grievances through workers' grievance committees, the promise of no discrimination against strikers, and new wage scales to compensate for the increased work under the stretch-out. Even though these leaderless strikes were settled for the present, others continued to flare up in various parts of South Carolina throughout the summer of 1929.

While the strikes in South Carolina were settled with comparative speed, those at Elizabethton and Gastonia, under the guidance of rival unions, continued with increased bitterness. Mothwurf announced that he would not recognize any union and, with the assistance of the militia and the injunction prohibiting all picketing, determined to open the two rayon plants at Elizabethton. Accordingly, on May 6 a force of 800 militiamen, deputy sheriffs, and police assembled at the Glanzstoff and Bemberg plants; but, in spite of this show of force, the Glanzstoff plant remained completely shut down, and the Bemberg plant was able to run at no more than 30 per cent normal. As the strikers continued to picket in defiance of the injunction, arrests were frequent; in all, hundreds were arrested, of whom 40 were found guilty of contempt of court and were given sentences ranging from a $10 fine to a $50 fine plus 10 days in jail.[22] Strikers were even arrested for picketing on the highway four miles away from the Glanzstoff properties.

When no cessation of the struggle could be seen, the U. S. Department of Labor sent Anna Weinstock to Elizabethton to attempt conciliation. On May 25 she succeeded in arriving at the following terms with Mothwurf: (1) all former employees were to register at once for reëmployment; (2) if an employee was not reinstated, reasons were to be given; (3) if the employee was dissatisfied with the reasons, the case was to be taken up with E. T. Wilson, personnel officer of the American Glanzstoff Corporation, who was to act as "an impartial person"; (4) Wilson was to be sole and final judge; (5) the corporation agreed not to discriminate against any former employee because of union affiliations, providing his activities were legitimate and were not carried on at the two plants; and (6) the management agreed to meet the grievance committees of the employees. The terms were presented by Miss Weinstock to a mass meeting of the strikers, who were at first unwilling to accept them, since they seemed to offer no concession whatever. Only when Vice-President W. F. Kelley of the United Textile Workers and President Paul Aymon of the Tennessee Federation of Labor pleaded for the acceptance of the settlement did the strikers vote to return to work under its terms. After the registration for reëmployment a "considerable number" of the former strikers, including the local union officers, failed to get back their positions.

At Gastonia no settlement could be reached. In fact, federal conciliator Charles G. Wood, as soon as he had arrived on the scene of the strike, had announced that "no conciliation is possible until the workers divest themselves from their communistic leaders." [23] But the strikers refused to renounce their leaders; instead, after the destruction of the National Textile Workers' Union headquarters on April 18, they leased a lot on the outskirts of Gastonia, where they erected new union headquarters and a relief store. On this lot there also grew up a tent colony of strikers, after some 200 families had been evicted from company houses. Guards were posted to prevent the recurrence of a raid; more organizers were sent by the National Textile Workers' Union; food was supplied by the Workers' International Relief; and the strikers settled down for a siege. The Loray mill and the other mills in the district, however, began to recruit a new working force and to resume operations gradually. The strike was doomed.

Many newspapermen and public officials attributed this failure to the Communist leadership of the strike, and talk arose that the southern mill owners, while they would never surrender to the Communist-led National Textile Workers' Union, might welcome the coöperation of the more conservative United Textile Workers. A number of observers were skeptical of this alleged change of heart toward the A. F. of L. United Textile Workers, among them Blanshard, who reported that:

. . . *the employers and the editors of the region have fallen back with touching solicitude upon the American Federation of Labor. Although no organizer of the United Textile Workers (representing the federation) is in the Carolinas at this writing [April 15], the newspapers have hailed with large headlines the statements emanating from New York that the regular union is to enter the field. The sincerity of the editors is questionable. In the long record of strikes conducted by the American Federation of Labor unions in Southern mills the orthodox leaders have been attacked with a ferocity almost equal to that now directed against the Communists. "Reds," "foreign agitators," and "emissaries of the Pope" are only a few of the phrases of the opposition which were hurled at the conservative leaders in the great Charlotte strike of 1921 which covered the area now captured by the Communists. The United Textile Workers is now honored in this region because it is weak and absent.*[24]

At any rate, President T. F. McMahon of the United Textile Workers announced the opening of a campaign to unionize the 300,000 textile workers in the South. He was accused by Albert Weisbord and other officers of the National Textile Workers' Union of attempting merely to undermine the organizational work already accomplished by the N.T.W.U. in North Carolina and of desiring to bring the strikers there the same "sell-out" settlement he had achieved at Elizabethton. The animosity between the two rival unions played into the mill owners' hands.

3. Gastonia's reign of terror

After the raid of April 18 the strikers at Gastonia never let up their armed guard over their tent colony, relief store, and union headquarters on the outskirts of the city. Their leader Beal, too, was never allowed, asleep or awake, to be without an armed guard to protect him from any possible violence. In this atmosphere charged with intimidation, hostility, and bitterness the strike at the Loray mill continued throughout the month of May and into early June. Even though their struggle seemed hopeless, the strikers maintained enough picketing to keep the mill from resuming normal operation. In such an atmosphere violence was inevitable, and on June 7 it occurred. Late that afternoon a parade of 150 strikers marched from the tent colony to the Loray mill to demonstrate there and call out the night shift, but it was attacked and dispersed by deputy sheriffs and police. On that same night Chief of Police Aderholt and four other policemen tried to invade the tent colony, and were met by the strikers' guard, which demanded a search warrant. Since the police had none, the strikers refused them entry. A policeman attempted to wrest a gun from one of the strikers, shooting began in the dark, and Aderholt fell mortally wounded. When he died the following day, the local press demanded swift retribution. The police arrested 71 persons; and the Gaston County grand jury indicted 16 of these for murder and seven for assault with a deadly weapon. Of the 16 who were indicted for murder eight were Gastonia strikers, while the rest, including Beal and three women, were either organizers for the National Textile Workers' Union or "outsiders" who had come from the North to assist the strikers. All 16 were held for trial without bail.

The trial was set for July 29, and Governor Gardner of North Carolina assigned Judge M. V. Barnhill to preside. State Solicitor J. G. Carpenter, in charge of the prosecution, announced that the death penalty would be asked for the 13 men defendants, but that southern chivalry would not permit asking the same for the three women. One reporter observed:

Maybe not. But I suspect that their charges were reduced to second-degree murder because the State knew that no jury, Southern, Northern, or Hottentot, would condemn the young women to the electric chair, and that the men, tried on identical charges, would have to be granted the same leniency. It took a long time for this chivalry to be resurrected. Where was it when the legionnaire deputies and the Gastonia police beat Bertha Thompkins in the face with their fists, and clubbed a number of other women strikers, and wrenched their arms, and pulled their hair? Was it chivalrous for displeased hearers to throw rotten eggs at Vera Bush while she was speaking, or for David Clark in the Southern Textile Bulletin *to refer to Miss Bush and Ellen Dawson, along with other strike leaders, as "cattle"?* [25]

The International Labor Defense took charge of the case for the strikers and appointed T. P. Jimison of Charlotte, North Carolina, to head the defense counsel. The first step of the defense was to demand a change of venue on the grounds that a fair trial could not be held in Gastonia; and when, at the opening of court on July 29, Jimison produced affidavits of threats against the defense counsel, Judge Barnhill ruled to move the trial to Charlotte, the seat of Mecklenburg County, 20 miles away, and set August 26 as the date for resumption.

This ruling was hailed by the press throughout the nation as a prelude to a fair trial. In an editorial, "A Just Judge," the *New York Times* wrote:

Mecklenburg is a much larger county, with a much larger city. Charlotte is not only more metropolitan than Gastonia, but has a press distinguished for broad viewpoint and a wish for fair play. Gastonia, where the Chief of Police was murdered, is naturally more stirred by the crime itself than by an attempt to get at the circumstances of guilt. Defense attorneys were abused in public places by citizens of the town, and at least one threat was made to kill one of them. In Charlotte no such local feeling is likely. With Judge Barnhill presiding, and a jury selected which will be undisturbed by the clamor and feeling of neighbors and relatives of the dead man, the trial should be as satisfactorily handled as the friends of the defendants could ask. Under the conditions, change of venue to Charlotte established the good faith of the judge and the State authorities.[26]

Nevertheless, even in Charlotte there was much evidence of prejudice against the defendants; the *Charlotte News*, for example, declared: "The leaders of the National Textile Workers' Union are communists, and are a menace to all that we hold most sacred. They believe in violence, arson, murder. They want to destroy our institutions, our traditions. They are undermining all morality, all religion. But nevertheless they must be given a fair trial, although everyone knows that they deserve to be shot at sunrise." [27] The International Labor Defense charged that another Sacco-Vanzetti case was being prepared by the State, and organized protest meetings and other forms of mass pressure to demand the release of the defendants.

When the trial was resumed on August 26 at Charlotte, a prosecution staff of 10 was assembled, including, besides Solicitor Carpenter, Clyde Hoey, a brother-in-law of Governor Gardner; Major A. L. Bulwinkle, special counsel for the Manville-Jenckes Company; and R. G. Cherry, state commander of the American Legion. Among the defense counsel were Dr. John R. Neal, who had been chief counsel for defense in the Scopes evolution trial at Dayton, Tennessee, and Arthur Garfield Hayes. The selection of the jury required a full week, and when completed it consisted of a steel worker, a news vender, a union carpenter, a grocer, a railroad clerk, a machinist, two cotton-mill workers, and four farmers. On September 5 the taking of evidence began. At the opening of court the prosecution wheeled into the court room a life-size plaster-of-Paris figure of Aderholt draped in a black shroud. Solicitor Carpenter removed the shroud to reveal "an exact reproduction of Aderholt in uniform, including hat and badge, complete to the shoestrings," while Aderholt's widow, dressed in black, sat weeping before the jury.[28] The defense, of course, protested, and Judge Barnhill instantly ordered the figure removed; but an effect had already been produced.

It was the contention of the prosecution that Aderholt's death was the result of a conspiracy which began April 1 when the strike was called at the Loray mill, and it wanted to introduce evidence regarding the communistic and atheistic beliefs of the defendants; Judge Barnhill, however, ruled: "I shall restrict the evidence to what happened on the grounds and will admit no evidence of any conspiracy except to resist the officers on the night of June 7." [29] As the trial continued, it became clear that the State was unable to present evidence of conspiracy, and the defense expected to win acquittal on a plea of self-defense. In fact, Policeman Roach under cross-examination made the very damaging admissions that he had been indicted earlier in the day on June 7 for assaulting a striker, and that he had worn civilian clothes and had possessed no warrant when he had tried to invade the strikers' colony. But unexpectedly on September 9 one of the jurors went violently insane. Judge Barnhill, to the disappointment of the defense, which felt certain of acquittal, declared a mistrial and ordered a new trial for September 30.

The news of the mistrial set loose a reign of terror in Mecklenburg, Gaston, and neighboring counties. On the night of September 9 a mob of 500 men raided strikers' headquarters at Gastonia and Bessemer City. Part of the mob surrounded the boarding house of Ben Wells, C. D. Saylor, and C. M. Lell, all members of the National Textile Workers' Union at Gastonia, kidnaped them, drove to Cabarrus County, and there flogged Wells severely. Another part drove to Charlotte and surrounded the county jail and the offices of the defense counsel, threatening to kill both defendants and counsel. Four attorneys of the defense counsel were forced to spend the night in the lobby of Hotel Charlotte under police protection. Wells, Saylor, and Lell, on their return to Gastonia the next day, filed complaints, and warrants were issued for 14 men, including several Loray mill officials and two or three Gastonia policemen. Only seven of the 14 were held for the grand jury on charges of kidnaping.

Meanwhile, the National Textile Workers' Union had announced a mass meeting for September 14 at South Gastonia. A mob collected to prevent the meeting. When a truck bearing 22 strikers and union members from Bessemer City tried to enter South Gastonia, it was turned back, and 10 or 15 autos set out in pursuit. After a five-mile chase one of the autos blocked the road and the truck was stopped. A volley of shots was fired into the unarmed strikers, and one of them, Mrs. Ella May Wiggins, mother of five children, was instantly killed. The following day Solicitor Carpenter held seven men on charges of murder, six of whom were employed by the Loray mill. Other terroristic acts were committed. On September 18, for example, Cleo Tessnair, an organizer for the National Textile Workers' Union, was kidnaped at King's Mountain by armed vigilantes, taken across the state line into South Carolina, and badly beaten. Several investigations were undertaken by the authorities, but no one was arrested. J. L. Engdahl, national secretary of the International Labor Defense, issued the following statement:

> *The events of Gastonia, the brutal killing of the widow, Mrs. Ella May Wiggins; the absolute Fascist reign of terror, prove our contention that the mill owners, the police and authorities are working hand in hand to terrorize the workers and union organizers, to intimidate the witnesses for the defense in the trial of the sixteen strikers that reopens Sept. 30 in Charlotte, N. C.*[30]

The American Civil Liberties Union called upon Governor Gardner for action against the terrorists, and offered a reward of $1,000 for information leading to the conviction of the person who murdered Ella May Wiggins.

After this sequence of kidnapings, floggings, and shootings, the trial of the defendants in the Aderholt killing reopened on September 30. By this time the prosecution had changed its tactics. It nol-prossed the charges against nine of the 16 defendants, including the three women, and reduced the charges against the remaining seven to second-degree murder. In this way, it not only bettered the chances for conviction, but also made it more difficult for the defense to obtain a favorable, even an unprejudiced, jury: while defendants charged with first-degree murder were allowed 12 peremptory challenges, those charged with second-degree murder had only four, and the defense found its peremptory challenges cut from 168 to 28. Of the seven who faced trial, four, including Beal, were northern organizers. When the jury was completed, it consisted of a non-union industrial worker, a retired wholesale grocer, a rural mail carrier, and nine farmers.

At first the legal issues for the jury were whether there had been a conspiracy, and whether the defendants, if they had fired the shots, were justified. In this second trial, as in the first, it was clear that the State was unable to establish a conspiracy, and once again the self-defense plea of the defendants appeared unshakable; for instance, under cross-examination both Roach and Hord, policemen who had accompanied Aderholt on the night of June 7, admitted that they had found everything peaceful on their arrival at the tent colony, and that they had brought with them, in addition to the regular police equipment, a number of rifles and shotguns.

The State then began to press for the admission of evidence regarding communism, atheism, and race equality. E. T. Cansler, of the prosecution, requested that Judge Barnhill grant the State the same permission granted the State in the Sacco-Vanzetti case and in the Haymarket case of 1886 to introduce the radical views of the defendants as evidence of conspiracy. Moreover, Cansler maintained that Beal, since he was an avowed Communist, was discredited as a witness, and that Carter, another of the defendants, was likewise discredited for having preached race equality. "If teaching racial equality does not tend to impeach a witness, I do not know what would," said Cansler.[31] Judge Barnhill yielded somewhat and permitted the political views of the defendants to be introduced; even more, on October 15 he impeached Mrs. E. S. Miller, wife of one of the defendants, as a witness because she denied the existence of "a Supreme Being who punishes for wrong and rewards for virtues." [32] Attorney Neal of the defense warned Judge Barnhill that the trial was being turned into a "political and heresy hunt."

Nevertheless, the intrusion of political and religious issues continued; and in the final summation on October 18 Solicitor Carpenter referred to the defendants as "devils with hoofs and horns, who threw away their pitchforks for shotguns," and appealed to the jury: "Men, do your duty; do your duty, men, and in the name of God and justice render a verdict that will be emblazoned across the sky of America as an eternal sign that justice has been done." Carpenter emphasized his plea "by lying down on the floor of the court to illustrate some of the testimony, kneeling and praying before the jury and holding the hand of Mrs. Aderholt, the slain chief's widow, who, attired in mourning, sat wiping her eyes before the jury box." [33] The jury was out 57 minutes and brought back a verdict of guilty. Judge Barnhill sentenced the four northern defendants to 17 to 20 years in the state prison; while two of the Gastonia men got 12 to 15 years, and the other, five to seven years. The defense filed notice of appeal and the seven defendants were released on bail totaling $27,000.

While the seven Gastonia defendants were convicted with dispatch and given severe sentences, all endeavors to convict the kidnapers of Wells and the slayers of Mrs. Wiggins ended in failure. The Gaston County grand jury refused to return indictments against the seven men held in the kidnaping of Wells, Saylor, and Lell. Four of the men, it is true, were brought to trial in Cabarrus County; but their counsel contended that Wells, Saylor, and Lell had "kidnaped themselves" in a "plot for advertising purposes," and the jury after 45 minutes brought in a verdict of not guilty. In the Wiggins case the Gaston County grand jury, despite the testimony of more than 75 witnesses, again returned no indictments on the grounds of "insufficient evidence." Protests poured in from every part of the country, and on November 3 Governor Gardner appointed Judge P. A. McElroy to reopen the investigation into the murder of Mrs. Wiggins. After conducting hearings, Judge McElroy issued warrants for the arrest of 16 men, most of them minor bosses and employees of the Loray mill. One of them, Horace Wheeler, was identified by witnesses as the man who fired the fatal shot. Judge McElroy decided to hold the accused men for the new Gaston County grand jury on January 1, 1930. At that time, five out of the 16 men were indicted. At the trial which followed, even though witnesses testified that Wheeler had fired the fatal shot and that the other four defendants had abetted the murder, the jury's verdict was not guilty. Thus, in no instance was anyone convicted of a crime against a striker in Gastonia and the surrounding region. As for the seven men convicted of Aderholt's murder, their sentences were upheld by the Supreme Court of North Carolina on August 20, 1930. In order to avoid serving the sentences, all seven jumped bail; two went into hiding in the United States, and the others, including Beal, escaped to Russia.

4. The United Textile Workers at Marion

The strikes in Gaston County, observed the press everywhere, had been attacked so brutally mainly because of the revolutionary leadership. As yet, the more conservative United Textile Workers had had no real opportunity—except for the inadequate test at Elizabethton—to learn whether its welcome in the South would be any different from that accorded the National Textile Workers' Union.

Consequently, when the United Textile Workers and the A. F. of L. in early summer, 1929, announced a campaign to unionize the southern cotton-mill workers, both the liberal and the conservative press prophesied greater success than that achieved by the radical National Textile Workers' Union. Representative of most newspaper opinion was the following statement by the *New York Times:*

The American Federation of Labor starts out on its self-imposed task of organizing the textile workers of the South with at least one advantage. This consists in the increasingly moderate tone of the Federation's policies, as formulated on various occasions. It should be difficult for any mill owner convincingly to charge Messrs. Green and Woll with Bolshevism. . . . Going to the South with a record for reasonable aims and law-abiding practice, the leaders of the unionizing movement cannot but profit in the public estimation by contrast with high-handed anti-labor methods like those of last Spring at Elizabethton, Tenn. . . .[34]

Accordingly, under the aegis of the United Textile Workers, local unions were organized in a number of southern textile mills, particularly in the Carolinas.

Among the locals thus organized were two at Marion, North Carolina—at the Marion Manufacturing Company and the Clinchfield mill. The growing discontent of the workers at these two plants brought Alfred Hoffman, southern organizer for the United Textile Workers, to Marion. He listened to complaints regarding a 12-hour day and the discharge of workers for union affiliation, but advised against a strike at that time, since he could obtain no financial aid from the national organization. In opposition to his advice, however, the workers at the Marion mill presented to its president, R. W. Baldwin, a list of demands calling for the 10-hour day and 55-hour week with no cut in wages, the reinstatement of 22 workers who had been discharged for union activity, and the recognition of the workers' grievance committee. Upon Baldwin's refusal to consider these demands, the entire force of 650 walked out on July 11. Two weeks later the 900 workers at the Clinchfield mill went on strike for similar demands, and the president, B. M. Hart, said: "I cannot see that there is any difference between this so-called conservative union and the Communist union in Gastonia." [35]

Both plants employed the customary measures to suppress the strikes. For instance, an injunction was obtained not only restraining strikers from assembling in the Marion mill village, but even restraining Hoffman from persuading strikers to picket.[36] Moreover, after an attempt to reopen the Clinchfield mill with strike-breakers failed, the National Guard was sent to Marion. There was little violence until August 31, when Clinchfield strikers prevented a non-union worker from moving into a house in the mill village and drove deputy sheriffs away with clubs and stones. Because of this, 74 strikers were arrested on the charge of "a rebellion against the constituted authority of the State of North Carolina." Soon afterwards, on September 11, a settlement was made at both mills through the mediation of an Asheville banker, and the United Textile Workers called off the strikes. This settlement granted the workers a 55-hour week, though with a corresponding reduction in pay, and with the understanding that at the end of six weeks the workers were to vote on the advisability of returning to the 60-hour week. In the meantime, there were to be no discriminations against the workers for union activity, except that Baldwin was given the right not to reëmploy 14 of the strikers.

On their return to work, the employees at the Marion mill found that not 14, but 102, of their number had been refused reinstatement by Baldwin. This breach of faith and, what was more, further efforts to make them disband their union heightened the dissatisfaction of the workers with the settlement of September 11. Apprehending another strike, Baldwin requested Sheriff O. F. Adkins on the afternoon of October 1 to come to the plant at the change of shifts. During the evening Sheriff Adkins and a number of deputies arrived, all heavily armed. For several hours, according to many accounts, the workers suffered provocation and abuse from the deputies and foremen.[37] Finally, at about 1:30 in the morning, the workers shut off the power and walked out. For the next five or six hours they waited outside the plant in order to notify the day shift of the strike. Toward 7 o'clock in the morning a crowd of 250 strikers had collected opposite the mill gate, where Sheriff Adkins, the deputies, and the foremen were lined up. When the crowd refused to disperse at his command, Sheriff Adkins exploded some tear gas into it. A striker attacked Adkins with a cane, a deputy fired, and the striker fell mortally wounded. Thereupon the deputies fired volley after volley into the crowd of unarmed strikers. By the time the shooting ended six strikers were killed and 18 wounded. Only one deputy sheriff was slightly injured; the others were untouched.

The news of the slaughter aroused the state. Baldwin, it is true, seemed unconcerned about the shooting, for on the following day he said in an interview for the *Asheville Citizen*:

I understand sixty or seventy-five shots were fired in Wednesday's fight. If this is true, there are thirty or thirty-five of the bullets accounted for. I think the officers are damned good marksmen. If I ever organize an army they can have jobs with me. I read that the death of each soldier in the World War consumed more than five tons of lead. Here we have less than five pounds and these casualties. A good average, I call it.[38]

Governor Gardner sent Judge W. F. Harding to conduct an inquiry. On October 3 Sheriff Adkins and 14 of the deputies and foremen were arrested on charges of murder, but Adkins and six others were immediately released. The remaining eight deputies were held for trial under bond of $3,000 each, which was furnished by Baldwin. Upon being released, Sheriff Adkins issued warrants against 32 strikers on charges of insurrection and riot.

With an injunction against picketing still in force, about 100 of the 650 employees at the Marion mill continued to work. As a stubborn struggle appeared to be developing, Vice-President F. G. Gorman of the United Textile Workers came to Marion to make overtures for a new settlement, but Baldwin declared that he would have nothing to do with unions. It was his intention to recruit a new force of non-union workers. First, however, it was necessary for him to rid the mill village of the strikers and their families. On October 7 he started legal action to evict them from the company houses. A month later the first evictions, involving 20 families, were carried out by Sheriff Adkins. At the same time more than 100 strikers were notified through letters sent by the Rev. S. J. McAbee that they were dropped from the rolls of the East Marion Missionary Baptist Church. By every means possible, the strikers were to be driven from the mill village.

While the mill was in this way gradually being manned with non-union workers, the cases against the strikers charged with "riot" and "rebellion" opened in court. Hoffman and three of the strikers were first selected to stand trial on the rebellion charge. The evidence, however, was so insufficient that Judge G. V. Cowper, after the State presented its case, pronounced a verdict of non-suit without waiting for the argument of the defense. At once the four defendants were arraigned on the charge of riot, and on

November 30 a verdict of guilty was returned. Because of his poor health, Hoffman was sentenced to only 30 days in the county jail and fined $1,000; the other three got six months on the public roads. In the meantime, the trial of the eight deputies charged with second-degree murder had been postponed until December 10. When it opened, the evidence produced against the deputies was damaging. A reporter for the *Asheville Citizen,* who had been an eye-witness of the shooting, testified that all the shots had come from the deputies and that he had seen no gun among the strikers. Furthermore, Sheriff Adkins admitted that he had deputized six non-union employees at the Marion mill, one of whom, Jim Owens, a defendant in the trial, was at the time out under $2,000 bond for shooting up the union headquarters. At no time did the defense deny that the deputies had fired the fatal shots; it rested its case on the plea that the defendants were officers of the law who had acted to suppress a riot. On December 22 the jury brought in a verdict of not guilty. Thus the strike at Marion under the guidance of the United Textile Workers was crushed in much the same manner as had been that at Gastonia. Against the anti-union policy of the southern mill owners the United Textile Workers, affiliated with the conservative A. F. of L., had fared no better than the National Textile Workers' Union, affiliated with the radical Red Trade Union International.

5. *The goose that laid the golden egg*

No matter how meager the concrete gains of the unions in the southern textile strikes of 1929, it had to be admitted that the principles of trade-unionism had got a foothold in the hostile South. Even though nearly all the strikes had been either badly defeated or settled by compromises little better than defeat, there remained nuclei of union members throughout the cotton-growing states. The United Textile

Workers, as a result of the southern campaign, acquired perhaps 25,000 members, and in 1929 could report 19 local unions in North Carolina, 11 in South Carolina, seven in Tennessee, seven in Georgia, and four in Alabama.[39] What was more, the textile workers of the South, despite their well-advertised tractability, had shown themselves ready to fight for improved working conditions. "The current strikes in the textile South have dispelled an illusion of the American industrial enterpriser. This was that the poor whites of the South, unlike labor elsewhere, never knew when they were put upon. They are, as has been widely advertised by southern chambers of commerce and power companies, 100 per cent native born; they are Protestants and religious; they do have in the main a rural background; but they are not utterly passive." [40] Indeed, the southern textile interests began to realize that they were "in danger of killing the goose that laid the golden egg," that is, the advantage they held over the North of lower labor costs and fewer labor troubles. Whereas the strikes, with the exception of that at Gastonia, arose originally over questions of wages, hours, the stretch-out, and other working conditions, in almost every instance they were converted finally into conflicts over union recognition. In other words, the southern textile workers were demanding the right to collective bargaining, rather than "kindly paternalism" or "philanthropy."

The smallness of the gains secured by unionism among the southern cotton-mill workers could be attributed in part to the powerful opposition of the textile interests, through whose influence many agencies united in putting down the strikes. Strikers were readily branded by the press as "radicals," and labor organizers as "foreign agitators." Wherever a strike broke out, state troops were immediately sent; and to this show of force were added police, deputy sheriffs, and bands of armed vigilantes. If this show of force failed to break the strike, then the strikers found themselves evicted from company-owned houses and villages, and saw the mills supplied with an entire new force of strike-breakers.

Moreover, there could be little doubt of the use of the courts to suppress the strikes. Not only were blanket injunctions issued to prohibit picketing and assemblies of strikers, but also a distinct lack of impartiality was shown in the handling of arrests arising from violence. In six major cases of violence directed against strikers not one conviction was obtained: the kidnapers of Hoffman and McGrady at Elizabethton on April 4 were never brought to trial; no indictments were returned against the mobs that wrecked the headquarters of the National Textile Workers' Union at Gastonia on April 18 and that raided union headquarters on September 9; no arrests were made in the kidnaping of Cleo Tessnair from King's Mountain; and verdicts of not guilty were voted in the trials of the kidnapers of Wells, Saylor, and Lell, of the murderers of Mrs. Wiggins, and of the deputies who killed six strikers and wounded 18 others at Marion on October 2. On the other hand, both the major cases of violence involving strikers resulted in convictions and severe sentences; thus the four strikers at Marion received sentences of 30 days in jail to six months of hard labor for "rioting and resisting officers," while seven strikers were convicted of the slaying of Aderholt and sentenced to terms of five to 20 years in the state prison. In an editorial summarizing the textile strikes, the *Greensboro Daily News* wrote: "In no case has a court found blood guilt when the blood shed was that of a striker or strike sympathizer; no officer or private citizen has been convicted of violation of law following any act of violence, whether pitched battle, assassination, assault, mob action in daytime or night time. *Per contra*, in no case has a group of strikers or strike sympathizers failed of the law's condemnation. . . ." [41]

The opposition of the employers to unionism, however, was not confined to the South alone, and was to be expected. Other more important factors contributed to the defeat of the southern textile strikes, factors that produced the general backwardness of all labor organization in the South. Chief among these factors was the plentiful reserve of surplus labor, with the result that workers could be obtained for any job under almost any conditions and trade-union members could be readily replaced. Furthermore, southern workers were, for the most part, unskilled, and therefore lacked the bargaining power which is essential to effective organization. In addition, poverty and instability hindered southern labor from becoming good trade-union material; for unless there was a fairly stable working force that could pay dues regularly, it was impossible to build up a treasury, develop responsible union officers, and educate the workers in the principles and methods of unionism.

Ignorance of these principles and methods, moreover, made the southern workers easy prey for propaganda directed against collective action; it was not difficult to arouse their prejudice against the North, their distrust of "outsiders," and their racial animosity. In particular, the racial problem, the attitude toward the Negro, involved great danger for the southern labor movement. Unless the Negro were unionized simultaneously with the white, he depressed wages, increased the potential labor reserve, acted as strike-breaker, and served to divert the white worker from the economic to the race issue. And yet, there was little prospect of uniting both races in a labor organization; for, while the National Textile Workers' Union admitted both Negro and white to its membership, the much more powerful United Textile Workers and the A. F. of L., except for occasional well-sounding resolutions, steadily evaded the issue. To the dangers of race prejudice and sectionalism was also added the confusion caused by southern "paternalism," by which part of the labor force was bound to the employers and rifts were created in the ranks of the workers. Considering all these factors, therefore, it was no easy task that the trade-unions faced in their attempts to organize the South.

Notwithstanding the difficulties to be overcome, the American labor movement in general—and the A. F. of L. and the United Textile Workers in particular—could not avoid undertaking the unionization of the South in order to protect its achievements in the rest of the country. Otherwise, the differentials in labor costs would force employers everywhere to crush the organizations of their workers so as to be able to meet the competition of the South. Consequently, it was partly for self-protection that the United Textile Workers, at the conclusion of the southern textile strikes, reiterated its intention to unionize the southern cotton-mill workers by means of a campaign whose immediate objectives were to be the 48-hour week, higher wages, and the abolition of night work. Southern textile labor, because of the recent strikes, appeared ready for such a campaign:

The impression seems to gain also in the South that it will be difficult to combat the advance of organized labor there. The employes in the textile industry are learning, as a result of the discussion of the strikes, that their wages are lower than those paid in the North; their temper is more congenial toward organization than formerly; and it is even possible for their attitude toward Northern organizers to become more friendly if relief does not come from other sources. If the owners of Southern textile mills have been able in the past to justify the low wages which they pay and to point to evidence of general industrial content, it will be more difficult to do so now or in the future. The recent strikes have been the means of educating the employes, employers, and the public generally on the subject. . . .[42]

Thus the spontaneous uprisings of the textile workers in the Carolinas and Tennessee, the organizational activities of the National Textile Workers' Union at Gastonia, and the subsequent entry of the United Textile Workers in the field made the first significant breach in southern anti-unionism.

X. LONGSHOREMEN ON THE WEST COAST

1. *The Blue Book*

Behind the longshoremen's strike on the west coast during the spring and summer of 1934—a strike which spread rapidly to the other maritime crafts, paralyzed shipping for nearly three months, and culminated in the great San Francisco general strike—lay principally the question of union control of hiring halls. For the preceding 15 years the longshoremen of the west coast, particularly at San Francisco, the chief Pacific port, had been hired through a company union, the Longshoremen's Association of San Francisco, known as the Blue Book. During an unsuccessful strike in 1919 a group of gang bosses had organized this as a schismatic union within the International Longshoremen's Association, and it had been promptly recognized by the Waterfront Employers' Union. Ever since, only holders of the Blue Book could get stevedore jobs, and, with a few exceptions on the northwest coast, the International Longshoremen's Association died away in the Pacific ports. So large, in fact, was the membership of the Blue Book that in 1929 the Central Labor Council of San Francisco accepted it as a "transformed" company union, but expelled it in 1931 when it was seen to be unregenerated.

Toward the end of 1932 the long-growing discontent with the Blue Book was focalized by a mimeographed bulletin, the *Waterfront Worker*, issued by a group of longshoremen, including a minority of Communist and other militant elements. Agitation developed for a new union which would be truly representative of the longshoremen, but no progress was made until the passage of the National Industrial Recovery Act several months later. Under the impetus of Article 7a of the N.I.R.A., which specifically guaranteed to workers the right to collective bargaining through representatives of their own choosing, the longshoremen in the Pacific ports joined the International Longshoremen's Association, affiliated with the American Federation of Labor. In July and August, 1933, nearly 95 per cent of the longshoremen deserted the Blue Book for the I.L.A.

Underlying this sudden movement to the I.L.A. was the acute dissatisfaction of the longshoremen with the conditions of their labor. An excess supply of labor in the ports produced casual and insufficient employment, long and often fruitless waits on the docks, unfair practices and graft in the procuring of jobs, and low earnings for the bulk of the longshoremen. While perhaps one-fourth of the longshoremen, those who received preference in the distribution of jobs, earned $40 a week or more, the remaining three-fourths averaged only $10 to $12 a week, even less. Boris Stern of the U. S. Bureau of Labor Statistics found in November, 1933: "In normal times, only a small part of this supply [of longshore labor] is earning what may be considered a decent wage. Probably a larger proportion is earning a subsistence wage, i.e., just about enough to make ends meet on a comparatively low standard of living. The balance is always on the brink of starvation and depends largely on outside support, chiefly charity. At the present time a very conservative estimate would probably place more than 50 percent of all the longshoremen on the relief rolls." [1] The longshoremen pointed with particular bitterness to the heavy subsidies that the shipping companies were receiving from the federal government: the Dollar Steamship Company, for example, under the Merchant Marine Act of 1928, was given ocean mail contracts totaling $15,896,516 for one line and $12,199,-336 for another during a period of 10 years with only 26 trips each per year required.[2] Yet at the same time the shipping companies kept the bulk of longshore wages at a starvation level.

More important to the men than the low wages was the unfairness which, they felt, resulted from the system of hiring halls then in force. These halls were the pool rooms, saloons, and cheap restaurants where the longshoremen gathered between periods of work. When a ship arrived in port, word was sent to the hiring halls and the hiring foreman (often the proprietor) would select a gang for the job. Under this system favoritism and discrimination were common: "The men have been unorganized for the last nineteen years, during which time employers have controlled these hiring halls, and have permitted vicious practices to creep in, such as permitting saloons, money lending and gambling schemes in the halls, and the men who patronized these saloons, gambling devices and money-lending schemes received the bulk of employment."[3] To the chaos caused by the irregularity of work, which depended on the weather and the vagaries of ship arrivals and departures, were thus added the dishonest and discriminatory practices resulting from the arbitrary power of the hiring foreman:

It is obvious that the hiring foreman occupies a position of the greatest importance on the water front. It is largely left to him to decide who shall be employed and who shall be left behind. He is seldom hampered in his choice, especially in regard to the more casual men. He can take them or reject them. He can call them to-day and ignore them to-morrow. It would indeed be strange if such concentration of autocratic power in the hands of a single person controlling the jobs of so many men did not result in some cases in the abuse of this power. This may be as mild as the acceptance of an occasional drink or a cigar, or it may go so far as to amount to a systematic sharing by the foreman in the earnings of the longshoreman as payment for the job. . . .[4]

The longshoremen maintained that union control, in place of employer control, of the hiring halls not only would put an end to the abuses of favoritism and discrimination, but also would rotate the available jobs and produce a more equitable division of earnings.

When the I.L.A. saw that practically all the west coast longshoremen, 12,000 in number, had become members, it undertook to alleviate some of the grievances of the men. In December, 1933, through the mediation of George Creel, National Recovery Administration director for California, negotiations were conducted between the I.L.A. and the waterfront employers. As a result, wages were increased from 75 to 85 cents an hour, and a verbal agreement was reached for joint control of the hiring halls, with the submission of disputes to whatever arbitration procedure would be set up by the Shipping Code of the N.R.A., then being formulated. However, this agreement was not satisfactory to the rank and file, who insisted that any sharing of the control of hiring halls would lead ultimately to the domination by the employers, the blacklisting of active union members, and the return of all the old abuses. There developed a triangular conflict among the employers, the conservative officials of the I.L.A., and the militant rank and file. Although the officials of the I.L.A. were willing to compromise on the question of the hiring halls, the rank and file refused to accept anything less than complete union control and the consequent destruction of the Blue Book.

The distrust of the longshoremen for the officials of the

I.L.A. led them to call a west coast rank-and-file convention in February, 1934, to which paid officers of the union could not qualify as delegates. The convention remained in session for about 10 days and adopted a number of demands: (1) recognition of the union; (2) union control of hiring halls; (3) a wage increase from 85 cents to $1 an hour, with $1.50 for overtime work; (4) a 30-hour week; and (5) a coastwide agreement with a uniform expiration date. Despite their exclusion from the convention as delegates, the union officials succeeded in winning the control of an Executive Board, which was to conduct negotiations with the shipowners. This conservative control, however, was neutralized by the adoption of a resolution that all settlement proposals were to be submitted to a rank-and-file vote for final decision. It was apparent that the longshoremen were suspicious of the intentions of the union officials and dubious of their methods; in fact, they ousted Lee Holman, district president of the I.L.A. in San Francisco, from the union for certain statements made by him against the militant elements in the rank and file.

In accordance with the decision of the convention, representatives of the I.L.A. entered into negotiations with the shipowners on March 5. The demands of the longshoremen were rejected outright. As no results were forthcoming, the San Francisco Bay district of the I.L.A. voted to strike beginning March 23 unless a settlement would be reached. Other locals along the Pacific coast voted similarly. On March 22, however, the day preceding the strike date, President Roosevelt sent a telegram to William J. Lewis, president of the west coast district of the I.L.A., requesting the longshoremen to postpone their strike until a fact-finding committee could make a report and the federal government could take due action. Because of the President's appeal, the strike was called off, and on March 28 new negotiations began.

The only product of these negotiations was an abortive agreement concluded secretly on April 3 between Lewis and the waterfront employers for joint control of the hiring halls, but it fell through because of a disagreement about dates. One Communist observer charged that "one of the prime objectives in postponing the struggle was to hold it until the college terms would end, so that a plentiful supply of student scabs might be obtained." [5]

After six weeks of fruitless waiting, it became clear to the longshoremen that neither the negotiations nor the President's fact-finding committee were producing any concrete results, and on May 7 the San Francisco local of the I.L.A. voted unanimously to strike on May 9. Telegrams from the U. S. Department of Labor and from Joseph P. Ryan, international president of the I.L.A., urged the men not to strike. Nevertheless, the longshoremen at San Francisco quit work on the appointed date, and Portland, Seattle, and other ports followed. Notwithstanding the fear of the conservative union officials that the strike would be broken by the thousands of unemployed for whom 85 cents an hour meant high wages, by May 11 the walkout had spread along the entire coast, and shipping was at a standstill. The only exception was Los Angeles, where the traditional open-shop policy prevented the development of a complete strike.

Evidently working conditions among marine labor were as unsatisfactory as among the longshoremen, for within a few days sympathetic walkouts broke out in the various maritime crafts, which immediately set up demands of their own. As ships touched port, entire crews deserted to join the longshoremen. The first maritime unions to call strikes were the Marine Workers' Industrial Union and the International Seamen's Union; the latter, affiliated with the A. F. of L., included the Sailors' Union of the Pacific; the Pacific Coast Marine Firemen, Oilers, Watertenders and Wipers' Association; and the Marine Cooks and Stewards' Association of the Pacific Coast. Other crafts quickly followed: the Marine Engineers' Beneficial Association; the Independent Union of Officers and Engineers; the West Coast Local no. 90 of the National Organization of Masters, Mates and Pilots of America; and the Ship Clerks' Association. Each submitted a list of grievances for redress: complaints about wages, hours, poor food aboard ships, discrimination, and, above all, forced membership in company unions. The shipowners refused to deal with the representatives of any of these striking marine crafts.

The strike leaders faced two critical problems. First, it was necessary to keep the various crafts unified. To prevent splits among them was not an easy task, since in previous strikes there had been strike-breaking by one craft against another; thus in 1919 the seamen had scabbed on the longshoremen, and in 1921 the longshoremen on the seamen. In order to attain unity, a Joint Strike Committee of 50 was formed, with Harry R. Bridges, of the San Francisco local of the I.L.A., as chairman. Each of the 10 unions involved in the strike, both maritime and shoreside, sent five delegates to the Joint Strike Committee, and all agreed to return to work only on a joint settlement for all. The second problem was to render the strike steadily more effective. In this problem the Teamsters' Union had a strategic position; for even if the employers succeeded in unloading the ship cargoes on the piers, they would be helpless unless the cargo could be moved from the piers to the warehouses, and from the warehouses to the railroad yards. Consequently, the strike of the longshoremen and marine workers achieved a firmer intrenchment when the Teamsters' Union, against the plea of Michael Casey, the local president, voted as early as May 13 not to haul scab cargo from the docks. The teamsters continued, however, to haul all freight from the warehouses, provided that the employers could get it there. Other locals of the Teamsters' Union followed the action of the San Francisco local. By the end of May the Joint Strike Committee was assured of both unity and effectiveness in the strike.

As soon as the strike of the longshoremen began, the waterfront employers advertised for strike-breakers. Several hundred were hired, and were kept in ships fitted out for the purpose. Many of the strike-breakers came from the universities. In fact, the strikers referred to the University of California, where Bill Ingram, the football coach, recruited students to act as strike-breakers, as a "scab incubator." [6] At the University of Washington a committee of students, appointed by President Hugo Winkenwerder to investigate the relation of the students to the strike, reported:

The first place employers went to obtain strike-breakers was the University of Washington. All fraternity houses were contacted and students requested to cut their classes and participate in a labor difficulty of which they had absolutely no knowledge. Employers guaranteed them board and room and wages higher than those offered longshoremen. Students were provided free taxi service to work. More enterprising employers sent boats to the University docks to pick up student strike-breakers, but the Dean of Men prevented the boats from docking.

Once on the waterfront, student strike-breakers were housed in boats tied to the docks. Excellent food, brand-new sheets and blankets and first-class Negro valet service convinced many that the life of the longshoreman was not so bad as they had believed.[7]

Other strike-breakers were also recruited, especially among the unemployed and the Negroes.

In the meantime, the strike continued to spread both geographically and by crafts. The *New York Times* reported

25,000 out by May 27. Along the entire Pacific coast shipping was tied up. In every port ships lay idle, unable to unload or take on cargo. Such cargo as was discharged remained piled up on the docks, since the teamsters refused to haul it to the warehouses. Cargo collected in ship holds, on docks, in warehouses; but there was no movement. Other industries were affected: lumber mills in Oregon had to shut down because of the shipping blockade. For the first time the west coast shipowners faced a solid front of all marine labor and a total paralysis of all shipping. The San Francisco port alone was losing $100,000 a day because of the strike.

2. The battle of Rincon Hill

Soon after the strike began, Assistant Secretary of Labor E. F. McGrady arrived at San Francisco to assist in the attempts at mediation. He succeeded in bringing together employers and labor leaders for a conference on May 19, but no agreement could be reached on the control of hiring halls. Upon the request of McGrady and other federal negotiators, President Ryan of the I.L.A. flew from New York to the west coast to induce the longshoremen to submit to arbitration. On May 28 Ryan proposed a settlement to the waterfront employers, the terms of which called for recognition of the I.L.A. without, however, the closed-shop provision; joint control of hiring halls; and arbitration of wages and hours. What Ryan failed to comprehend in submitting this settlement plan was the temper of the longshoremen. The strikers refused to accept any compromise whatever on the hiring-hall question, and despite Ryan's tour of the ports to plead for the peace plan, they instantly and crushingly rejected it. By mass picketing the strikers continued to keep shipping tied up. Even though at San Francisco between 300 and 500 strike-breakers were at work under police protection, such cargo as was unloaded could not, because of the teamsters' sympathetic action, be moved from the piers. In fact, on June 12 the teamsters decided not to haul scab cargo anywhere. The Portland and Seattle harbors were also locked tight.

Negotiations continued in secret until June 16, when Ryan —contrary to the decision of the February convention that no settlement was to be authentic and binding unless voted on by the entire body of strikers—signed an agreement with the Waterfront Employers' Union in the office of Mayor Angelo J. Rossi of San Francisco. The terms were almost exactly the same as those of the May 28 proposal, including again joint control of the hiring halls. Moreover, there was no provision for the 13,000 marine workers who had joined the strike of the longshoremen. When, therefore, mass meetings of the strikers were called on June 17 at San Francisco, Portland, Tacoma, and other ports to consider Ryan's settlement, it was unanimously repudiated. What was more, Ryan was booed off the platform at San Francisco; and the strikers decided to take the right to negotiate away from the Executive Board, made up of I.L.A. officials, and turn it over to the rank-and-file Joint Strike Committee. Front-page announcements appeared in the newspapers that an agreement had been signed and that the strike was over; nevertheless, picketing went on and cargoes remained unmoved. The rift between the officialdom and the rank and file of the I.L.A. grew more apparent every day.

As it became clear that the strikers would not submit to any arbitration of the crucial question of hiring-hall control, the San Francisco Chamber of Commerce invited the Industrial Association, which represented the principal industrial and financial interests throughout the city, to assist in opening the port. According to the Chamber of Commerce, $40,000,000 worth of goods was piled up in ship holds and on piers, while an equal amount was diverted to other ports because of the strike. The Industrial Association accepted the invitation and on June 23 announced definite plans to open the port by force if necessary. Trucks were hired, a warehouse leased, strike-breakers and armed guards imported. Chief of Police W. J. Quinn, after a conference with representatives of the Industrial Association, the State Harbor Board, and the Chamber of Commerce, declared: "If necessary every available police officer in San Francisco will be detailed to the waterfront to give necessary protection and prevent violence from either side." [8] On the same day Acting Governor Frank F. Merriam of California said: "This strike isn't going to last all Summer," and "If the State cannot settle through negotiations, I shall take steps to force the issue and open up State property on the water front to the resumption of commerce." [9] To the strikers these pronouncements portended a concerted attack upon them by employers and the public authorities.

While the Industrial Association prepared to break the strike, federal arbitrators and labor officials continued their efforts to settle the dispute before violence was resorted to. Under the provisions of the Wagner Labor Disputes Bill, President Roosevelt appointed a National Longshoremen's Board of three—Archbishop Edward J. Hanna of San Francisco, Assistant Secretary of Labor McGrady, and O. K. Cushing, a San Francisco attorney—to investigate the strike and, upon the request of both sides, to arbitrate. The waterfront employers were willing to arbitrate, but not the strikers, who held to their original decisions not to compromise on the control of hiring halls and not to settle unless all the maritime crafts were included. President Andrew Furuseth of the International Seamen's Union came to San Francisco to urge arbitration upon the strikers. On June 27 the Joint Strike Committee met with Mayor Rossi, Furuseth, and

McGrady, who importuned the strikers to return to work under the terms of the June 16 pact. It was no use. On two points the strikers remained unyielding: they believed that anything less than absolute union control of hiring halls and a joint coastwide settlement meant actual defeat for them. When these new attempts at mediation failed, Managing Director Albert Boynton of the Industrial Association announced that the drive to open the port would begin immediately. However, at the request of Mayor Rossi the drive was postponed to the noon of July 3.

At the scheduled time the Industrial Association made its first effort to transport goods from the docks to a warehouse near the passenger terminal of the Southern Pacific Coast Line. A barricade of freight cars of the state-owned Belt Line Railway was drawn around Pier 38, from which a lane of police cars was formed to the warehouse. In this safety lane trucks moved with the cargo. On the outside of the lane the strikers were attacked by police with clubs, guns, and tear gas. The strikers retaliated with bricks and railroad spikes. All afternoon the fighting continued. One striker was killed and a score badly injured. At the close of the day the Industrial Association declared: "The port is opened. It will stay open." [10] For the following day, since it was Independence Day, a truce was declared, but cargo moving was to be resumed on Thursday, July 5. Acting Governor Merriam, on July 4, ordered the National Guard to be ready to enter the waterfront area; and the State Board of Harbor Commissioners, in charge of the Belt Line Railway, which connected all the waterfront piers with the terminals of the transcontinental railroads, got ready 14 freight cars to handle cargoes of the Matson Navigation Company.

The resumption of cargo transportation on July 5 brought a renewal of violence. The entire police force of San Francisco was ordered to the waterfront. The first attack occurred in the morning, when police charged 2,000 strikers who had gathered to stop the procession of trucks from Pier 38 to the Industrial Association's warehouse. After an hour and a half of fighting the strikers were dispersed. But even fiercer fighting broke out in the afternoon as police tried to drive strikers from Rincon Hill, overlooking the waterfront and the Belt Line Railway. The battle raged all afternoon, strikers' spikes and bricks against the guns, clubs, tear gas, and vomiting gas of the police. Cargo was moved, but only after much bloodshed. It was "bloody Thursday" in San Francisco. Two strikers and one sympathizer were killed, and at least 115 strikers, policemen, and bystanders were wounded seriously enough to be taken to hospitals for treatment. Immediately after the battle the Joint Strike Committee wired to President Roosevelt:

Pickets on San Francisco waterfront being attacked by police. Vomiting gas, revolvers, projectiles and hand grenades being used freely. Reign of terror inaugurated at the request of the Industrial Association, which is attempting to open the port.

The undersigned committee protests most vigorously against this uncalled-for action by the police. As American citizens we urge you to take necessary action to eliminate this terrorism and bring pressure to bear on the ship owners, who are attempting to crush our unions and are fighting us with money borrowed from the government.[11]

The corner of Steuart and Mission Streets, where the two strikers had been shot down, was banked with flowers by the longshoremen and was chalked with the inscription: "Two men killed here, murdered by police."

That night Acting Governor Merriam pronounced the San Francisco waterfront in a "state of riot," and on his orders 1,700 National Guardsmen marched in. The Embarcadero, the street along the waterfront, was enclosed with barbed wire, machine-gun nests were set up, armored cars patrolled the area. Admission was by pass only, and the troops were instructed to shoot to kill. Under this military protection, freight was moved steadily from waterfront to warehouse, although there it was again stranded by the refusal of the Teamsters' Union to handle scab cargo. Notwithstanding the freight movements under the bayonets of the National Guard, there was no loosening of the grip on shipping. The strike was still solid. About 250 ships lay idle along the coast from San Diego to Seattle. The cost to the west coast shipping lines had risen to $1,000,000 a day.[12] The Industrial Association undertook further action to break the deadlock. It sent letters to employers throughout the city soliciting funds for crushing the strike:

The port of San Francisco must be opened immediately. We must retrieve control of our waterfront from the Communistic leadership of the Longshoremen's Union and restore to the people of this community the security to which they are entitled in the transaction of their business and daily affairs.

An adequate sum of money must be made available at once to the Industrial Association of San Francisco to permit it to meet the responsibilities it has assumed in this public service. The need is urgent and imperative.[13]

In addition, the public was prepared for the contemplated attack on the strikers through a series of full-page advertisements in the San Francisco newspapers. The shipowners stated in these again and again their willingness to arbitrate and asserted that the strikers' rejection of the June 16 "settlement" was the result of Communist agitation.

In the meantime, San Francisco was stirred by the funeral procession in honor of the two strikers who had been killed on "bloody Thursday." Fifteen thousand strikers and representatives of local trade-unions marched in the simple, but impressive parade up Market Street. There could be little doubt of the sentiment aroused in the workingmen of San Francisco by the brutality employed to open the port. From outside the city and state, too, protests were sent in. President Green of the A. F. of L. telegraphed to Mayor Rossi protesting against the use of the police to assist in strike-breaking. To this Mayor Rossi replied: "The police of San Francisco were never the aggressors. They fought only to protect life and property and to suppress rioting and violence." [14] However, many observers disagreed with Mayor Rossi's assertion; one eye-witness, for example, reported:

> . . . I am led to conclude, not only that Mayor Rossi is inaccurate in saying that "the police were never the aggressors"—as has been said above, I know that to be untrue—but also that the actual story of "bloody Thursday" would show that the police were always the aggressors. "They fought," says Mr. Rossi, "only to protect life and property and to suppress rioting and violence." The facts are that they damaged property at the Seaboard and at half a dozen other points along the Embarcadero; that they destroyed life at Steuart and Mission, if nowhere else; that repeatedly they were guilty of initiating violence; and that such rioting as occurred was the direct product of their own aggression.[15]

It was clear that the news of the police violence had increased the sympathy of the workers of San Francisco for the strikers.

Because of this sympathy, there began to spread through the body of San Francisco labor a growing desire to support the longshore and marine strikes. It is true that after the battles of "bloody Thursday" President Ryan of the I.L.A.

issued a statement to the press that denounced equally the strike leaders and the employers:

There are three elements which are preventing the settlement of the strike. One is that the Communist party, led by Harry Bridges, is in control of the San Francisco situation.

Secondly, our longshoremen, who had nerve enough to strike on May 9 to rid themselves of this hiring hall system, have had foisted on their shoulders a group of other marine craft, who did not have nerve enough to go on strike with the longshoremen.

The third reason is that the employers have delegated their case to a small committee of their own group to handle for them, and this small committee is dominated by the Industrial Association of San Francisco, an American plan organization, and the Manufacturers Association of Los Angeles, an avowed "open shop" organization.

These two groups will not let the steamship companies settle, and the Communists and marine craft will not allow our association to settle.[16]

But Ryan, by this time thoroughly discredited among the strikers, was practically alone in his attack upon the strike leaders. In fact, a number of trade-unions threatened sympathy strikes. The machinists and welders decided not to work on ships with scab crews. More important, the powerful Teamsters' Union on July 8 voted 1,220 to 217 to go on strike July 12 if there was no sign of a definite settlement between the waterfront employers and the strikers. On both sides—capital and labor—the struggle was rapidly being broadened. In an attempt to avert the impending widespread conflict, the National Longshoremen's Board opened public hearings on July 9, and begged both sides to submit to arbitration. Neither side, however, was willing to yield on the decisive question of hiring-hall control. The basis of the struggle remained unchanged.

3. General strike

Even as early as June the feeling had spread among the trade-union members in San Francisco that, unless a fair settlement was reached in the longshore and marine strikes, a general strike would be unavoidable. It was not only necessary to protest against the use of police for strike-breaking, it was also necessary to protect the very existence of the trade-unions against the developing employer-offensive. If the longshoremen and marine workers were defeated, then the trade-unions foresaw a series of attacks to crush them one after another. It was not safe, the trade-unions believed, to let the longshoremen and marine workers alone face the combination of industry and finance represented in the Industrial Association. Accordingly, in the middle of June the Painters Local 1158 circulated among all the other A. F. of L. local unions a letter requesting the support of a general strike if it proved necessary. This action was followed on June 20 by the vote of the Machinists Local 68 to join such a strike when called.

At first the San Francisco Central Labor Council, composed of the most conservative trade-union elements, underestimated the growing demand for a general strike and failed to realize the widespread sympathy among the workingmen for the longshore and marine strikes. In fact, on June 23 it passed a resolution condemning the "Communist" leadership of these strikes. After the battles of July 5, however, it could no longer ignore the general-strike movement. The police attacks and the entry of the National Guard intensified the fear of the trade-unions that a city-wide employer-offensive was being planned, and a dozen local unions voted to join the Painters and Machinists. In order to seize control of the general-strike movement, the Central Labor Council appointed a Strike Strategy Committee of seven, headed by Edward D. Vandeleur, president of the Council, to investigate the advisability of a general strike. "The action of the conservative element in the labor council in naming the strike strategy committee . . . successfully sidetracked the plan of more radical groups to incite and promote a general walkout immediately." [17] S. Darcy, a Communist, charged that the Strike Strategy Committee was "appointed to kill the strike, and not to organize it." [18]

During the week following the battle of Rincon Hill the general-strike movement gained momentum, particularly when the hearings conducted by the National Longshoremen's Board achieved no material results. On July 11 the Teamsters' Union reaffirmed its vote for a sympathy strike, and the next morning 4,000 truck drivers in San Francisco and Oakland walked out. Gasoline deliveries ceased and taxis remained in their garages. Only emergency trucks—fire trucks, hospital service, scavengers, etc.—were permitted to operate. Other sympathetic strikes were called by the ship boilermakers, machinists, welders, butchers, laundry workers. By July 13 there were 13 unions, with 32,000 members, on strike; while 60 other local unions had agreed to wait for whatever recommendation would be made by the Strike Strategy Committee. A mass meeting on this day at the Labor Temple showed conclusively that the unions were overwhelmingly in favor of an immediate general strike, and the Strategy Committee called a convention of accredited delegates on July 14. The convention, representing 115 unions and 65,000 members, voted 315 to 15 for a general strike to begin at 8 A.M. Monday, July 16. A General Strike Committee was chosen, with Vandeleur as chairman. A similar vote by the Oakland Central Labor Council, embracing 40,000 members, set a general strike for Tuesday morning, July 17. More than 100,000 organized workers were directly involved in the Bay area, and another 47,000 unorganized workers indirectly.

On Monday morning, July 16, transportation in San Francisco and the Bay area was badly crippled, in fact, almost completely paralyzed. There were six main inlets to the city: the Bay Shore highway, the U. S. 101 highway, the Skyline Boulevard, the sea, the ferries, and the railroads. All but the ferries and the railroads were picketed and tied up; for some reason the Ferryboatmen did not join the strike, although their president, C. W. Deal, was vice-chairman of the General Strike Committee. Within the city itself traffic was likewise halted. The Market Street Railway, the cable cars, and the municipal street cars were not running. Private automobiles could obtain no gasoline. Since most deliveries were stopped, many retail trades and businesses had to shut down. All such services as laundry, tailoring, and barbering ceased. The General Strike Committee, however, aware of its serious responsibility in the conduct of the strike, adopted a plan for rationing food and gasoline supplies by districts. Milk and bread deliveries were not interrupted; while food trucks were given special permits to enter the city, and care was taken to prevent profiteering in the distribution of food. Gasoline was brought in to supply physicians' automobiles and other essential services. At first, 19 restaurants were allowed to stay open to serve the public, but this number was soon increased to 51. Moreover, when the General Strike Committee learned on the first day that the municipal carmen were in danger of losing their civil service rating because of their walkout, it sent them back to work and restored the municipal railway service. In every way it tried to reduce the hardships that the general public might suffer because of the strike.

As soon as the general strike was called, it was vehemently

denounced by the public authorities as a revolutionary plot, and instant action was taken to suppress it. Mayor Rossi issued a proclamation that a state of emergency existed, and blamed the "Communists" for the situation. In a letter to Acting Governor Merriam, requesting additional troops, he wrote: "I am convinced the situation above described is largely due to the efforts and activities of Communists who have no regard for our American form of government and are desirous of breaking down and destroying law observance." [19] On Monday night, at the close of the first day of the general strike, Merriam delivered a radio address to the people of the state, in which he accused "alien counsels" and professional agitators of having fomented the strike: "From the inception of the strike of longshoremen and through many weeks of fruitless efforts to reach a settlement fair to all, the fact has been evident—increasingly evident— that destructive and subversive influences have been working against an agreement on any basis whatsoever. . . . Fully as much as the employers in this State, the workers have been handicapped and exploited by known Communists and professional agitators—men and women who cloak their sinister purposes under hypocritical appeals for human rights, but whose actual purpose is revolution, violent, bloody and destructive." [20] Both the mayor and the Governor demanded that transportation be resumed at once. Mayor Rossi organized a Committee of 500, made up of business and professional men, to assist in moving trucks. Chief of Police Quinn augmented his force by 500 special police and established a new anti-radical bureau. Acting Governor Merriam ordered more troops to the waterfront—infantry, machine-gun, tank, and artillery units. There were now 1,800 policemen and 4,500 National Guardsmen in San Francisco.

In conjunction with the public authorities, the newspapers also organized to crush the strike. On the eve of the general strike there was a meeting of newspaper publishers: C. R. Lindner, general manager of the *San Francisco Examiner;* G. T. Cameron, publisher of the *San Francisco Chronicle;* R. O. Holliday, publisher of the *San Francisco Call-Bulletin;* J. R. Knowland, publisher of the *Oakland Tribune;* and R. A. Carrington, Jr., publisher of the *Oakland Post-Enquirer.* The leadership of the group was given to John F. Neyland, general counsel for the Hearst newspapers.[21] Offices were opened in the Palace Hotel and plans were laid to break the strike. In unison, the newspapers fulminated against the general strike as a "revolution against constituted authority." William Randolph Hearst telephoned from London to say that a story was being cabled about the crushing of the 1926 general strike in England. On July 16 the *San Francisco Examiner* carried a front-page article headed *General Strike in England Crushed When Government Took Control of Situation,* and a front-page editorial, "A Lesson from England":

But if the small group of Communists, starting with their control of the longshore and maritime unions, extend their power over the community of the bay area—and thence into the whole, or even part of the State—California would be no more fit to live in than Russia.[22]

A "red" scare was being deliberately drummed up. Other newspapers in the state took up the theme of the San Francisco press; the *Los Angeles Times,* for example, wrote:

The situation in San Francisco is not correctly described by the phrase "general strike." What is actually in progress there is an insurrection, a Communist-inspired and led revolt against organized government. There is but one thing to be done—put down the revolt with any force necessary and protect the right of ordinary people to conduct their ordi-

*nary occupations in security. They move about on foot in
peril of a rioting mob or stray bullet or brick. And for what?
Not because there is any labor dispute, but in order that Red
leaders of waterfront unions may dominate water-borne commerce of the Pacific Coast and say who shall earn a living
and not. These Red leaders will not arbitrate. They insist on
rule or ruin.*[23]

At the same time, the council of newspaper publishers endeavored to split the ranks of the strikers by distinguishing
continually between "conservative leaders" and "radicals."
"Mr. Neyland entered into negotiations with conservative
labor leaders. . . . Newspaper editorials built up the
strength and influence of the conservative leaders and aided
in splitting the conservative membership away from the radicals. . . .[24]

The generation of the "red" scare and the incitement of the
subsequent reign of terror were promoted, whether deliberately or not, by General Hugh S. Johnson, National Recovery Administrator, who came to San Francisco as semi-
official mediator. On July 17, the second day of the general
strike, he delivered an address at the University of California. He did, it is true, assert the right of labor to collective bargaining and spoke of the denial of that right by the
waterfront employers: "Now I think that labor is inherently
entitled to bargain collectively through representatives of its
own choosing. I think that the employer who denies or even
obstructs that right is anti-social. . . . I will go a step
further and say that in the American shipping industry, including the loading and unloading of ships, the right has not
been justly accorded. . . . If the shipping industry does not
fully and freely accord these rights, on its head lies every
ounce of responsibility for whatever may happen here." [25]
Yet he went on to pronounce the general strike a "threat to

the community," a "menace to the Government," and "civil war." Moreover, he attributed the strike to "subversive influences." The people, he said, "would act to wipe out this subversive element as you clean off a chalk mark on a blackboard with a wet sponge." And he urged "responsible" labor organization to "run these subversive influences out from its ranks like rats." He concluded: "Let's settle this thing, and let's do it now." The newspapers gave wide publicity to this speech, which seemed to lend semi-official sanction to what ensued.

It was not surprising, after the incitement by public officials, the newspapers, and General Johnson, that on July 17 an organized reign of terror opened. Groups of vigilantes raided strikers', radical, and Communist headquarters, clubbing people and smashing furniture and office equipment. Police "mopped up" after them and arrested more than 300 "radicals" in one day. The *New York Times* reported:

A series of raids on known Communist "hot spots" were under way here today. The police are determined to smash the radical element in San Francisco. Youthful civic Vigilantes aided them.

The first indication of the concerted drive against radicals came from Charles Wheeler, vice president of the McCormick Steamship Line, who said in a talk at the Rotary Club here today [July 17] that the raids would start soon. He intimated government consent had been obtained for the raids.[26]

It was the intention of the police and the vigilantes to leave the impression that the raids on radical headquarters were conducted by the strikers themselves, who thus showed their hatred for their "radical leadership." To further this impression, the vigilantes often dressed like workers, and the San Francisco press referred to raids by "union labor." But the pretense was not kept up long, and the general opinion was, according to the *New York Times*, that the vigilantes "were connected with the Committee of 500 organized by prominent citizens yesterday at the behest of Mayor Angelo J. Rossi." [27] On July 17 and 18 raids were made on the *Western Worker*, the Ex-Service Men's League, the Workers' School, the Mission Workers' Neighborhood House, the Marine Workers' Industrial Union, the International Seamen and Harbor Workers' Union, and many other organizations and private dwellings where radicals and strikers were known to gather. The raids spread to Berkeley and Oakland, and soon all along the west coast a clean-up drive was on against Communists and radicals.

Throughout the period of the raids, the Industrial Association was in close touch with the police, and on at least two occasions received confidential reports on raids before they occurred. [28] Much later, the responsibility of the police and public authorities for some of the raids was legally established in suits won by the American Civil Liberties Union against the cities of Richmond, Berkeley, and San Francisco. [29] Not only police and vigilantes took part in the raids; federal agencies were also involved. Those persons arrested during the raids were subjected to scrutiny by immigration officials and U. S. Army officers, and a number were held for possible deportation. Indeed, to a request from Acting Governor Merriam for federal aid in deportations, Secretary of Labor Perkins replied: ". . . I assure you that the Department of Labor will coöperate with California officials to the full extent authorized by law." [30]

Under the widespread reign of terror, the general strike began to weaken. However, more important than the reign of terror in bringing about the ultimate defeat of the strike was a defect in the policy of the General Strike Committee itself. Although the success of the general strike depended mainly on its thoroughness, at no time was it complete in San

Francisco and the Bay area. Not only did the General Strike Committee relax its grip on transportation the first day by allowing the municipal carmen to return to work, but it also failed entirely to bring out certain strategic crafts, such as the Ferryboatmen, the printing trades, the electricians, and the telephone and telegraph workers. As a result, the newspapers were not hampered in their campaign against the strike, and the General Strike Committee had no control over the crucial communications and power systems. Moreover, the General Strike Committee failed to spread the strike along the west coast by appealing to Seattle and Portland to join. Particularly in Portland there arose a strong general-strike movement. On July 15 the Central Labor Council, representing 60 unions, voted for a general strike, but left the date to be set by a Strategy Committee. Only the arrival of Senator Robert F. Wagner, sent by the National Labor Relations Board, averted the spread of the strike to Portland.

The first step in the retreat of the General Strike Committee was taken on July 17, the second day of the strike. In opposition to the wishes of the longshoremen and marine workers, who were, of course, a minority in the General Strike Committee, a resolution was passed urging that the mayors and governors of the west coast appeal to President Roosevelt to intervene in the waterfront struggle, and that "all waterfront employers and recognized organizations of the employes be requested immediately to submit to arbitra‹ tion all questions involved in the dispute between them, which for months has remained unsolved, to the President's longshore board and that their decision shall be accepted by all parties." [31] The vote was close, 207 to 180. What the longshore and marine strikers had steadfastly rejected, arbitration of the question of hiring-hall control, they were now committed to by the resolution of the General Strike Committee. They had been out-maneuvered by the conservative officials of the Central Labor Council. "All indications were that the conservative labor leaders, who formerly could not control a rank and file which had been urged to drastic action by radical leaders, had regained control and were now firmly in the saddle." [32]

Once the conservative element in the General Strike Committee found itself in control, it moved rapidly to end the strike. On July 18, the third day of the strike, the embargo was lifted on all foods, gasoline, and fuel oil, and all restaurants were permitted to reopen. Intimations of the end of the strike were to be found also in the conferences between General Johnson and the General Strike Committee. What was more, a hard blow was dealt the general strike by President Green of the A. F. of L. in a statement to the press on July 18. Even though he said: "When working people are engaged in an economic life-or-death struggle it does not seem appropriate for their friends to engage in comment which might be used against them by their enemies," still he declared that the "American Federation of Labor neither ordered the strike nor authorized it." [33] By this statement Green publicly censored the Central Labor Council of San Francisco, a member of the A. F. of L., for calling the general strike. In every way the termination of the strike was prepared for. It was not unexpected, therefore, that on the afternoon of July 19, after a turbulent session at the Labor Temple, the General Strike Committee called off the strike. Again the vote was extremely close, 191 to 174. Later in the day the general strike was called off in Oakland and the other cities across the Bay.

That same night Mayor Rossi spoke over a nation-wide radio hook-up: "I congratulate the real leaders of organized labor on their decision and the part they have played in ending the general strike. San Francisco has stamped out without bargain or compromise an attempt to import into its life the very real danger of revolt." He added: "We will deal effectively with the small group who opposed peace and plotted revolution." [34] After three and a half days the general strike called in sympathy with the longshoremen and marine workers was at an end. One hundred thousand trade-union members in the San Francisco Bay cities were ordered back to work. Only the longshoremen, the maritime crafts, and the teamsters still remained out on strike.

4. The National Longshoremen's Board arbitrates

With the collapse of the general strike in the San Francisco Bay area and with the spread of the "red" scare, waterfront employers and public officials all along the west coast began a new drive to open the ports and smash the stubborn strike of longshoremen and marine workers. In fact, on July 18, as soon as the termination of the general strike was foreseen, President W. P. Roth of the Matson Navigation Company announced: "Our vessels will be brought to their berths in San Francisco immediately. We have radioed the captains to alter their courses immediately. The citizens of San Francisco have again shown us a city that knows how." And President H. S. Dollar of the Dollar Steamship Company: "We have radioed our captains afloat to lay a course for San Francisco. As we understand it, San Francisco has answered the threat of insurrection. This is our home port, and is going to continue to be." [35] The other ports on the Pacific coast, which had been watching the outcome in San Francisco, now made determined efforts to unload and load the long-idle ships with strike-breakers. At Seattle on July 20 Chief of Police G. F. Howard, who had persistently refused to employ the police to assault pickets, was forced to resign; and Mayor C. L. Smith himself led a police attack on 2,000 strikers and drove them from the docks with gas and guns. At Portland, on the demand of the shipowners, Governor E. L. Meier of Oregon ordered out 1,000 National Guardsmen; but the troops remained camped on the outskirts of the city after the Portland Central Labor Council threatened an immediate general strike if they were moved in on the waterfront.

It was principally the desertion of the teamsters, however, not the renewal of force, which presaged the end of the longshore and maritime strikes. Without the support of a general walkout, the Teamsters' Union could not continue long its sympathy strike, for fear that the Industrial Association and Mayor Rossi's Committee of 500 would man all trucks with strike-breakers, replace all the teamsters in the city, and thus crush their union. On July 20 the Teamsters' Union of San Francisco voted 1,138 to 283 to return to work and to haul all goods, including scab cargo. J. F. Vizzard, president of the Draymen's Association, issued the following statement to the press:

> This vote means that the teamsters will return to work 100 per cent, including the transportation of merchandise and freight to and from the docks. More than 70 per cent of the teamsters' work is on the waterfront.
>
> This vote is a blow at Harry Bridges, chairman of the Maritime Strike Committee. He has been the fly in the ointment and now he is through. The longshoremen, acting sanely, will recognize proper leadership. Bridges is too radical; he doesn't want to settle anything. Why, even now he's going around with eight bodyguards.
>
> It was agreed between me and Michael Casey, president of the Teamsters Union, that if the men voted to return to work, it would mean all work, including that on the docks.
>
> I predict that the longshoremen will now choose new leaders and settle their troubles by arbitration.[36]

The action of other ports copied that in San Francisco. In Oakland, Seattle, and other cities where the teamsters had struck in sympathy, they now returned to work unconditionally.

The strike of the teamsters was essential to the success of the longshoremen and marine workers. After the decision of the Teamsters' Union to return to work and handle all cargo, the Joint Strike Committee realized that there was little hope of winning the strike. Furthermore, the final resolution of the General Strike Committee bound the maritime strikers to arbitration. On July 21, therefore, after the shipowners pledged themselves to arbitrate the grievances of the marine workers, the Joint Strike Committee agreed to let the National Longshoremen's Board conduct a vote in all the west coast ports to see if the longshoremen were willing to submit to arbitration. The qualification for voting was a membership card in the I.L.A. Tabulation of the ballots on July 25 showed 6,378 to 1,471 for arbitration. Less than two-thirds of the total I.L.A. membership had voted.

After its success in getting itself recognized as mediator by both longshore strikers and employers, three problems still faced the National Longshoremen's Board: what to do with the strike-breakers, how to settle the grievances of the marine workers, and how to return the longshoremen to work. But all three were soon solved. On July 27 the Waterfront Employers' Union agreed to discharge all men hired since the inception of the strike and not to discriminate against any worker for union affiliation or for strike activity; the seamen voted on July 30 for arbitration, as did the other maritime crafts; and it was agreed that, pending the arbitration proceedings, both the National Longshoremen's Board and the I.L.A. were to have observers in the hiring halls to see that the employment of longshoremen was fair and without discrimination. Accordingly, on July 31, after nearly three months of strike, 12,000 longshoremen and 13,000 marine workers returned to their jobs.

With the decision finally of the strikers to arbitrate all their grievances and the conclusion of the strike in sight, there was no longer any need for the troops. On July 26 the last of the National Guard withdrew from the Bay area. That the business interests of San Francisco understood the important rôle of the National Guard in breaking the strike was indicated several weeks later; to wit, on October 10 the *San Francisco Daily News* reported: "Very quietly, the bigger business men of the town have been gathering up a fund to buy something for the National Guard. You may hear about it later because two points of view have developed concerning the move. The group behind it considers the contribution a tangible appreciation of the way Guard members have met the duties of citizenship. The opposition snorts that it's a tip to the guard for strike service." Concerning this appeal for funds, the *Nation* commented:

It is headed "An Appreciation of Good Citizenship" and bears the names of important figures in the social and economic life of the Bay region who "are sponsoring a popular subscription the proceeds of which will be expended in a manner yet to be determined, but which will be of the greatest benefit in the development of the National Guard service." "Good citizenship" comes high, but no one knows better than the "bigger business men" of San Francisco and their company union, the Industrial Association, how well it pays.[37]

Meanwhile, the National Longshoremen's Board was at work on a settlement for the longshore dispute. On August 7 it succeeded in getting both the I.L.A. and the waterfront employers of San Francisco, Seattle, Portland, and Los Angeles to agree that whatever decision it made would be binding until September 30, 1935, and would be renewed from year to year unless terminated by written notice 40 days prior to the expiration date. Two months later, on October 10, 1934, it announced its award: (1) an increase of straight-time pay from 85 to 95 cents an hour and of overtime from $1.25 to $1.40, retroactive to July 31, 1934, when the longshoremen returned to work; (2) a five-day 30-hour week to replace the 48-hour week; and (3) joint operation of the hiring halls by the I.L.A. and the respective employers. Qualifying the last decision were several provisions. There was to be a central hiring hall in each Pacific coast port, under the control of a Labor Relations Committee representing the I.L.A. and the employers; and branch halls were to be opened as the Committee found them necessary. Longshoremen, whether union or non-union, were to be hired without favoritism or discrimination. While the award specifically provided that hall dispatchers, who assigned the workers to the various docks, were to be appointed by the union, it also permitted the employers to select their men freely from all those available. The Labor Relations Committee was to investigate and adjudicate any disputes that arose.

Thus the struggle between the longshoremen and the waterfront employers was brought to a temporary termination. On two of their demands—wages and hours—the longshoremen won a substantial victory. On the third they suffered a partial defeat, for although they were granted recognition of their union, they failed to achieve either the closed shop or the absolute control of hiring halls. Nevertheless, the gains of the strike gave the west coast longshoremen much satisfaction. For one thing, they had secured wage and hour advantages. For another, they had destroyed the Blue Book and had built up a powerful coastwide organization in the I.L.A. Finally, in opposition to the more conservative labor officials, they had succeeded in calling a general strike—the second in the history of the country—and had in this way shown that widely different trade-unions could be cemented together in sympathetic action.

NOTES AND REFERENCES

CHAPTER I

[1] An editorial, "Is It a Drawn Battle?" The *New York Times,* July 27, 1877.

[2] Russell, C. E., *Railroad Melons, Rates and Wages* (Chicago: Charles H. Kerr & Co., 1922), p. 27-28.

[3] The *Commercial and Financial Chronicle,* Aug. 18, 1877, p. 149.

[4] *Ibid.,* July 14, 1877, p. 30.

[5] *Ibid.,* Aug. 11, 1877, p. 126.

[6] The *New York Times,* July 22, 1877.

[7] *Ibid.,* July 25, 1877.

[8] Reprinted, *ibid.,* July 22, 1877.

[9] Hungerford, E., *The Story of the Baltimore & Ohio Railroad, 1827-1927* (New York: G. P. Putnam's Sons, 1928), vol. 2, p. 140.

[10] The *New York Times,* July 21, 1877.

[11] *Ibid.,* July 26, 1877.

[12] *Ibid.,* July 22, 1877.

[13] *Ibid.,* July 29, 1877.

[14] *Ibid.,* July 24, 1877.

[15] *Ibid.,* July 25, 1877.

[16] *Ibid.,* July 25, 1877.

[17] *Ibid.,* July 28, 1877.

[18] *Ibid.,* July 29, 1877.

[19] *Ibid.,* July 26, 1877.

[20] Lewis, L., and Smith, H. J., *Chicago: The History of Its Reputation* (New York: Harcourt, Brace and Co., 1929), p. 150-151.

[21] *Ibid.,* p. 152.

[22] The *New York Times,* July 27, 1877.

[23] *Ibid.,* an editorial paragraph, July 30, 1877.

[24] An editorial, "The Late Riots," The *Nation,* Aug. 2, 1877.

[25] Commons, J. R., and associates, *History of Labour in the United States* (New York: The Macmillan Co., 1921), vol. 2, p. 191.

[26] Robbins, E. C., *Railway Conductors: A Study in Organized Labor (Studies in History, Economics and Public Law, vol. 61, no. 1;* New York: Columbia University, 1914), p. 21-22.

[27] Commons and associates, *op. cit.,* vol. 2, p. 191.

[28] An editorial, "The Rioters and the Regular Army," The *Nation,* Aug. 9, 1877.

[29] The *New York Times,* July 30, 1877.

ADDITIONAL REFERENCES EMPLOYED IN THE PREPARATION OF THIS CHAPTER

"Railroad Wages," The *Nation,* Aug. 16, 1877.

Scharf, J. T. *History of Saint Louis City and County.* Philadelphia: Louis H. Everts & Co., 1883.

Schotter, H. W. *The Growth and Development of the Pennsylvania Railroad Company.* Philadelphia: Allen, Lane & Scott, 1927.

Scott, T. A. "The Recent Strikes," The *North American Review,* September, 1877.

Sharfman, I. L. *The American Railroad Problem.* New York: The Century Co., 1921.

Stevens, F. W. *The Beginnings of the New York Central Railroad.* New York: G. P. Putnam's Sons, 1926.

CHAPTER II

[1] Illinois Bureau of Labor Statistics, "The Eight-Hour Movement of 1886," *Fourth Biennial Report* (Springfield, Illinois, 1886), p. 474. Cf. Public laws of Minnesota, 1885, chap. 206, p. 277.

[2] March 13, 1880, cited by Bogart, E. L., and Thompson, C. M., *The Industrial State, 1870-1893 (The Centennial History of Illinois, vol. 4;* Springfield, Illinois: Illinois Centennial Commission, 1920), p. 163.

[3] Commons, J. R., and associates, *History of Labour in the United States* (New York: The Macmillan Co., 1921), vol. 2, p. 361.

[4] *Ibid.,* vol. 2, p. 376.

[5] *Ibid.,* vol. 2, p. 381.

[6] Reprinted in *Public Opinion,* May 8, 1886.

[7] Powderly, T. V., *Thirty Years of Labor, 1859 to 1889* (Columbus, Ohio: Excelsior Publishing House, 1890), p. 496.

[8] *Bradstreet's*, May 15, 1886.

[9] Commons and associates, *op. cit.*, vol. 2, p. 290-300.

[10] Nov. 1, 1884, reprinted by Gary, J. E., "The Chicago Anarchists of 1886: The Crime, the Trial, and the Punishment," The *Century Magazine*, April, 1893.

[11] Chicago *Vorbote*, Oct. 4, 1885, quoted by Commons and associates, *op. cit.*, vol. 2, p. 391.

[12] *Bradstreet's*, May 15, 1886.

[13] *Ibid.*, May 8, 1886.

[14] Bogart and Thompson, *op. cit.*, p. 167-168.

[15] Photographic reprint in Schaack, M. J., *Anarchy and Anarchists: A History of the Red Terror and the Social Revolution in America and Europe* (Chicago: F. J. Schulte & Co., 1889), p. 130.

[16] Altgeld, J. P., *Reasons for Pardoning Fielden, Neebe, and Schwab* (A pamphlet, 1893), p. 49.

[17] *Ibid.*, p. 38-39.

[18] Associated Press dispatch, *Terre Haute Evening Gazette*, May 5, 1886.

[19] Bogart and Thompson, *op. cit.*, p. 172.

[20] Gary, *loc. cit.*, p. 831.

[21] *Cf. Public Opinion*, May 15, 1886.

[22] The *Chicago Daily News*, May 10, 1889. *Cf.* Altgeld, *op. cit.*, p. 51.

[23] Altgeld, *op. cit.*, p. 8.

[24] *Ibid.*, p. 50.

[25] *Cf.* Parsons, A. R., *Anarchism: Its Philosophy and Scientific Basis* (Chicago: Mrs. A. R. Parsons, Publisher, 1887), p. 53.

[26] *Famous Speeches of the Eight Chicago Anarchists in Court* (Chicago: Lucy E. Parsons, Publisher, 1910), p. 24.

[27] *Ibid.*, p. 40.

[28] *Ibid.*, p. 36.

[29] Parsons, *op. cit.*, p. 200.

[30] Quoted by Gary, *loc. cit.*, p. 837.

[31] *Bradstreet's*, June 12, 1886.

[32] Powderly, *op. cit.*, p. 533.

[33] An editorial, "The Supreme Court and the Anarchists," The *Nation*, Oct. 27, 1887.

[34] Lombroso, C., "Illustrative Studies in Criminal Anthropology.

III. The Physiognomy of the Anarchists," The *Monist,* April, 1891.

[35] Schwab, M., "A Convicted Anarchist's Reply to Professor Lombroso," The *Monist,* July, 1891.

[36] Browne, W. R., *Altgeld of Illinois: A Record of His Life and Work* (New York: B. W. Huebsch, Inc., 1924), p. 107.

ADDITIONAL

Adams, H. C. "Shall We Muzzle the Anarchists?" The *Forum,* July, 1886.

"Coquetting with Anarchy," The *Nation,* Sept. 9, 1886.

"The Execution of the Anarchists," The *Nation,* Nov. 10, 1877.

Hill, F. T. *Decisive Battles of the Law.* New York: Harper & Brothers, 1907.

U. S. Commissioner of Labor. "Strikes and Lockouts," *Third Annual Report, 1887.* Washington: Government Printing Office, 1888.

Zenker, E. V. *Anarchism: A Criticism and History of the Anarchist Theory.* London: Methuen & Co., 1898.

CHAPTER III

[1] Carnegie, A., "An Employer's View of the Labor Question," The *Forum,* April, 1886.

[2] Carnegie, A., "Results of the Labor Struggle," The *Forum,* August, 1886.

[3] Bridge, J. H., *The Inside Story of the Carnegie Steel Company* (New York: The Aldine Book Co., 1903), p. 186.

[4] *Ibid.,* p. 204.

[5] Associated Press dispatch, *Terre Haute Evening Gazette,* July 13, 1892.

[6] U. S. House of Representatives, *Employment of Pinkerton Detectives,* 52nd Congress, 2nd Session, Report no. 2447 (Washington: Government Printing Office, 1893), p. 23.

[7] *Ibid.,* p. 108.

[8] *Ibid.,* p. xi.

[9] *Ibid.,* p. 31.

[10] *Ibid.,* p. xi.

[11] The *New York Daily Tribune,* July 7, 1892.

[12] *Ibid.,* July 8, 1892.

[13] *Ibid.,* July 7, 1892.

[14] "The Merits of the Homestead Trouble," The *Nation,* July 14, 1892.

[15] Oates, W. C., "The Homestead Strike. I. A Congresional View," The *North American Review,* September, 1892, p. 362.

[16] U. S. House of Representatives, *op. cit.,* p. 59.

[17] The *New York Daily Tribune,* July 8, 1892.

[18] U. S. House of Representatives, *op. cit.,* p. 50.

[19] Associated Press dispatch, *Terre Haute Evening Gazette,* July 12, 1892.

[20] *Ibid.,* July 16, 1892.

[21] Statement by Lewis S. Gillette, president of the Gillette-Herzog Manufacturing Company, The *New York Daily Tribune,* July 9, 1892.

[22] Curtis, G. T., "The Homestead Strike. II. A Constitutional View," The *North American Review,* September, 1892, p. 366.

[23] U. S. House of Representatives, *op. cit.,* p. 30.

[24] Byington, M. F., *Homestead: The Households of a Mill Town* (*The Pittsburgh Survey;* New York: Charities Publication Committee, 1910), p. 172.

[25] *Ibid.,* p. 180.

[26] *Ibid.,* p. 181.

ADDITIONAL

Black, C. F. "The Lesson of Homestead: A Remedy for Labor Troubles," The *Forum,* September, 1892.

Burgoyne, A. G. *Homestead: A Complete History of the Struggle of July, 1892, between the Carnegie Steel Company, Limited, and the Amalgamated Association of Iron and Steel Workers.* Pittsburgh, 1893.

"Congressman Oates's Report," The *Nation,* Aug. 11, 1892.

Powderly, T. V. "The Homestead Strike. III. A Knight of Labor's View," The *North American Review,* September, 1892.

"The Striking Fever," The *Nation,* July 2, 1891.

"Warring Protectionists at Homestead," The *Nation,* July 21, 1892.

CHAPTER IV

[1] Carwardine, W. H., *The Pullman Strike* (Chicago: Charles H. Kerr and Co., 1894), p. 54-55.

[2] U. S. Senate, *Report on the Chicago Strike of June-July, 1894,*

by the United States Strike Commission, 53d Congress, 3d Session, Ex. Doc. no. 7 (Washington: Government Printing Office, 1895), p. xxxiv.

[3] *Cf.* Russell, C. E., *Railroad Melons, Rates and Wages* (Chicago: Charles H. Kerr and Co., 1922), p. 253-271.

[4] U. S. Senate, *op. cit.,* p. xxi.

[5] Carwardine, *op. cit.,* p. 69. *Cf.* U. S. Senate, *op. cit.,* p. xxxiii *ff.*

[6] U. S. Senate, *op. cit.,* p. xxxv.

[7] *Ibid.,* p. xxii.

[8] Reprinted by the Pullman Company in a pamphlet, *The Strike at Pullman* (No date), p. 26.

[9] U. S. Senate, *op. cit.,* p. xxxv.

[10] *Ibid.,* p. xxxviii.

[11] *Ibid.,* p. xxiv.

[12] *Ibid.,* p. xlii.

[13] *Ibid.,* p. 250.

[14] Associated Press dispatch, *Terre Haute Evening Gazette,* June 30, 1894.

[15] *Public Opinion,* July 5, 1894.

[16] "The Boycott of the Pullman Company," *Harper's Weekly,* July 7, 1894.

[17] Lloyd, C. A., *Henry Demarest Lloyd* (New York: G. P. Putnam's Sons, 1912), vol. 1, p. 152.

[18] *Bradstreet's,* July 14, 1894, p. 436-437.

[19] *Public Opinion,* July 12, 1894.

[20] "Gov. Altgeld and the President," The *Nation,* July 12, 1894.

[21] An editorial paragraph, The *Nation,* July 12, 1894.

[22] *Terre Haute Evening Gazette,* July 7, 1894.

[23] *Ibid.,* June 30, 1894.

[24] *Ibid.,* July 9, 1894.

[25] Cleveland, G., "The Government in the Chicago Strike of 1894," *McClure's Magazine,* July, 1904, p. 232.

[26] Frankfurter, F., and Greene, N., *The Labor Injunction* (New York: The Macmillan Co., 1930), p. 17-24. *Cf.* Commons, J. R., and associates, *History of Labour in the United States* (New York: The Macmillan Co., 1921), vol. 2, p. 502-509.

[27] Frankfurter and Greene, *op. cit.,* p. 254-255.

[28] U. S. Senate, *op. cit.,* p. xl.

[29] *Public Opinion,* July 19, 1894.

[30] U. S. Senate, *op. cit.,* p. xviii.

[31] *Bradstreet's,* July 28, 1894, p. 467.

[32] Associated Press dispatch, *Terre Haute Evening Gazette,* July 17, 1894.

[33] *The Strike at Pullman,* p. 38.

[34] U. S. Senate, *op. cit.,* p. xxvi-xxvii.

[35] *Bradstreet's,* July 21, 1894, p. 450.

[36] U. S. Senate, *op. cit.,* p. xviii.

ADDITIONAL

Bogart, E. L., and Mathews, J. M. *The Modern Commonwealth, 1893-1918. The Centennial History of Illinois,* vol. 5. Springfield, Illinois: Illinois Centennial Commission, 1920.

Burns, W. F. *The Pullman Boycott: A Complete History of the Great R. R. Strike.* St. Paul: The McGill Printing Co., 1894.

Day, S. A. "A Celebrated Illinois Case That Made History," *Transactions of the Illinois State Historical Society for 1917,* vol. 23, p. 99-108.

"The Debs Case," The *Nation,* Sept. 13, 1894.

Grant, T. B. "Pullman and Its Lessons," The *American Journal of Politics,* August, 1894.

McElroy, R. McN. *Grover Cleveland: The Man and the Statesman.* New York: Harper & Brothers, 1923.

Mason, J. W. "Pullman and Its Real Lessons," The *American Journal of Politics,* September, 1894.

Painter, F. R. *That Man Debs and His Life Work.* Bloomington, Indiana: Indiana University, 1929.

von Holst, H. "Are We Awakened," The *Journal of Political Economy,* September, 1894.

Wright, C. D. "The Chicago Strike," *Publications of the American Economic Association,* 1894, vol. 9, p. 503-522.

CHAPTER V

[1] *Report to the President on the Anthracite Coal Strike of May-October, 1902, by the Anthracite Coal Strike Commission* (Washington: Government Printing Office, 1903), p. 17-26. *Cf.* Roberts, P., *Anthracite Coal Communities* (New York: The Macmillan Co., 1904), p. 3-25.

[2] Jones, E., *The Anthracite Coal Combination in the United States* (Cambridge: Harvard University Press, 1914), p. 52.

[3] *Report* of the Anthracite Coal Strike Commission, p. 22

[4] Jones, *op. cit.*, p. 50.

[5] Roberts, *op. cit.*, p. 19.

[6] *Bradstreet's*, May 17, 1902, p. 305.

[7] *Report* of the Anthracite Coal Strike Commission, p. 50.

[8] *Ibid.*, p. 27.

[9] Walsh, W. J., *The United Mine Workers of America as an Economic and Social Force in the Anthracite Territory* (Washington: The Catholic University of America, 1931), p. 83-84.

[10] *Report* of the Anthracite Coal Strike Commission, p. 70.

[11] *Ibid.*, p. 68-69.

[12] *Ibid.*, p. 33.

[13] The *New York Times*, May 1, 1902.

[14] *Ibid.*, May 4, 1902.

[15] *Report* of the Anthracite Coal Strike Commission, p. 35.

[16] The *New York Times*, May 16, 1902.

[17] *Ibid.*, July 13, 1902.

[18] *Ibid.*, an editorial, "Mine Coal," June 28, 1902.

[19] *Ibid.*, July 18, 1902.

[20] Mitchell, J., *Organized Labor* (Philadelphia: American Book and Bible House, 1903), p. 380-381.

[21] The *New York Times*, July 27, 1902.

[22] *Ibid.*, Aug. 16, 1902.

[23] *Ibid.*, July 31, 1902.

[24] *Ibid.*, Aug. 4, 1902.

[25] *Ibid.*, Aug. 21, 1902.

[26] *Ibid.*, Sept. 23, 1902.

[27] The *Nation*, June 19, 1902.

[28] The *New York Times*, Sept. 11, 1902.

[29] Bishop, J. B., *Theodore Roosevelt and His Time* (New York: Charles Scribner's Sons, 1920), vol. 1, p. 203.

[30] Roosevelt, T., *An Autobiography* (New York: The Macmillan Co., 1913), p. 513-516.

[31] The *New York Times*, Oct. 10, 1902.

[32] Lloyd, C. A., *Henry Demarest Lloyd* (New York: G. P. Putnam's Sons, 1912), vol. 2, p. 196-197.

[33] The *New York Times,* Oct. 13, 1902.

[34] *Ibid.,* Oct. 21, 1902.

[35] *Report* of the Anthracite Coal Strike Commission, p. 61.

ADDITIONAL

Cummings, J. "The Passing of the Coal Strike," The *Journal of Political Economy,* December, 1902.

Glück, E. *John Mitchell, Miner.* New York: The John Day Co., 1929.

Hinrichs, A. F. *The United Mine Workers of America and the Non-Union Coal Fields. Studies in History, Economics and Public Law,* vol. 110, no. 1. New York: Columbia University, 1923.

Roberts, P. "The Anthracite Coal Situation," *Yale Review,* May, 1902.

Roberts, P. "The Anthracite Conflict," *Yale Review,* November, 1902.

Shalloo, J. P. *Private Police: with Special Reference to Pennsylvania.* Philadelphia: The American Academy of Political and Social Science, 1933.

Spahr, C. B. "The Miners' Strike: Impressions in the Field," The *Outlook,* May 31, 1902.

Suffern, A. E. *The Coal Miners' Struggle for Industrial Status.* New York: The Macmillan Co., 1926.

Sydenstricker, E. *Collective Bargaining in the Anthracite Coal Industry.* Bulletin of the United States Bureau of Labor Statistics, whole number 191. Washington: Government Printing Office, 1916.

Warne, F. J. "The Real Cause of the Miners' Strike," The *Outlook,* Aug. 30, 1902.

Wellman, W. "The Settlement of the Coal Strike," *Review of Reviews,* November, 1902.

Williams, T. "A General View of the Coal Strike," *Review of Reviews,* July, 1902.

CHAPTER VI

[1] U. S. Senate, *Report on Strike of Textile Workers in Lawrence, Mass., in 1912,* 62nd Congress, 2nd Session, Doc. no. 870 (Washington: Government Printing Office, 1912), p. 19.

[2] *Ibid.,* p. 20.

[3] *Ibid.,* p. 28.

[4] Rowell, W. E., "The Lawrence Strike," The *Survey*, March 23, 1912.

[5] U. S. Senate, *op. cit.*, p. 27.

[6] *Ibid.*, p. 149.

[7] *Ibid.*, p. 154-157.

[8] *Cf.* U. S. House of Representatives, *The Strike at Lawrence, Mass.*, Hearings before the Committee on Rules, 62nd Congress, 2nd Session, House Doc. no. 671 (Washington: Government Printing Office, 1912), p. 35.

[9] U. S. Senate, *op. cit.*, p. 27.

[10] *Ibid.*, p. 63-64.

[11] *Ibid.*, p. 39-40.

[12] *Ibid.*, p. 41.

[13] An editorial, "Pity for the Poor," The *New York Times*, Jan. 26, 1912.

[14] U. S. Senate, *op. cit.*, p. 44.

[15] *Ibid.*, p. 45.

[16] The *New York Times*, Feb. 1, 1912.

[17] O'Sullivan, M. K., "The Labor War at Lawrence," The *Survey*, April 6, 1912.

[18] The *Survey*, Feb. 24, 1912, p. 1792.

[19] U. S. House of Representatives, *op. cit.*, p. 89.

[20] Carstens, C. C., "The Children's Exodus from Lawrence," The *Survey*, April 6, 1912.

[21] U. S. House of Representatives, *op. cit.*, p. 24.

[22] U. S. Senate, *op. cit.*, p. 57-58.

[23] *Ibid.*, p. 57.

[24] *Ibid.*, p. 56.

[25] *Ibid.*, p. 58.

[26] Woods, R. A., "The Breadth and Depth of the Lawrence Outcome," The *Survey*, April 6, 1912.

[27] The *Survey*, April 6, 1912, p. 80.

[28] Ebert, J., *The Trial of a New Society* (Cleveland, Ohio: I.W.W. Publishing Bureau, 1913), p. 73.

[29] The *New York Times*, Nov. 25, 1912.

[30] Quoted by Ebert, *op. cit.*, p. 148.

ADDITIONAL

Adams, J. A. "Clod or Brother?" The *Survey*, March 30, 1912.

Brissenden, P. F. *The I.W.W.: A Study of American Syndicalism. Studies in History, Economics and Public Law*, vol. 83. New York: Columbia University, 1919.

Cole, J. N. "The Issue at Lawrence. The Manufacturers' Point of View: A Reply," The *Outlook*, Feb. 24, 1912.

Deland, L. F. "The Lawrence Strike: A Study," The *Atlantic Monthly*, May, 1912.

Haywood, W. D. *Bill Haywood's Book*. New York: International Publishers, 1929.

Heaton, J. P. "The Legal Aftermath of the Lawrence Strike," The *Survey*, July 6, 1912.

Heaton, J. P. "The Salem Trial," The *Survey*, Dec. 7, 1912.

Lauck, W. J. "The Significance of the Situation at Lawrence," The *Survey*, Feb. 17, 1912.

Leupp, C. D. "The Lawrence Strike Hearings," The *Survey*, March 23, 1912.

Lovejoy, O. R. "Right of Free Speech in Lawrence," The *Survey*, March 9, 1912.

Palmer, L. E. "A Strike for Four Loaves of Bread," The *Survey*, Feb. 3, 1912.

Vorse, M. H. "The Trouble at Lawrence," *Harper's Weekly*, March 16, 1912.

Weyl, W. E. "It Is Time to Know," The *Survey*, April 6, 1912.

Weyl, W. E. "The Strikers at Lawrence," The *Outlook*, Feb. 10, 1912.

Woods, R. A. "The Clod Stirs," The *Survey*, March 16, 1912.

CHAPTER VII

[1] Davis, W. T., "The Strike War in Colorado," The *Outlook*, May 9, 1914.

[2] U. S. Commission on Industrial Relations, *Report on the Colorado Strike* (by George P. West; Washington, 1915), p. 59. *Cf. Report of Vice-President Frank J. Hayes, Twenty-fourth Consecutive and First Biennial Convention of United Mine Workers of America*, January, 1914, p. 14.

[3] U. S. Senate, *The Colorado Coal Miners' Strike, Report of the Commission on Industrial Relations*, 64th Congress, 1st Ses-

sion, Senate Doc. no. 415 (Washington: Government Printing Office, 1916), vol. 9, p. 8781-8782.

[4] U. S. Commission on Industrial Relations, *op. cit.*, p. 16.

[5] Figures of James Dalrymple, State Inspector of Mines in Colorado, U. S. Senate, *op. cit.*, vol. 7, p. 6463.

[6] U. S. Commission on Industrial Relations, *op. cit.*, p. 81-82.

[7] *Ibid.*, p. 33.

[8] *Ibid.*, p. 34.

[9] U. S. Senate, *op. cit.*, vol. 9, p. 8416.

[10] *Ibid.*, vol. 7, p. 6800-6802.

[11] U. S. Commission on Industrial Relations, *op. cit.*, p. 32.

[12] *Ibid.*, p. 62.

[13] *Ibid.*, p. 63.

[14] U. S. Senate, *op. cit.*, vol. 9, p. 8741-8744.

[15] U. S. Commission on Industrial Relations, *op. cit.*, p. 68-69.

[16] U. S. Senate, *op. cit.*, vol. 7, p. 6554-6555.

[17] U. S. Commission on Industrial Relations, *op. cit.*, p. 69.

[18] U. S. Senate, *op. cit.*, vol. 9, p. 8501.

[19] *Ibid.*, vol. 9, p. 8500.

[20] *Ibid.*, vol. 9, p. 8492.

[21] *Ibid.*, vol. 9, p. 8492-8493, 8499.

[22] U. S. Commission on Industrial Relations, *op. cit.*, p. 41.

[23] *Ibid.*, p. 42.

[24] *Ibid.*, p. 43-44. Also U. S. Senate, *op. cit.*, vol. 8, p. 7117.

[25] U. S. Senate, *op. cit.*, vol. 9, p. 8416.

[26] *Ibid.*, vol. 7, p. 6455-6456.

[27] *Ibid.*, vol. 9, p. 8419-8420.

[28] *Ibid.*, vol. 9, p. 8426.

[29] The *New York Times*, April 7, 1914.

[30] U. S. Commission on Industrial Relations, *op. cit.*, p. 22.

[31] *Ibid.*, p. 102.

[32] *Ibid.*, p. 106.

[33] *Ibid.*, p. 104.

[34] U. S. Senate, *op. cit.*, vol. 9, p. 8421-8422.

[35] U. S. Commission on Industrial Relations, *op. cit.*, p. 108.

[36] U. S. Senate, *op. cit.*, vol. 9, p. 8424.

[37] *Ibid.*, vol. 8, p. 7118.

[38] *Ibid.,* vol. 7, p. 6707.

[39] *Militarism in Colorado, Report of the Committee Appointed at the Suggestion of the Governor of Colorado to Investigate the Conduct of the Colorado National Guard During the Coal Strike of 1913-1914* (Denver, 1914), p. 9.

[40] *Ibid.,* p. 9.

[41] *Ibid.,* p. 11.

[42] *Ibid.,* p. 12.

[43] U. S. Senate, *op. cit.,* vol. 7, p. 6810.

[44] U. S. Commission on Industrial Relations, *op. cit.,* p. 125.

[45] U. S. Senate, *op. cit.,* vol. 9, p. 8429-8430.

[46] U. S. Commission on Industrial Relations, *op. cit.,* p. 126.

[47] *Ibid.,* p. 127.

[48] *Ibid.,* p. 127.

[49] The *New York Times,* April 22, 1914.

[50] An editorial, "When Peace Comes to Colorado," The *Survey,* May 16, 1914.

[51] The *New York Times,* April 23, 1914.

[52] U. S. Senate, *op. cit.,* vol. 9, p. 8439.

[53] Fitch, J. A., "Law and Order: The Issue in Colorado," The *Survey,* Dec. 5, 1914, p. 244-245. *Cf.* Creel, G., "Poisoners of Public Opinion," *Harper's Weekly,* Nov. 7 and 14, 1914. Also U. S. Commission on Industrial Relations, *op. cit.,* p. 151-152.

[54] Fitch, *loc. cit.,* p. 241. *Cf.* U. S. Commission on Industrial Relations, *op. cit.,* p. 23-24.

[55] U. S. Senate, *op. cit.,* vol. 8, p. 7176.

[56] Fitch, *loc. cit.,* p. 242.

[57] Weyl, W. E., "Three Years' Truce for the Colorado Coal Strike," The *Survey,* Sept. 19, 1914.

[58] U. S. Senate, *op. cit.,* vol. 7, p. 6688.

[59] U. S. Commission on Industrial Relations, *op. cit.,* p. 18.

[60] Letter by President J. F. Welborn to the *Nation,* Nov. 12, 1914.

[61] U. S. Commission on Industrial Relations, *op. cit.,* p. 153.

[62] U. S. Senate, *op. cit.,* vol. 9, p. 8442.

[63] *Ibid.,* vol. 7, p. 6680.

[64] *Ibid.,* vol. 7, p. 6692.

[65] *Ibid.,* vol. 7, p. 6693.

[66] *Ibid.,* vol. 7, p. 6693-6694.

[67] *Ibid.,* vol. 9, p. 8773.

[68] U. S. Commission on Industrial Relations, *op. cit.,* p. 185.

[69] Selekman, B. M., and Van Kleeck, M., *Employes' Representation in Coal Mines: A Study of the Industrial Representation Plan of the Colorado Fuel and Iron Company* (New York: Russell Sage Foundation, 1924), p. 27, 80.

[70] Rockefeller, J. D., Jr., "Labor and Capital—Partners," The *Atlantic Monthly,* January, 1916, p. 21.

[71] *Report of International Vice-President Frank J. Hayes, Twenty-fifth Consecutive and Second Biennial Convention of the United Mine Workers of America,* 1916, p. 12-13.

[72] U. S. Commission on Industrial Relations, *op. cit.,* p. 156-157.

[73] *Ibid.,* p. 186.

[74] Selekman and Van Kleeck, *op. cit.,* p. 188.

ADDITIONAL

An Answer to the Report of the Commanding General to the Governor for the Use of the Congressional Committee on the Military Occupation of the Coal Strike Zone by the Colorado National Guard 1913-1914. Issued by District No. 15, U. M. W. of A.

A Strike Breaker. United Mine Workers of America. A leaflet. Denver, 1913(?).

Atkinson, H. A. "Why the Miners Struck," *Harper's Weekly,* May 23, 1914.

Bowden, W. "Two Alternatives in the Settlement of the Colorado Coal Strike," The *Survey,* Dec. 20, 1913.

Bowden, W. "New Developments in the Colorado Strike Situation," The *Survey,* Feb. 14, 1914.

Davis, W. T. "The Southern Colorado Coal Strike," The *Outlook,* Jan. 3, 1914.

Dunn, R. W. *Company Unions.* New York: Vanguard Press, 1927.

Fitch, J. A. "The Colorado Strike," The *Survey,* Dec. 20, 1913.

Louis Zancanelli, of the United Mine Workers of Trinidad, Colorado, Found Guilty April 9, 1915. United Mine Workers of America. A leaflet. No date. (1915?)

McGregor. "The Way Rockefeller Looks at It," *Harper's Weekly,* May 23, 1914.

Proceedings of the Special Convention to Consider President Wilson's Proposition for Settlement of Colorado Coal Strike. District 15, U. M. W. of A. Held at Trinidad, Colorado, September 15, 16, 1914.

Report of the Medical & Sociological Departments of the Colorado Fuel & Iron Company. 1913-1914.

The Struggle in Colorado for Industrial Freedom. Bulletins nos. 1, 2, and 4, issued August 12, 20, and 28, 1914, respectively. United Mine Workers of America. Denver, Colorado.

CHAPTER VIII

[1] U. S. Senate, *Report on Conditions of Employment in the Iron and Steel Industry in the United States,* 62nd Congress, 1st Session, Senate Doc. no. 110 (Washington: Government Printing Office, 1913), vol. 3, p. 118-119.

[2] *Report on the Steel Strike of 1919 by the Commission of Inquiry, the Interchurch World Movement* (New York: Harcourt, Brace and Howe, 1920), p. 44, 55-56.

[3] *Ibid.,* p. 48-49.

[4] U. S. Senate, *Report Investigating Strike in Steel Industries,* 66th Congress, 1st Session, Senate Reports, vol. A, no. 289 (Washington: Government Printing Office, 1919), p. 14.

[5] Reprinted, Interchurch *Report,* p. 63-64.

[6] U. S. Senate, *Report Investigating Strike in Steel Industries,* p. 15.

[7] *Ibid.,* p. 15.

[8] *Current Opinion,* January, 1920, p. 122.

[9] Interchurch *Report,* p. 102-103.

[10] *Ibid.,* p. 97.

[11] *Ibid.,* p. 95.

[12] *Ibid.,* p. 100-101.

[13] The *New York Times,* Oct. 3, 1919.

[14] Interchurch *Report,* p. 104.

[15] *Ibid.,* p. 106-107.

[16] Fitch, J. A., *The Steel Workers (The Pittsburgh Survey;* New York: Charities Publication Committee, 1910), p. 6.

[17] The *New York Times,* Oct. 3, 1919.

[18] Foster, W. Z., *The Great Steel Strike and Its Lessons* (New York: B. W. Huebsch, Inc., 1920), p. 18.

[19] *Ibid.,* p. 21.

[20] Shaw, S. A., "Closed Towns," The *Survey,* Nov. 8, 1919.

[21] U. S. Senate, *Report Investigating Strike in Steel Industries,* p. 2.

[22] Interchurch *Report,* p. 210.

[23] *Ibid.,* p. 213.

[24] The *New York Times,* Aug. 28, 1919.

[25] *Ibid.,* Sept. 11, 1919.

[26] Foster, *op. cit.,* p. 90-91.

[27] U. S. Senate, *Report Investigating Strike in Steel Industries,* p. 13-14.

[28] Foster, *op. cit.,* p. 100 *ff.*

[29] Wisehart, M. K., "The Pulpit and the Strike," *Public Opinion and the Steel Strike, Supplementary Reports of the Investigators to the Commission of Inquiry, the Interchurch World Movement* (New York: Harcourt, Brace and Co., 1921), p. 278-280.

[30] *Ibid.,* p. 280.

[31] Wisehart, M. K., "The Pittsburgh Newspapers and the Steel Strike," *Public Opinion and the Steel Strike,* p. 99.

[32] U. S. Senate, *Report Investigating Strike in Steel Industries,* p. 14.

[33] Interchurch *Report,* p. 20, 43.

[34] Littell, R., "Report on Under-Cover Men," *Public Opinion and the Steel Strike,* p. 35-36.

[35] Interchurch *Report,* p. 240.

[36] *Ibid.,* p. 238.

[37] The *New York Times,* Oct. 18, 1919.

[38] Interchurch *Report,* p. 230.

[39] Littell, R., *loc. cit.,* p. 57.

[40] The *New York Times,* Oct. 19, 1919.

[41] Foster, *op. cit.,* p. 141-142. *Cf.* The *New York Times,* Oct. 10, 1919.

[42] Wisehart, M. K., "The Pittsburgh Newspapers and the Steel Strike," *loc. cit.,* p. 134-136.

[43] Littell, R., *loc. cit.,* p. 28.

[44] Wisehart, M. K., "The Pittsburgh Newspapers and the Steel Strike," *loc. cit.,* p. 113.

[45] *Ibid.,* p. 153.

[46] Foster, *op. cit.,* p. 235.

[47] *Ibid.*, p. 220. *Cf.* Interchurch *Report*, p. 196.

[48] Interchurch *Report*, p. 169.

[49] Littell, R., *loc. cit.*, p. 45.

[50] *Public Opinion and the Steel Strike*, p. 334.

[51] *Ibid.*, p. 335, 338.

[52] Foster, *op. cit.*, p. 191.

[53] Interchurch *Report*, p. 177.

[54] The *Survey*, Jan. 17, 1920, p. 421.

[55] Foster, *op. cit.*, p. 209.

[56] An editorial, " 'Guildsman' and 'Red,' " The *New York Times*, Aug. 22, 1920.

[57] *Public Opinion and the Steel Strike*, p. 320.

[58] *Ibid.*, p. vi.

ADDITIONAL

Address of Mr. John Fitzpatrick. Report of Proceedings of the Thirty-ninth Annual Convention of the American Federation of Labor, p. 419-421.

Fitch, J. A. "A Strike for Freedom," The *Survey*, Sept. 27, 1919.

Fitch, J. A. "The Closed Shop," The *Survey*, Nov. 8, 1919.

Kellogg, P. U. "Frick—and After," The *Survey*, Dec. 13, 1919.

Merz, C. "The A. F. of L. Moves Forward," The *New Republic*, June 7, 1919.

Mussey, H. R. "The Steel-Makers," The *Nation*, May 1, 1920.

Olds, M. *Analysis of the Interchurch World Movement Report on the Steel Strike*. New York: G. P. Putnam's Sons, 1923.

Saposs, D. J. "How the Steel Strike Was Organized," The *Survey*, Nov. 8, 1919.

Shaw, S. A. "Steel-Making," The *Survey*, Aug. 2, 1920.

Taylor, G. "At Gary," The *Survey*, Nov. 8, 1919.

Vorse, M. H. "Aliens," The *Outlook*, May 5, 1920.

Vorse, M. H. "Civil Liberty in the Steel Strike," The *Nation*, Nov. 15, 1919.

Vorse, M. H. "Derelicts of the Steel Strike," The *Survey*, Dec. 4, 1920.

Vorse, M. H. "The Steel Strike," The *Liberator*, January, 1920.

CHAPTER IX

[1] Murchison, C. T., "Southern Textile Manufacturing," The *Annals of the American Academy of Political and Social Science*, January, 1931, p. 30.

[2] Mitchell, B., and Mitchell, G. S., *The Industrial Revolution in the South* (Baltimore: The Johns Hopkins Press, 1930), p. 168.

[3] "What's the Matter in North Carolina?" The *Business Week*, Oct. 12, 1929.

[4] U. S. Senate, *Working Conditions in the Textile Industry in North Carolina, South Carolina, and Tennessee, Report by the Committee on Manufactures*, 71st Congress, 1st Session, Senate Report no. 28 (Washington: Government Printing Office, 1930), vol. A, part 2, p. 4-5.

[5] *Ibid.*, part 2, p. 5-6.

[6] Stark, L., "The Meaning of the Textile Strike," The *New Republic*, May 8, 1929.

[7] U. S. Senate, *op. cit.*, part 2, p. 3.

[8] Murchison, *loc. cit.*, p. 31.

[9] Otey, E. L., "Women and Children in Southern Industry," The *Annals of the American Academy of Political and Social Science*, January, 1931, p. 164.

[10] Evans, M. G., "Southern Labor Supply and Working Conditions in Industry," The *Annals of the American Academy of Political and Social Science*, January, 1931, p. 160-161.

[11] Mitchell and Mitchell, *op. cit.*, p. 183.

[12] Lemert, B. F., *The Cotton Textile Industry of the Southern Appalachian Piedmont* (Chapel Hill: The University of North Carolina Press, 1933), p. 52.

[13] Edmonds, R. W., *Cotton Mill Labor Conditions in the South and New England* (Baltimore: Manufacturers' Record Publishing Co., 1925), p. 9-10.

[14] *Ibid.*, p. 9.

[15] Stewart, E., "Present Situation in Textiles," *American Federationist*, June, 1929, p. 689.

[16] The *New York Times*, May 19, 1929. *Cf.* Stark, *loc. cit.*

[17] McGrady, E., "Conciliation Proposals," *American Federationist*, June, 1929.

[18] Milton, G. F., "The South Fights the Unions," The *New Republic*, July 10, 1929.

[19] Quoted by Blanshard, P., "Communism in Southern Cotton Mills," The *Nation*, April 24, 1929.

[20] Blanshard, P., "One-Hundred Per Cent Americans on Strike," The *Nation*, May 8, 1929.

[21] The *Commercial and Financial Chronicle*, May 11, 1929, p. 3107.

[22] McCracken, D., *Strike Injunctions in the New South* (Chapel Hill: The University of North Carolina Press, 1931), p. 103-106.

[23] The *New York Times*, April 7, 1929.

[24] Blanshard, "Communism in Southern Cotton Mills," *loc. cit.*

[25] Porter, P., "Justice and Chivalry in Carolina," The *Nation*, Aug. 28, 1929.

[26] The *New York Times*, Aug. 3, 1929.

[27] Quoted by Porter, *loc. cit.*

[28] The *New York Times*, Sept. 6, 1929.

[29] Lewis, N. B., "Tar Heel Justice," The *Nation*, Sept. 11, 1929.

[30] The *New York Times*, Sept. 16, 1929.

[31] *Ibid.*, Oct. 12, 1929.

[32] *Ibid.*, Oct. 16, 1929.

[33] *Ibid.*, Oct. 19, 1929.

[34] *Ibid.*, an editorial, "Labor in the South," July 16, 1929.

[35] *Ibid.*, Sept. 2, 1929.

[36] McCracken, *op. cit.*, appendix xviii, p. 223-224.

[37] *Cf.* Stolberg, B., "Madness in Marion," The *Nation*, Oct. 23, 1929.

[38] Oct. 4, 1929, quoted by Stolberg, *loc. cit.*

[39] Lemert, *op. cit.*, p. 60-61.

[40] Mitchell, B., "Taking a Stand in Dixie," The *Commonweal*, June 5, 1929.

[41] Dec. 23, 1929, quoted by Schwenning, G. T., "Prospects of Southern Textile Unionism," The *Journal of Political Economy*, December, 1931, p. 807.

[42] Knight, E. W., "The Lesson of Gastonia," The *Outlook and Independent*, Sept. 11, 1929.

ADDITIONAL

Bailey, F. "Gastonia Goes to Trial," The *New Republic*, Aug. 14, 1929.

Bonner, M. "Behind the Southern Textile Strikes," The *Nation*, Oct. 2, 1929.

Bowen, M. "The Story of the Elizabethton Strike," *American Federationist,* June, 1929.

Britten, R. H., Bloomfield, J. J., and Goddard, J. C. *The Health of Workers in a Textile Plant.* U. S. Treasury Department: Public Health Bulletin no. 207, July, 1933.

Eberling, E. J. "The Strikes Among Textile Workers in the Southern States," *Current History,* June, 1929.

Ethridge, M. "The South's New Industrialism and the Press," The *Annals of the American Academy of Political and Social Science,* January, 1931.

Googe, G. L. "Textile Workers Organize," *American Federationist,* July, 1929.

Jones, W. "Southern Labor and the Law," The *Nation,* July 2, 1930.

Kelley, F. "Our Newest South," The *Survey,* June 15, 1929.

Larkin, M. "Ella May's Songs," The *Nation,* Oct. 9, 1929.

Larkin, M. "Tragedy in North Carolina," The *North American Review,* December, 1929.

Lewis, N. B. "Anarchy vs. Communism in Gastonia," The *Nation,* Sept. 25, 1929.

MacDonald, L. "Normalcy in the Carolinas," The *New Republic,* Jan. 29, 1930.

Matthews, T. S. "Gastonia in Court," The *New Republic,* Sept. 18, 1929.

Mitchell, G. S. "Organization of Labor in the South," The *Annals of the American Academy of Political and Social Science,* January, 1931.

Nelson, F. "North Carolina Justice," The *New Republic,* Nov. 6, 1929.

Patterson, D. "Organization Possibilities in South Carolina," *American Federationist,* June, 1929.

Shaplen, J. "Strikes, Mills and Murder," The *Survey,* Sept. 15, 1929.

Vorse, M. H. "Gastonia," *Harper's Magazine,* November, 1929.

Wharton, D. "Poor-White Capitalists," The *Outlook and Independent,* Oct. 16, 1929.

CHAPTER X

[1] "Longshore Labor Conditions and Port Decasualization in the United States," *Monthly Labor Review,* December, 1933.

[2] Saugstad, J. E., *Shipping and Shipbuilding Subsidies* (U. S. Department of Commerce, Bureau of Foreign and Domestic Commerce, Trade Promotion Series, no. 129), p. 67-68.

[3] Statement by Joseph P. Ryan, The *New York Times*, July 6, 1934.

[4] U. S. Bureau of Labor Statistics, *Cargo Handling and Longshore Labor Conditions*, Bulletin no. 550 (Washington: Government Printing Office, 1932), p. 72.

[5] Darcy, S., "The Great West Coast Maritime Strike," The *Communist*, July, 1934, p. 668.

[6] Seeley, E., "San Francisco's Labor War," The *Nation*, June 13, 1934.

[7] Letter by W. H. Washington, chairman of the student committee, The *New Republic*, June 6, 1934.

[8] The *New York Times*, June 24, 1934.

[9] *Ibid.*, June 24, 1934.

[10] *Ibid.*, July 4, 1934.

[11] *Ibid.*, July 7, 1934.

[12] *Ibid.*, July 9, 1934.

[13] The *San Francisco Examiner*, July 11, 1934.

[14] *Ibid.*, July 11, 1934.

[15] Hedley, G. P., *The San Francisco Strike as I Have Seen It: An Address before the Church Council for Social Education, Berkeley, California, July 19, 1934* (A pamphlet), p. 5.

[16] The *New York Times*, July 6, 1934.

[17] *Ibid.*, July 8, 1934.

[18] Darcy, S., "The San Francisco Bay Area General Strike," The *Communist*, October, 1934, p. 991.

[19] The *New York Times*, July 17, 1934.

[20] *Ibid.*, July 17, 1934.

[21] *Cf.* Burke, E., "Dailies Helped Break General Strike," *Editor & Publisher*, July 28, 1934.

[22] The *San Francisco Examiner*, July 16, 1934.

[23] Reprinted in the *New York Times*, July 17, 1934.

[24] Burke, *loc. cit.*

[25] The *New York Times*, July 18, 1934.

[26] *Ibid.*, July 18, 1934.

[27] *Ibid.*, July 18, 1934.

[28] *Cf.* "A Report on the Industrial Association," The *Nation,* Oct. 10, 1934.

[29] Letter from the Northern California branch of the American Civil Liberties Union, July 24, 1935.

[30] The *New York Times,* July 19, 1934.

[31] *Ibid.,* July 18, 1934.

[32] *Ibid.,* July 19, 1934.

[33] *Ibid.,* July 19, 1934.

[34] *Ibid.,* July 20, 1934.

[35] *Ibid.,* July 19, 1934.

[36] *Ibid.,* July 21, 1934.

[37] The *Nation,* Oct. 31, 1934, p. 493.

ADDITIONAL

Barnes, C. B. *The Longshoremen.* New York: Survey Associates, Inc., 1915.

Brown, D. M. "Dividends and Stevedores," *Scribner's Magazine,* January, 1935.

Cantwell, R. "San Francisco: Act One," The *New Republic,* July 25, 1934.

Cantwell, R. "War on the West Coast. I. The Gentlemen of San Francisco," The *New Republic,* Aug. 1, 1934.

Crook, W. H. "Social Security and the General Strike," *Political Science Quarterly,* September, 1934.

De Ford, M. A. "Riot Guns in San Francisco," The *Nation,* July 18, 1934.

De Ford, M. A. "San Francisco: An Autopsy on the General Strike," The *Nation,* Aug. 1, 1934.

Dickinson, R. "Show-Down Time," *Printers' Ink,* July 19, 1934.

Dunne, W. F. "Fascism in the Pacific Coast Strike," *New Masses,* July 31, 1934.

Hamilton, I. "General Strike," *New Masses,* July 24, 1934.

Hamilton, I. "Longshoremen on the Pacific," *New Masses,* June 5, 1934.

Hamilton, I. " 'Shoot to Kill!' on the Coast," *New Masses,* July 17, 1934.

Laski, H. J. "The Problem of the General Strike," The *Nation,* Aug. 15, 1934.

Levenson, L. "California Casualty List," The *Nation,* Aug. 29, 1934.

Levenson, L. "The Case of Thomas Sharpe," The *Nation,* Sept. 5, 1934.

Mettee, G. "Zero Hour on the Coast," The *Nation,* July 25, 1934.

Seeley, E. "War on the West Coast. II. Journalistic Strikebreakers," The *New Republic,* Aug. 1, 1934.

Taylor, P. S. "The San Francisco General Strike," *Pacific Affairs,* September, 1934.

Taylor, P. S., and Gold, N. L. "San Francisco and the General Strike," *Survey Graphic,* September, 1934.

"Who Owns the San Francisco Police?" The *Nation,* Aug. 29, 1934.

Winter, E. "Stevedores on Strike," The *New Republic,* June 13, 1934.

INDEX

RELATED READING

The Changing Face of U.S. Politics
Working-Class Politics and the Trade Unions
Jack Barnes

A handbook for workers coming into the factories, mines, and mills, as they react to the uncertain life, ceaseless turmoil, and brutality of capitalism in the closing years of the twentieth century. It shows how millions of workers, as political resistance grows, will revolutionize themselves, their unions, and all of society. $19.95

Labor's Giant Step
The First Twenty Years of the CIO: 1936-1955
Art Preis

The story of the explosive labor struggles and political battles in the 1930s that built the industrial unions. And how those unions became the vanguard of a mass social movement that began transforming U.S. society. $26.95

Trade Unions in the Epoch of Imperialist Decay
Leon Trotsky, Karl Marx

"Apart from their original purposes, the trades unions must now learn to act deliberately as organizing centers of the working class in the broad interest of its complete emancipation. . . . They must convince the world at large that their efforts, far from being narrow and selfish, aim at the emancipation of the downtrodden millions." —Karl Marx, 1866.

In this book, two central leaders of the modern communist workers movement outline the fight for this revolutionary perspective. $14.95

The History of American Trotskyism
James P. Cannon

Origins of the communist movement in the United States, told by one of its central leaders, from the impact of the Russian revolution on militants in the Industrial Workers of the World and Socialist Party, to the struggle of the Left Opposition against Stalin, to the formation of the Socialist Workers Party in 1938. $18.95

PATHFINDER

Available from Pathfinder

The Bolivian Diary of Ernesto Che Guevara

Guevara's account, newly translated, of the 1966-67 guerrilla struggle in Bolivia. A day-by-day chronicle by one of the central leaders of the Cuban revolution of the campaign to forge a continent-wide revolutionary movement of workers and peasants capable of contending for power. New translation includes material published in English for the first time. $21.95

Nelson Mandela Speaks

Forging a Democratic, Nonracial South Africa

Mandela's speeches from 1990 through 1993 recount the course of struggle that put an end to apartheid and opened the fight for a deep-going political, economic, and social transformation in South Africa. $18.95

To Speak the Truth

Why Washington's 'Cold War' against Cuba Doesn't End

Fidel Castro and Che Guevara

Why the U.S. government is determined to destroy the example set by the socialist revolution in Cuba and why its effort will fail. Introduction by Mary-Alice Waters. $16.95

The Eastern Airlines Strike

Accomplishments of the Rank-and-File Machinists

Ernie Mailhot and others

The story of the 1989-91 strike in which rank-and-file resistance by Machinists prevented Eastern's antiunion onslaught from becoming the road to a profitable nonunion airline. $9.95

The History of the Russian Revolution

Leon Trotsky

The social, economic, and political dynamics of the first victorious socialist revolution. The story is told by one of the revolution's principal leaders, writing in exile in the early 1930s, with these historic events still fresh in his mind. Unabridged edition, 3 vols. in one. 1,358 pp. $35.95

The Communist Manifesto

Karl Marx and Frederick Engels

Founding document, published in 1848, of the modern working-class movement. Explains how capitalism arose as a specific stage in the economic development of class society and how it will be superseded through revolutionary action on a world scale by the working class. Booklet. $2.50

February 1965: The Final Speeches

Malcolm X

Speeches from the last three weeks of Malcolm X's life, presenting the accelerating evolution of his political views. A large part is material previously unavailable, with some in print for the first time. The inaugural volume in Pathfinder's selected works of Malcolm X. $17.95

Cosmetics, Fashions, and the Exploitation of Women

Joseph Hansen, Evelyn Reed, and Mary-Alice Waters

How big business promotes cosmetics to generate profits and perpetuate the oppression of women. In her introduction, Mary-Alice Waters explains how the entry of millions of women into the workforce during and after World War II irreversibly changed U.S. society and laid the basis for a renewed rise of struggles for women's equality. $12.95

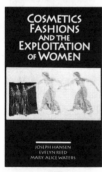

Notebook of an Agitator

From the Wobblies to the Fight against the Korean War and McCarthyism

James P. Cannon

Articles spanning four decades of working-class battles—defending IWW frame-up victims and Sacco and Vanzetti; 1934 Minneapolis Teamsters strikes; battles on the San Francisco waterfront; labor's fight against the McCarthyite witch-hunt; and much more. $21.95

A Political Biography of Walter Reuther: The Record of an Opportunist

Beatrice Hansen

A case history of the formation of a union bureaucrat, the former president of the United Auto Workers union. Booklet. $2.50

WRITE FOR A FREE CATALOG. SEE FRONT OF BOOK FOR ADDRESSES.

Farmers Face the Crisis of the 1990s

Doug Jenness Examines the deepening economic and social crisis in the capitalist world and explains how farmers and workers can unite internationally against the mounting assaults from the billionaire bankers, industrialists, and merchants of grain. Booklet. $3.50

The Frame-Up of Mark Curtis
A Packinghouse Worker's Fight for Justice

Margaret Jayko The story of the frame-up of unionist and political activist Mark Curtis on rape and burglary charges. His real crime, in the authorities' eyes, is that he is part of a layer of young workers active in supporting the rights of immigrants, strengthening the unions, and campaigning against U.S. government intervention from Cuba to the Mideast. Booklet. $5.00

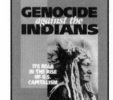

Genocide against the Indians

George Novack "The conflict between the red man and the white is usually represented as essentially racial in character. But their war to the death was at bottom a social struggle," Novack explains. "The scramble for wealth was at its root. In this case, the chief prize was individual ownership of the land." Booklet. $4.00

Racism, Revolution, Reaction, 1861-1877
The Rise and Fall of Radical Reconstruction

Peter Camejo The achievements of the Radical Reconstruction state governments that arose in the South following the Civil War, the challenges they faced, and the counterrevolution that overthrew them. $17.95

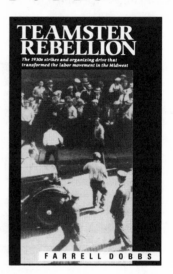

New International

A MAGAZINE OF MARXIST POLITICS AND THEORY

No. 10

Imperialism's March toward Fascism and War *by Jack Barnes* • What the 1987 Stock Market Crash Foretold • Defending Cuba; Defending Cuba's Socialist Revolution *by Mary-Alice Waters* $14.00

No. 7

Opening Guns of World War III: Washington's Assault on Iraq *by Jack Barnes* • 1945: When U.S. Troops Said 'No!' *by Mary-Alice Waters* • Lessons from the Iran-Iraq War $12.00

No. 9

The Triumph of the Nicaraguan Revolution • Washington's Contra War and the Challenge of Forging Proletarian Leadership • The Political Degeneration of the FSLN and the Demise of the Workers and Farmers Government $14.00

No. 8

The Politics of Economics: Che Guevara and Marxist Continuity *by Steve Clark and Jack Barnes* • Che's Contribution to the Cuban Economy *by Carlos Rafael Rodríguez* • On the Concept of Value and The Meaning of Socialist Planning *by Ernesto Che Guevara* $10.00

No. 6

The Second Assassination of Maurice Bishop *by Steve Clark* • Washington's 50-Year Domestic Contra War *by Larry Seigle* • Land, Labor, and the Canadian Socialist Revolution *by Michel Dugré* • Renewal or Death: Cuba's Rectification Process *two speeches by Fidel Castro* $10.00

No. 5

The Coming Revolution in South Africa *by Jack Barnes* • The Future Belongs to the Majority *by Oliver Tambo* • Why Cuban Volunteers Are in Angola *two speeches by Fidel Castro* $9.00

No. 1

Their Trotsky and Ours: Communist Continuity Today *by Jack Barnes* • Lenin and the Colonial Question *by Carlos Rafael Rodríguez* • The 1916 Easter Rebellion in Ireland: Two Views *by V.I. Lenin and Leon Trotsky* $8.00

Eugene V. Debs Speaks

Speeches by the pioneer U.S. socialist agitator and labor leader, jailed for opposing Washington's imperialist aims in World War I. Debs speaks out on capitalism and socialism, anti-immigrant chauvinism, how anti-Black racism weakens the labor movement, Rockefeller's massacre of striking miners at Ludlow, Colorado, and more. $19.95

Marx and Engels on the United States

Articles and letters from 1846 to 1895 examine the rise of U.S. capitalism and the challenges facing the emerging working-class movement. Indispensable for understanding the economic roots and consequences of the Civil War. $15.95

The Wages System ■ FREDERICK ENGELS

Is "a fair day's wages for a fair day's work" possible? Should workers build their own political party? Can trade unions play a revolutionary role? A series of articles written for the labor press in Britain. Booklet. $2.00

Revolutionary Continuity ■ FARRELL DOBBS
Marxist Leadership in the United States

Forging a leadership to advance the class interests of the toilers in the United States. From pre–Civil War struggles by workers and small farmers, to Radical Reconstruction and the labor battles of the 1870s and '80s. From the efforts to build a Marxist left wing in the pre–World War I Socialist Party to the Russian revolution and formation of the Communist Party.

REVOLUTIONARY CONTINUITY: THE EARLY YEARS, 1848-1917 $16.95

REVOLUTIONARY CONTINUITY: BIRTH OF THE COMMUNIST MOVEMENT, 1918-1922 $16.95